DISCOVERING THE
ITALIAN BAROQUE

The Denis Mahon Collection

Sponsored by Guinness Mahon/Henderson Crosthwaite

DISCOVERING THE ITALIAN BAROQUE

The Denis Mahon Collection

GABRIELE FINALDI AND
MICHAEL KITSON

*With contributions by Christopher Brown, Humphrey Wine
and Denis Mahon*

National Gallery Publications, London

Distributed by Yale University Press

Authors' Acknowledgements

We have benefited from the assistance and good will of a large number of people. First to be thanked, of course, is Sir Denis Mahon himself, whose research lies behind much of what is presented here. He has been immensely generous in sharing his learning and experience and it has been the greatest honour to work closely with him. We are grateful to all the staff and colleagues at the National Gallery who have made the exhibition possible.

Thanks are also due to the following: Julian Agnew, Jack Baer, Alexander Bell, Emily Black, Father James Boner OFM, Duncan Bull, Hugo Chapman, Irene Cioffi, the staff of the Courtauld Institute Library, Angela Delaforce, David Ekserdjian, Caroline Elam, Marta Maria Finaldi, Jennifer Fletcher, Donald Garstang, John Harris, Michael Helston, Christopher Kingzett, Patrick Matthiesen, John Morton Morris, Gabriel Naughton, Francis Russell, Thomas Schneider, Jonathan Scott, Robert Wenley, Clovis Whitfield, in London; and to Joseph Baillio, Rosanna Barbiellini Amidei, Sergio Benedetti, Jean-Claude Boyer, Xanthe Brooke, Francesca Cappelletti, Keith Christiansen, Sarah M. Crawford, Peter Day, Gosem C. Dullaart, Andrea Emiliani, Maurizio Fagiolo dell'Arco, Richard L. Feigen, Revd. James Finnemore, Burton Fredericksen, Maria L. Gilbert, Colin Harrison, Rüdiger Klessmann, Rebecca Lawton, Adrian Le Harivel, Silvia Mascalchi, Patrick Michel, Serena Mormone, Raffaella Morselli, Eduardo Nappi, Stephen Pepper, Lunk Pijl, Catherine R. Puglisi, Wolfgang Prohaska, Mauro Riccomini, Erich Schleier, Nicola Spinosa, Katherine Stainer-Hutchins, Claudio Strinati, Carol Togneri, Rossella Vodret, Natalie Voural, Aidan Weston-Lewis, Catherine Whistler, Jon Whiteley, Lucy Whitaker, Daniel Wildenstein.

Special thanks are due to María Inés Finaldi.

This book was published to accompany an exhibition at:
The National Gallery, London
26 February – 18 May 1997

© National Gallery Publications Limited 1997

First published in Great Britain in 1997 by
National Gallery Publications Limited
5/6 Pall Mall East, London SW1Y 5BA

ISBN 1 85709 177 9 hardback

British Library Cataloguing-in-Publication Data
A catalogue record is available from the British Library
Library of Congress Catalog Card Number: 96–71403

EDITORS Felicity Luard and Diana Davies
EDITORIAL ASSISTANT Katharine Eyston
DESIGNER Andrew Shoolbred
PRINTED AND BOUND IN GREAT BRITAIN BY Butler and Tanner, Frome and London

FRONT JACKET
Guercino, *Elijah fed by Ravens* (cat. 43)
BACK JACKET
Donato Creti, *Artemisia drinking the Ashes of Mausolus* (cat. 18)
FRONTISPIECE
Johann Liss, *The Fall of Phaeton*, detail (cat. 52)

Contents

Sponsor's Preface

Guinness Mahon and Henderson Crosthwaite are delighted to be sponsoring *Discovering the Italian Baroque: The Denis Mahon Collection* at the National Gallery. It is particularly apt that this, the Guinness Mahon Group's first association with the National Gallery, is in support of an exhibition highlighting the achievements of Sir Denis Mahon as he is a direct descendant of the family which established Guinness & Mahon in 1836.

The Group is a wholly owned subsidiary of the Bank of Yokohama. The Group specialises in providing top quality services to its clients in the distinct areas of Merchant Banking, Private Banking, Stockbroking, Asset Management and Development Capital. The Group has representatives or affiliates in Switzerland, The Channel Islands, USA, Hong Kong, Bahamas, India, Monaco and Mexico.

Guinness Mahon and Henderson Crosthwaite are committed to continuing to support and encourage the promotion of the visual arts in Britain and hope that this impressive collection, on public display in its entirety for the first time, will be widely enjoyed.

David Potter
Chief Executive

Foreword

This exhibition is a celebration of the art of seventeenth-century Italy, but it is also a tribute to Sir Denis Mahon. And it is, I think, fitting that this tribute should take the form of simply allowing the public to enjoy free of charge some of the finest achievements of the artists to whom Sir Denis has devoted most of his life; for all his activities – as scholar and collector, critic and political campaigner – have been informed by the belief that everybody can, and should, be free to share the pleasure of looking at pictures.

It is a conviction that has marked him deeply as an art historian and led him to argue consistently that the understanding of the art of the past is above all an affair of the eye, that we must first look at how painters painted and only then think about how painters thought. His great contribution to our understanding of Poussin, for example, has been to insist that, painter-philosopher though he may have been, it is the study of Poussin's technique, his handling of oil and colour, his control of composition and light, that will reveal both the sequence of his development and his full stature as an artist. And time after time, his pragmatic British approach to this quintessentially French intellectual artist has been vindicated and proved right.

Denis Mahon put together his collection in forty odd years, from the mid-1930s to the early 1970s. It is an anthology of seventeenth-century Italian painting which any museum would be proud to own, but which few in this century have come close to equalling. I doubt if it is possible anywhere in the world, for example, to follow the whole career of Guercino through such distinguished works; and I doubt if anybody following that career could fail to see that we are in the presence of a supremely gifted artist.

Our ability to see and grasp that is, in large measure, also the achievement of Denis Mahon, because the collector-pragmatist has at the same time been one of the most influential theoretical and critical writers of recent art history. He more than anyone else has enabled us to see once again how moving and beautiful these paintings are. After Ruskin's dazzling polemic against the Italian Baroque in the middle of the last century, it became more or less impossible to enjoy these pictures, or to discern through the conventions and rhetoric they rely on a sincere expression of feeling or belief. Denis Mahon not only collected and studied these works. He set about persuading a whole generation of curators, scholars and critics that they can still speak to us.

Largely thanks to his efforts, the seventeenth-century Italian rooms in museums across Britain and America are now a central and popular part of the collection in a way that would have been unthinkable fifty years ago. A major element of the European tradition, neglected for a century, has been recovered for our enjoyment.

In his introductory essay, Michael Kitson outlines Denis Mahon's hardly less remarkable political achievements. Decade after decade, he has persistently reasoned and argued, hectored and blustered in defence of the museums of the United Kingdom. Astonishingly, in almost every case he has ultimately persuaded governments of all colours to face up to their duty to preserve and enrich public collections for future generations, always coming back to the point that if governments want private support for museums, they must unequivocally demonstrate their own.

We are grateful to Guinness Mahon/Henderson Crosthwaite for so generously providing the private support that allows us to present this exhibition to the public, who, Sir Denis hopes, will one day be able to enjoy it in perpetuity. The National Gallery, like museums and galleries across the country, has too many debts of gratitude to Denis Mahon to list them here. We hope he will find in this exhibition a proper expression of our thanks.

Neil MacGregor
Director

Sir Denis Mahon
Art Historian and Collector

MICHAEL KITSON

Britain has a long tradition of collecting, and has been fortunate in producing in this century perhaps more art historian-collectors than any other country. Generally speaking, it would be invidious to mention some names rather than others, but one clearly stands out above the rest: that of Sir Denis Mahon (fig.1).

Sir Denis is undoubtedly the greatest art historian-collector of our time or almost of any time; to find an adequate precedent one would have to go back to such figures, now known only to specialists, as the Boisserée Brothers in Germany at the beginning of the nineteenth century, or the Milanese collector of drawings, Padre Resta, more than a century before, or, to take a still earlier example, Nicolas Poussin's patron and friend (and one of Sir Denis's heroes), Cassiano dal Pozzo. Like those forebears, Sir Denis has made his collecting the visual counterpart of his scholarship. As this exhibition and catalogue show, his interests have lain principally in the field of seventeenth-century Bolognese painting, and above all in the work of Guercino. In pointing to the merits of this School in the early part of his career, during the 1930s and 1940s, he was the prime mover in Britain of the revival of interest in the Italian Baroque.

There is also something else which should be mentioned at once. Whereas most British collectors in this century, whether art historians or not, have felt a lingering regret at the steady shift of works of art from private hands to ownership by museums, Sir Denis has long been an ardent and resolute champion of the interests of the public. This has shown itself not only in his often stated intention to bequeath most of his collection to museums and galleries in Britain and the Republic of Ireland, the largest part of it to the National Gallery in London, but also in his campaigns, often conducted single-handedly, to shame the Government into fulfilling its duties towards the national heritage. This alone, apart from the pleasure the exhibition gives, is justification for showing the Mahon collection of paintings in its entirety, together with a selection of his drawings by Guercino, in the National Gallery.

The great stylistic movement which we call the Baroque began in Italy around 1600, dominated Italian painting, sculpture and architecture for the next hundred and fifty years, and produced echoes of varying intensity in the art of all other European countries, and also in Latin America. However, by the mid-eighteenth century the Baroque had more or less run its course, to be replaced by its antithesis, Neo-classicism. The leading theorist of this, who was also the first real historian of ancient Greek art, J.J. Winckelmann,[1] attacked the Baroque not only in its later, declining phase, which might have been expected, but also in the period of its greatest strength, the mid- and later seventeenth century, represented by the architecture of Bernini, Borromini and Guarini. According to Winckelmann, this architecture – and by implication Bernini's sculpture too – was extreme, ill-proportioned,

bizarre (indeed this was the original definition of 'baroque'). More than this, it was in bad taste. Classicism – meaning by that, adherence to the laws of clarity, harmony and proportion established for art in classical antiquity – was 'good taste'; everything else was 'bad taste', or aesthetically negligible. Winckelmann, however, was not quite the first to express this point of view, although he did so more forcefully than any predecessor. Something of the same concern about the issues of classicism and anti-classicism was felt by a number of artists and critics – Poussin, for instance, and his supporter Bellori – even at the height of the Baroque period itself. Indeed, the heritage of Antiquity, and the art of Raphael which was perceived to be its modern equivalent, were never forgotten, and practically no seventeenth-century artist or architect (Caravaggio was perhaps an exception) spoke out against either. It was just that Baroque artists departed more or less widely from both ideals in practice.

Winckelmann said comparatively little about painting but he was responsible for one insidious interjection: the naming of the three revolutionary Bolognese painters, Ludovico, Agostino and Annibale Carracci, as 'eclectics'.[2] Because they were supposed to have worked to a programme of combining the best qualities of various earlier artists – the purity of Raphael and the ancients, the knowledge of Michelangelo, the richness and exuberance of the Venetians, etc. – the Carracci were characterised by Winckelmann as mere imitators and hence by definition as decadents. A generation later, in the early nineteenth century, this judgement was introduced into English criticism by Henry Fuseli.[3] The label 'eclectic' pinned to the Carracci was not only to serve as a proof of their inferiority in the eyes of hostile nineteenth-century critics; it also remained an embarrassment to those early twentieth-century scholars engaged in restoring the good reputation of Seicento painting as a whole. Beginning in 1947, it has been a major concern of Sir Denis Mahon's[4] to show that the Carracci were not eclectics, nor did they try to be.

As the nineteenth century wore on, the whole of Italian art since the Renaissance came to be regarded as decadent, on the principle that, if the Renaissance represented the summit of art, everything that followed it must be a decline. In addition, Seicento painting was perceived, especially in England, as shallow and insincere. Possibly as early as about 1800, Fuseli averred: 'The gods of Guido [Reni] have the air of ancient courtiers... The Christ of Guido is a well suspended corpse'[5] – and this at a time when Reni was still prized by collectors above pretty well all other artists except Raphael. Then, in the 1840s and 1850s, in *Modern Painters*, Ruskin went much further. His maledictions read absurdly today and were perhaps never taken entirely seriously by his contemporaries, even in Puritan Britain and America. Writing of Domenichino, he observed: 'The man who painted the Madonna del Rosario and Martyrdom of St. Agnes in the gallery

Fig.1 Sir Denis Mahon.

Fig.2 Annibale Carracci, *The Dead Christ Mourned* ('*The Three Maries*'), c.1604. Oil on canvas, 92.8 x 103.2 cm. London, National Gallery.

of Bologna is palpably incapable of doing anything good, great or right in any field, way, or kind, whatsoever.' As for Guercino:

The grief of Guercino's Hagar, in the Brera Gallery at Milan, is partly despicable, partly disgusting, partly ridiculous; it is not the grief of the injured Egyptian, driven forth into the desert with the destiny of a nation in her heart, but of a servant of all work turned away for stealing tea and sugar.

And Ruskin summed the whole thing up by declaring roundly: 'The Venetian school of landscape expired with Tintoret, in the year 1594; and the sixteenth century closed, like a grave, over the great art of the world. There is *no* entirely sincere or great art in the seventeenth century.'[6]

As an aside to this, however, we should note that there was a wide gap between, on the one hand, the pronouncements of scholars and critics, who had been accumulating arguments against the Baroque for more than fifty years, and the taste of collectors and the general public on the other. As late as 1857, the most popular painting on view in the huge Manchester *Art Treasures* exhibition was Annibale Carracci's '*The Three Maries*' now in the National Gallery (fig.2).[7] Moreover, only four years earlier the 4th Duke of Northumberland acquired an important group of Bolognese paintings from a collection in Rome (see cat.7). Even after this, isolated examples of the School continued to find their way into the National Gallery, usually by gift or bequest. After 1864, however, the Gallery stopped buying Seicento pictures, and those that it owned were relegated to a kind of ghetto removed from the rest of the Italian Schools.[8] When the Baroque came to be reinstated during the first half of the twentieth century, there was a similar mismatch at the outset between advanced opinion and popular taste, and the process of running ahead by one group and catching up by the other was repeated, this time in reverse.

Apart from Guercino's *Incredulity of Saint Thomas* and Pietro da Cortona's *Saint Cecilia* (acquired as a Domenichino), purchased respectively in 1917 and 1941, the National Gallery did not recommence buying Seicento pictures until 1957 (with Reni's large *Adoration of the Shepherds*, fig.3, the acquisition of which was advocated by Denis Mahon as a Trustee).[9]

It is not the place here to recount in detail the intellectual rehabilitation of Italian Baroque art, beginning in the 1880s, in the universities of Germany and Austria. However, it should be noted that revolutions in interpreting the art of the past were now no longer a matter for independent thinkers like Winckelmann and Ruskin, but had become the province of art historians. As a concomitant of this, art history as an academic subject had by then been established in German and Austrian universities for many years, although not as yet anywhere else. Moreover, the way it was conceived and taught was more or less strongly under the influence of the German philosophical tradition, particularly Hegel's philosophy of history, and the powerful scholarship of historians such as Leopold von Ranke.

As with the reaction *against* the Baroque in the second half of the eighteenth century, the revival began with the re-evaluation of architecture and was only afterwards extended to sculpture and painting. The first scholar to recognise the importance of Italian Baroque painting was Alois Riegl,[10] partly because he was the first to treat Baroque art as a style in its own right, not as a deviation from the art of the Renaissance, and partly because he went back to the early biographical sources, Baglione, Bellori, Passeri and Baldinucci. Admittedly his account is fairly summary – it is also, for Riegl, surprisingly unphilosophical – but it found an interesting echo a few years afterwards in the brief surveys of early seventeenth-century painting in Rome included in the two pioneering monographs on Nicolas Poussin, by Walter Friedländer and Otto Grautoff, which were published in Munich in 1914.

During the course of this phase there were naturally shifts in both method and interpretation. One of these shifts was the exchange of a formalist for a contextual approach, which led to an association of the Baroque with the Counter-Reformation. Another shift – or rather, several shifts – occurred in the supposed chronological limits of the style. There were further changes resulting from the 'discovery' of Mannerism around the time of the First World War. There was also a steady advance in the quantity and quality of research.

Something must be said here in particular about Wölfflin's major book, *Kunstgeschichtliche Grundbegriffe* (*Principles of Art History*), first published in 1915, because the author's method of stylistic analysis was to be taken up and used in a more refined way by Denis Mahon. Moreover, this book, which became a bestseller in Germany, was the only foreign text relating to Baroque art to be translated into English (in 1932) until the 1950s.[11] To the modern reader, Wölfflin's *Principles* has some odd features.[12] First, it treats the Baroque as beginning in the 1520s with Michelangelo's Medici Chapel and Laurenziana Library, though that is perhaps chiefly a matter of terminology. More importantly, the words 'Renaissance' and 'Baroque' are not used, as most art historians have always used them, as terms defining cultural periods or indicating the work of large groups of artists doing broadly similar things but all in slightly different ways. Instead, these words are made to stand for independent entities with minds of their own: the Renaissance 'does' this, the Baroque 'does' that; and whatever the Renaissance does, the Baroque does the opposite – there is no transitional phase between them. Thirdly, though this again is minor but curious in the present context, while Wölfflin used Italian examples throughout for his discussion of architecture, almost all the Baroque paintings he chose were Dutch or Flemish, with the strongest emphasis on Rubens.

However, while these aspects of the book may be controversial or out of date, Wölfflin's methods of formal analysis can still seem very striking, and they were enormously influential at the time and for many years afterwards. Famously, Wölfflin organises his material in pairs of contrasting concepts, one illustrating a Renaissance approach to form, the other a Baroque. What is more, he insists that the concepts he uses for painting are equally applicable to sculpture and architecture. They are grouped under five headings (in each case, the Renaissance approach is the one mentioned first): linear and painterly; surface and depth (this pair refers to an arrangement of the composition in planes parallel to the surface, as opposed to one that plunges diagonally into depth); closed and open compositions (which have to do with, respectively, regard for, and defiance of, the frame); multiplicity (building a composition out of distinct but related parts) and unity (blending everything together); and clarity and obscurity, or perhaps more accurately, determinate and indeterminate.

Now, in adapting this method, Denis Mahon discards a good deal. He betrays no sympathy for Wölfflin's attribution of creative powers to abstract forces, and no desire to employ the comparative method to characterise whole artistic epochs. On the other hand, he acknowledges that on certain levels – that of national or local tradition, for example – shared stylistic characteristics self-evidently exist, even if we cannot always define them or know what ultimately caused them. Thus there are Venetian characteristics, Bolognese characteristics, Roman characteristics, etc., and Sir Denis handles these with great finesse. An analogous shift occurs in the case of Wölfflin's Renaissance/Baroque antithesis, which Sir Denis redefines as Classical/Baroque, or Classical/Anti-classical – and in so doing he draws on the debates about these matters within the seventeenth century itself. In sum, it is Sir Denis's habit to focus on particulars rather than generalities, and, in so far as he makes use of Wölfflin's methods of comparison, it is not so much to separate or connect large groups of works by different artists as to establish fine distinctions between one painting and another by the *same* artist.

What he perhaps takes most directly from Wölfflin, though he develops it in his own way, is an acute sensitivity to the way an artist organises a picture. This sensitivity is surely Wölfflin's most remarkable gift, whether one agrees with his precise terminology – linear *versus* painterly, etc. – or not. Denis Mahon's approach, typically, is less schematic and he employs only those criteria that are relevant to the case in hand. But to follow him as he analyses a painting, for example when discussing Guercino's change of style in the mid-1620s or Poussin's in the mid-1630s, is an object lesson. Sometimes the key to an understanding of the picture lies in the artist's use of horizontals, verticals or diagonals. Or it may lie in his placing of the main emphasis on straight or curved lines; or perhaps in the presence of movements on the surface or into

Fig.3 Guido Reni, *The Adoration of the Shepherds, c.*1640. Oil on canvas, 480 x 321 cm. London, National Gallery.

depth, or in the depiction of the figures as overlapping or separate from one another, and so on. Other crucial factors may be the smoothness or roughness of the brushwork, or the depth or lightness of the chiaroscuro and how it is used to unite or break up the forms. The ability to 'read' all these signs with the utmost subtlety and penetration has been central to Sir Denis Mahon's work as an art historian throughout his life.

At the same time, however, Sir Denis has also owed much to the Italian tradition of art history which, in its concentration on formal minutiae and qualities of aesthetic expression, was not in fact so very far from the Wölfflinian practice of stylistic analysis. But it lacked the same basis in a theoretical explanation of the origins of creativity that Wölfflin's method had (though Mahon's did not). An emphasis on intuition in the Italian approach to art history is hardly surprising, given that the leading Italian philosopher of the first half of the twentieth century was Benedetto Croce, for whom intuition, and only intuition, was the mainspring of art. This in turn was reflected in a high value being placed by Italian art historians on connoisseurship and on the hunt for forgotten and previously unknown pictures. For Denis Mahon, however, connoisseurship has always been a tool, not an end in itself, and he has explained that he made a decision early in his career to avoid becoming entangled in the type of obsessive searching after everything, akin to stamp-collecting, of which Bernard Berenson was the past-master.[13]

Probably the most brilliant Italian art historian of the first half of the twentieth century was the scholar, intuitive critic (he was a disciple of Croce) and connoisseur, Roberto Longhi. He was also one of the first in Europe to focus on the work of Caravaggio and his circle, whereas German and Austrian scholars tended to emphasise the Bolognese. Longhi dominated Caravaggio studies from his first articles in the periodical *L'Arte* in 1913–16 to the epoch-making *Mostra del Caravaggio e dei Caravaggeschi* at Milan in 1951, which he organised; he also published a monograph on the artist in 1952.[14] An original contribution of a different kind was made by a large survey exhibition of Seicento and Settecento painting held in the Pitti Palace in Florence in 1922.[15] The Italian custom of frequently putting on major Old Master exhibitions (which were less common in Germany and Austria, where the permanent museum collection reigned supreme) is a further illustration of the strongly visual bias of Italian art history;[16] it is also another example of Denis Mahon's affinity with the Italian outlook, for he too, as we shall see, has for many years been closely involved with exhibitions. The Pitti Palace exhibition not only drew attention to these pictures in a way that their long-standing, undisturbed presence in churches and palaces had not but was a demonstration by a major national museum that Seicento and Settecento painting once more had official approval.

In England, where there was still no academic centre for the study of art history,[17] the art world was dominated by amateurs. They were the collectors, critics and dealers of their day, with, standing somewhat warily to one side of them, the museum curators. All were primarily connoisseurs, intensely concerned with attributions but possessing only a general knowledge of the historical development of art. However, among all these groups, during the 1920s, a cautious interest in the Seicento began here and there to emerge. There was also one eager champion of the style – Sacheverell Sitwell – whose *Southern Baroque Art* (1924) enjoyed a fashionable success for several years. This was a sort of conjuring-trick of a book, in that it managed to communicate a modish enthusiasm for Baroque art without actually discussing it in visual terms. It also had the unusual characteristic for the time of approaching the Baroque from the wrong end, as it were; that is, starting not from the point of view of the emergence of a Baroque style around 1600 in Bologna and Rome, but focusing rather on the more extravagant, flamboyant art and architecture of Southern Italy, Spain and Mexico a hundred years later.

More typical, however, of the attitude of English amateurs between the wars is the patronising comment of Sir Robert Witt in his introduction to the catalogue of the enormous *Exhibition of Italian Art 1200–1900* at the Royal Academy in 1930. Referring to the small section devoted to the Seicento in this exhibition, he wrote: 'Although the present generation cannot even contemplate the abandonment of the early (i.e. the painting of the *primitivi* and the Renaissance) in favour of the late, it may perhaps throw a more sympathetic glance upon the indisputable skill of the Academies of the Bolognese Eclectics.'[18] The record of the *Burlington Magazine* in the first thirty years of the century is also revealing. There was a good though by modern standards superficial article by the architectural historian Martin Briggs on 'The Genius of Bernini' in 1914;[19] a sympathetic and intelligent review by Roger Fry of the fourth German edition of Wölfflin's *Principles of Art History* in 1921[20] (Fry also published a longer but more confused essay on 'The Seicento' in *Transformations*, published in 1926);[21] and a brief survey of the subject (not a review) entitled 'The Seicento and Settecento Exhibition in Florence', by the Italian art historian Carlo Gamba, in 1922.[22] And this was about all – until Denis Mahon's first article in the Magazine, 'Notes on the Young Guercino', in 1937.[23] In the opening paragraph of this, Sir Denis summed up the situation up to that time with characteristic precision: '...in England it [Seicento painting] is still something of the neglected Cinderella of Italian art, *perhaps not so much from the point of view of appreciation as from that of art-history*' (present writer's italics).

Strictly true as that was, however, it is fair to say that, in the previous few years, the character of art history in general in England had at last begun to change and to become more professional. In 1931, the Courtauld Institute of Art was founded as a new School of the University of London, but what really transformed the situation, as everyone agrees, was the arrival of the Warburg Institute in London from Hamburg in December 1933. This was an institution comprising both a great library and a staff of dedicated scholars trained in the humanities, of which art history was only a part, though in their case an important one, in the universities of Germany and Austria. Among these scholars were the Director, Fritz Saxl, whose wide-ranging interests inspired everybody, and two specialists in the Italian Baroque. One was Otto Kurz, who had recently written his doctoral dissertation at the University of Vienna on Guido Reni and whose professional life for the next twenty years was to be closely connected with Denis Mahon's. The other was Rudolf Wittkower; at this stage, however, his publications were almost exclusively on architecture and sculpture and he added painting only later.[24]

Simultaneously, a small group of young English-born art historians, Oxbridge-educated, energetic, ambitious and highly intelligent although not professionally trained, was beginning to appear and to take advantage of what the Warburg had to offer. They included a tiny sub-group with a special interest in the Seicento: Ellis Waterhouse who, after a short spell on the staff of the National Gallery, was Librarian of the British School in Rome from 1933 to 1936 and, in 1937, published *Baroque Painting in Rome*;[25] Anthony Blunt, who included a section on Seicento artistic theory as part of his Fellowship dissertation for Trinity College, Cambridge, in 1932; and, the youngest of the three, born in 1910, Denis Mahon himself. Another name should also be mentioned in this context: that of the art historian and collector, Brinsley Ford (now Sir Brinsley), although his interests lay more in the Settecento than the Seicento and he did not begin publishing until after the war.

Sir Denis has explained in a published interview how he first came to take up Italian seventeenth-century painting in general and to specialise in Guercino in particular.[26] After finishing a history degree at Oxford, he stayed on for a further year to study art history informally under Kenneth Clark, who was then Keeper of Western Art and Director of the Ashmolean Museum. Asked by Mahon to recommend a field that was still under-studied, Clark suggested the Seicento.[27] Coming down from Oxford in 1933, Sir Denis next attended lectures on Seicento painting at the Courtauld Institute given by Nikolaus Pevsner – another scholar recently arrived in London from Central Europe. Pevsner was the most adventurous and intellectually ambitious young scholar of the Italian Baroque in Europe at the time, although he was soon to give up this field in favour of the history of English architecture.[28] His lectures at the Courtauld must have gone clean over the heads of most of the not very serious students who attended the Institute in its early days, but they fascinated Denis Mahon. He took private lessons with Pevsner, who taught him the rudiments of scholarly method as well as much about the Seicento. He also asked Pevsner for suggestions for a research topic. Important work had already been done or was in progress on the Continent on Caravaggio by Roberto Longhi, on Annibale Carracci by Hans Tietze, on Ludovico Carracci by Heinrich Bodmer, on Guido Reni by Otto Kurz, and on Pietro da Cortona by Hans Posse.[29] There was even an old, inadequate monograph in Italian on Domenichino by Luigi Serra.[30] So – 'Why not Guercino?', said Pevsner.

And Guercino it was, which, in Sir Denis's own words, 'attracted me very much'. He had now sought out the best scholarly advice, he had a considerable literature on the Seicento in German and Italian at his disposal and, not least, he had the seventeenth-century biographical sources, above all the *Felsina Pittrice: Vite dei pittori bolognesi* of Count Carlo Cesare Malvasia, published in Bologna in 1678, which contained by far the most important *Life* of Guercino. He also had, in the Seicento, a field on which almost nothing had yet been written in English 'from the point of view of art history', and, in Guercino, an artist of great strength and beauty on whom little had been published in any language. In fact, there was only a long essay by Matteo Marangoni, 'Il vero Guercino', and the article on Guercino by Hermann Voss in Thieme-Becker's *Künstlerlexikon*.[31] Coinciding with the commencement of Denis Mahon's studies, however, Roberto Longhi brought his formidable intellectual armoury to bear on Guercino, stressing the Ferrarese roots of the artist's style, in *Officina Ferrarese* (Florence, 1934), and repeating this in an article published the following year, 'Momenti della pittura bolognese'.[32]

Not long after starting work, Sir Denis bought his first painting by the artist, *Jacob blessing the Sons of Joseph* (cat.44), which he acquired during a visit to Paris in 1934, and two years later bought a second, similar picture, *Elijah fed by Ravens* (cat.43), from the Barberini family in Rome. Both paintings were executed in 1620, when Guercino was twenty-nine. To a modern viewer, they are perhaps not 'easy' works; that is to say, they are not lyrical, elegiac or tender, as are some of Guercino's other paintings and many of Guido Reni's; nor, on the other hand, are they tense and violent, like Caravaggio's. The colours are subdued, the tones predominantly dark, and the principal figures are bearded, balding, large-boned elderly men whose knees and feet project outwards towards the spectator's space.

Like all the great Italian figure painters from Giotto to Raphael, and then again, following the Mannerist interlude, from the Carracci onwards, Guercino centres his works on the telling of an important story, paying due attention to the demands of both narrative and psychology, so that, whatever else the painting may be 'about', the episode depicted is clear to the viewer. And Guercino does this more conscientiously than most, not only in his early works but throughout his career. What is more, he does it without frills. However great his inventive powers – and they are very great – however unfailing his technical abilities and however bold his compositions, there is a down-to-earth, essentially workmanlike quality to Guercino; indeed, one can fairly add the word 'businesslike', as his careful keeping of accounts, recording the prices paid for his pictures and the names of those for whom the pictures were painted, in his later years shows.

It is not surprising that Guercino appeals so strongly to Denis Mahon, who has, if one may be permitted to say so, a similar clarity of purpose, singleness of mind, capacity for attending to detail, and shrewd sense of the practical. Although his collection includes some pictures whose charm any uninstructed art-lover can readily respond to – such as the late *Cumaean Sibyl* (cat.48) by Guercino – his taste is a highly educated one, based on a thorough understanding of the artistic values that were prized by artists and patrons of the Seicento itself. And what were those values – besides clarity of narrative and the rendering of human feeling by means of gestures and expressions? Here are some of them: nobility of form which is nevertheless dependent on knowledge of the structure of actual human bodies; the power of making the transcendental physically credible; the capacity to organise a composition; the belief that the gamut of human emotions and experiences – love in all its forms, ecstasy, terror, awe, curiosity, resignation, and so on – is best rendered in terms of biblical narratives, classical history and mythology.

The visitor to this exhibition must therefore be prepared to make an effort to sympathise with the artist's aims, enjoying as well the pleasure of being knocked off his or her feet from time to time by some flash of painterly virtuosity or poignant expression of sentiment. Whenever Sir Denis speaks about the paintings he owns, one is very aware, too, of his satisfaction in the fact that many of them are securely anchored in the documentation of their time; we know, because he has been able to find out, exactly when, where and for whom these paintings were executed. Such an ability to recreate the circumstances in which a given painting was produced, combined with the presence of the painting itself on his walls, is what, for Sir Denis, makes art history 'come alive'.

It is also no surprise to learn that, having first done the preliminary reading, he set off in or about 1935 to tour Britain and the Continent in search of Guercino's paintings and drawings. He went as far as Russia, though naturally concentrated on the area including Cento, Ferrara and Bologna. As guide and travelling companion, he took with him Otto Kurz, and Sir Ernst Gombrich has described in a charming memoir of Kurz[33] how their journeys were of great benefit to both scholars. The results, both appearing in 1937, were Kurz's fundamental study of Guido Reni in the Vienna *Jahrbuch*[34] and Mahon's 'Notes on the Young Guercino' in the *Burlington Magazine*.[35] In this article, Sir Denis analyses some of the paintings, including frescoes, produced by Guercino in and near Cento around 1614, and shows precisely how they were

Fig.4 Guercino, *The Burial and Reception into Heaven of Saint Petronilla*, 1623. Oil on canvas, 720 x 423 cm. Rome, Capitoline Gallery.

materials and stylistic analysis must be made to work together, and finally his conviction that what ultimately matters is the character of the work of art and how it came to have that character. This is, of course, an empiricist, profoundly English kind of approach. The theoretical armature of Hegelian determinism that sustained the Austro-German tradition of art history, with which Mahon had become familiar through his reading and through listening to Pevsner's lectures, has been silently dropped.

Seicento painting at last began to receive its due in England in 1938, with an important *Exhibition of 17th Century Art in Europe* at the Royal Academy,[36] organised chiefly by Ellis Waterhouse; to it Denis Mahon lent his *Elijah fed by Ravens* – the first of countless loans from his collection to exhibitions. Then, in 1939, he bought the warmly coloured, richly toned and classically composed *Coronation of the Virgin* by Annibale Carracci, which is datable to just after the artist's arrival in Rome in 1595 (cat.8; now in the Metropolitan Museum, New York – it is one of the very few paintings which Sir Denis has sold); and in 1941 he was able to buy Guercino's large painting, *Saint Gregory the Great with Saints Ignatius Loyola and Francis Xavier* (cat.47). In the six years before the war, Sir Denis also acquired a dozen Guercino drawings, including a powerful study (cat.94) for the artist's painting, *The Assassination of Amnon*, and another (cat.97) for *The Martyrdom of Saints John and Paul*, now in Toulouse.

Both the *Elijah fed by Ravens* and the *Saint Gregory* were to feature in Denis Mahon's ground-breaking book, *Studies in Seicento Art and Theory*, which was published by the Warburg Institute in 1947. It is worth looking at this book at some length. Its basic plan is lucid, even simple. Part I deals with Guercino's change of style from a dynamic, painterly 'Baroque' manner in his early period to a quieter, more orderly and more 'classical' manner characteristic of his later years. This change is plotted by the author by means of a series of comparative analyses of 'early' and 'late' paintings, analyses which are carried out on Wölfflinian lines. Guercino's change of style did not complete itself overnight, of course, but its beginning can be assigned to a definite period and indeed to a specific picture: the immense altarpiece representing *The Burial of Saint Petronilla* (fig.4), which the artist painted for St Peter's during the last six months of his stay in Rome from the summer of 1621 to the summer of 1623.

Sir Denis's analysis – to keep to examples included in the present exhibition – runs roughly as follows. The *Elijah*, painted in Ferrara in 1620, is characterised by scattered lights, spontaneous movements, and diagonals both on the surface and extending into depth – diagonals made up of the figure's limbs, the tilt of his head, the awkward twist of his body, and the contrasting angles of the stone slab and the scroll at the lower right. Moreover, although the composition itself is not unbalanced, the action – the dropping of the food by the ravens into Elijah's outstretched cloak – takes place off-centre, at the top right. Compare this with *The Presentation of Jesus in the Temple* (cat.45), painted only three years or so later, just after Guercino's return from Rome. The figure of Joseph, with his jutting-out knee and sharply turned body, still has something of the appearance of Elijah, but he is at once smaller and set further back in space, so that he becomes part of the line-up of figures stretched across the composition in a more-or-less single plane parallel to the picture surface. The

indebted to, and differed from, the work of, on the one hand, Ludovico Carracci in Bologna and, on the other, that of the Ferrarese artist, Lo Scarsellino. He remarks on the 'vivacity and easy fluidity of movement' of Guercino's forms at this early date and makes the important point that the artist's lighting, which had often been supposed to derive from Caravaggio, in fact does nothing of the kind but stems ultimately from the North Italian tradition of Correggio and the Venetians. What is equally striking about this article, however, is the degree to which Denis Mahon's methods as an art historian are already apparent, almost fully formed. Here we find his erudition, his thoroughness, his acute visual sense, his intolerance of hasty judgements and loose thinking, his insistence that every statement must be backed up by solid evidence, either verbal or visual, his belief – which is perhaps another way of putting the same thing – that documentary source

Christ Child and the extended hands of the priest, which together comprise the focus of the action, are now centrally placed and come somewhere near the apex of a stable pyramid whose base is defined by the steps. This painting has an almost Annibale Carracci-like compactness and harmony, as several scholars have observed.

The *Saint Gregory* of 1625 is also a more symmetrically arranged and more firmly constructed composition than Guercino's pre-Roman works. The great bulk of the three principal figures and the fact that they occupy the front plane of the picture, filling almost the entire space, make this in some ways a less 'advanced' and more Baroque work than the *Presentation*, where the figures are calmer and have more room to breathe; they are also more evenly lit. Yet no one ever said that Guercino's stylistic development had to progress in a straight line, and the differences can be accounted for by the difference in purpose: the *Saint Gregory* is an altarpiece, and the artist, at this stage of his career, may be said to have instinctively given it a certain Baroque strength in order to make a sufficient impact, whereas the *Presentation* was for a private collector and could therefore be more restrained.

After the *Saint Gregory*, there is a twenty-six-year gap in the sequence of paintings by Guercino in the Mahon collection until *The Cumaean Sibyl with a Putto* (cat.48), dating from 1651, and the sequence is completed by *The Angel appears to Hagar and Ishmael* (cat.49) of two years later. By now, the change in the artist's style is, of course, fully realised – indeed, Sir Denis believes this to have occurred by the mid-1630s. The main differences lie in the greater degree of idealisation and simplification. The poses are elegant, the bodies are svelte, and the draperies smoothly flow. The figures are self-contained instead of being partially dissolved into a larger whole, and the light tends to define forms rather than break them up. The dramatic temperature is lowered, and the protagonists appear to 'bottle up' their emotions rather than express them openly by extravagant gestures and expressions.

The principal point made in Part I of *Studies in Seicento Art and Theory*, after the analysis of Guercino's change of style itself, is that that change, starting in 1623, had an external cause. While in Rome, that is to say, Guercino is overwhelmingly likely to have met and thence to have come under the influence of Monsignor Giovanni Battista Agucchi, the Secretary to the newly elected Pope Gregory XV.[37] Agucchi was a passionate devotee of the arts and a dedicated exponent of the classic-idealist theory of painting. He was also a long-standing protector of Domenichino, who had been in Rome (not quite continuously) since the beginning of the century. Mahon proposes that it was in response to the example of Domenichino's work as praised and provided with a theoretical justification by Agucchi that Guercino consciously reorientated his style in a classicising direction. Furthermore, he argues that, in doing so, Guercino was going against the grain of his own nature – a hypothesis supported by the fact that his drawings do not share the same classicising tendency. The 'true' Guercino was thus the early, progressive, 'Baroque' artist, the one that chiefly appealed to Sir Denis's own taste, at any rate in the first instance.[38] This was not, incidentally, a novelty, for most critics since the seventeenth century had expressed the same preference, and Marangoni's two articles of 1920 were explicitly designed to show that only in his early work was Guercino true to himself, whereas

in later years he was conforming to what patrons expected of him.

In Part II of the book, Agucchi takes centre stage as the author of the *Trattato della Pittura*, written in about 1615 and printed in an incomplete form as an anonymous insertion in the preface to a rare book published in 1646,[39] fourteen years after his death. Sir Denis discusses the contents of this treatise, the details of which need not concern us here except to note that they contradict the anti-naturalist trend of late sixteenth-century treatises on art and anticipate the more normative (though still idealising) theory expounded in Bellori's *Idea*. In Part III, Sir Denis looks at the records of the Accademia di San Luca in the 1590s, and finds that, despite the efforts of the *Principe*, Federico Zuccaro, to establish an interest in theory in that institution, he apparently failed, and thus there was no body of official doctrine to oppose the artistic innovations of the anti-academic Caravaggio.

It was Part IV, entitled 'The Construction of a Legend: The Origins of the Classic and Eclectic Misinterpretations of the Carracci', that had the most far-reaching impact. This is Sir Denis's famous demolition of the traditional view that a conscious programme of eclecticism underlay the approach to art of Ludovico, Agostino and Annibale Carracci, and, in assessing the value of Mahon's campaign today, it is important to appreciate the background against which it was carried out. The term 'eclectic' was first linked to the Carracci in the late eighteenth century, as we have seen, and its use persisted right into the twentieth century even among art historians endeavouring to rehabilitate the Seicento as a whole.[40] Thus the Carracci were always being dragged down, as it were, by comparison with other Seicento painters. There was undoubtedly a real abuse here for Denis Mahon to abuse. And because the leading modern authority on the humanistic, or 'classic-idealist', theory of art, Rensselaer Lee, had attempted in his review of *Studies in Seicento Art and Theory*[41] to reinstate the use of 'eclectic', albeit in a modified way, Sir Denis returned to the question, adducing additional evidence, in a long article in 1953.[42]

The evidence and the arguments involved in interpreting Sir Denis's position are necessarily complex, but the basic issues, as so often with him, are relatively simple. The objections to 'eclectic' or 'eclecticism' as a label to attach to the Carracci are twofold. First, it is inherently implausible as a description of how a sixteenth- or seventeenth-century artist went about painting a picture. It is as if he were a cook aiming to produce the best possible dish by throwing into the pot a variety of ingredients that were delicious in themselves but disastrous as a mixture. That the Carracci were supposed to have done just this is based on a passage in the eulogy delivered by the writer Lucio Faberio at the funeral of Agostino Carracci in 1602. Agostino, he said, was gifted with 'The energy and assurance of Michelangelo, the softness and delicacy of Titian, the grace and majesty of Raphael, and the beauty and fluency of Correggio.'[43] However, it was one thing for Faberio to assert, with the exaggeration appropriate to a funeral address, that Agostino *possessed* these qualities; it was another for later critics to infer from this that he or any of the Carracci deliberately adopted a programme of combining the qualities of other artists as a theoretical doctrine.

The second objection is that, in Denis Mahon's view, no reliable evidence exists that any such doctrine was associated with any artist at the time. None of the seventeenth-century biographers mentions one, for example; and, while it is true that a sonnet published by Malvasia conveying a similar idea to Faberio's oration was once believed to have been written by Agostino Carracci about Niccolò dell'Abate, his authorship of this sonnet has since been questioned. Mahon also reveals that Faberio's speech, which was published in 1603 and reprinted by Malvasia, was adapted from the work of another author who used it in a different context, and emphasises that, although Faberio was secretary to the Carracci Academy in Bologna in the 1580s, he was a man of letters and not someone professionally concerned with the visual arts. In fact, the positive evidence that Sir Denis found for the working practices of the Carracci all points the other way, and suggests that they – and above all Annibale – were not self-consciously 'intellectual' artists at all; without being simply unreflecting craftsmen who produced imaginative results merely by instinct, they were men who did their thinking as part of the process of painting itself.

In 1977, a rejoinder to this interpretation appeared in the form of a short book by Charles Dempsey, *Annibale Carracci and the Beginnings of Baroque Style*.[44] Its argument is that, in relieving the Carracci of an inappropriate label, Sir Denis also deprived them of the power of reflecting on the wider problems of art as a whole, and in particular of the intellectual capacity first to perceive and then to find a way out of the impasse into which art in Northern Italy had fallen in the third quarter of the sixteenth century. However, it is Mahon's contention that, although theorists may have been affected by previous tendencies in artistic practice, artists – particularly during the crucial period from about 1580 to 1630, when so many fundamental innovations occurred – achieved their ends without the assistance of formalised theoretical doctrines; or, if they were influenced by theory, as in Guercino's case when he was affected by the stance of Agucchi, the results were not beneficial. The truth here may be that Mahon and Dempsey have a different idea of what constitutes artistic theory. For the former it is a rigid, abstract and ultimately impotent system, capable at best of responding intelligently to what had already happened (as Bellori did in his essay *Idea*). For the latter it is a body of general principles pointing to the exalted purposes which art could fulfil and with which the artist had the right, and even the duty, to associate himself. In the light of this conception, Dempsey makes a good deal of the role of the Carracci Academy in Bologna, seeing it as a forcing-house of ideas in which a whole community of young artists played their part under the leadership of Ludovico, Agostino and Annibale; in other words, it was far more than a mere drawing school. It is true that Malvasia's account gives some vague support to this interpretation, but one cannot help feeling that there is an element of wishful thinking, as well as guesswork, in the lengths to which Dempsey takes it. For Mahon, on the other hand, who followed a lead from Heinrich Bodmer,[45] the Carracci Academy was 'a very flourishing joint workshop at Bologna, frequented by numerous pupils and amateur admirers'.[46] Their conclusions reflect an absolute difference of method. For Sir Denis Mahon, as we have seen repeatedly, nothing can be assumed to be true unless it is supported by evidence. For Professor Dempsey, truth need not, or perhaps should not, be measured by such essentially pragmatic criteria. For all this, the

relationship between practice and theory remains one of the most perplexing problems in the study of seventeenth-century art, and not just of Italian art at that.

Studies in Seicento Art and Theory was the single most important influence, as Charles Dempsey himself has generously pointed out, in winning over the institutions of art history in Britain to the acceptance of Italian seventeenth-century painting as a major school of art. At the Courtauld Institute in the early 1950s, as the present writer can testify, the seventeenth century was *the* Special Period to study, although the fact that this was so was also due to the influence of Anthony Blunt, who invited Denis Mahon and Otto Kurz to give joint classes at the Institute. Carrying folders of black-and-white photographs, the two scholars were an unforgettable double act, for ever politely deferring to each other ('As Mr Mahon says...'; 'As Dr Kurz says...'). Another 'cell' of the new enthusiasm for the Seicento was the *Burlington Magazine* under its recently appointed editor, Benedict Nicolson, whose main field of interest was Caravaggism, and the Magazine has given constant support to Seicento studies under successive editors ever since. *Apollo Magazine* under Denys Sutton was not far behind. Important purchases of Seicento pictures were made by the Ashmolean and Fitzwilliam Museums and by the Birmingham City Art Gallery, though it took a little while longer for the National Gallery to come round. The publication of catalogues of the Bolognese drawings in the Royal Collection at Windsor Castle, beginning with John Pope-Hennessy's *The Drawings of Domenichino* (1948), was another sign of the times.[47] One could go on.

Directly the Second World War was over, Sir Denis's collection started to expand rapidly. In 1945, he bought the sublime late Guido Reni of the *Rape of Europa* (cat.63), which has been newly cleaned for the present exhibition. In the following year, he added Domenichino's *Landscape with a Fortified Town* (cat.22), also a late work of its creator and a painting which combines nobility of form with a sense of the freshness of nature; Sir Denis bought this together with a small *Holy Family* (cat.74) by Bartolomeo Schedoni, a Modenese artist who was an older contemporary of Guercino, at a sale of Seicento paintings from the famous Bridgewater Collection, which had been on view to the public until 1939. In 1946, too, he acquired the very early Guercino, *Madonna of the Sparrow* (cat.39) – a painting of unusual intimacy for the Seicento. His first 'late' Guercino, the *Hagar and the Angel*, which he bought in 1948, and the elegant, dignified and richly coloured *Cumaean Sibyl*, acquired in 1954, have already been mentioned. He also acquired a further 34 drawings by the artist to add to the dozen he bought before the war.[48]

Two other Bolognese paintings of his are worth describing briefly: Reni's *Saint Francis consoled by the Musician Angel* (cat.61) and Domenichino's *Vision of Saint Jerome* (cat.20). Although they are by different artists, by coincidence they have a number of similarities. Both were painted in Rome between about 1605 and 1610; both are on copper and of about the same size; and both show a seated or kneeling saint in the lower left 'triangle' with, in the opposite 'triangle', a flying angel (or two angels). A diagonal caesura running from lower right to top left separates the earthly and heavenly figures, and in the background of both compositions there is a rocky landscape. Both paintings show the influence of Annibale Carracci, indeed, Reni's *Saint Francis consoled by the Musician Angel* was once attributed to him. The two pictures are not, of course, identical in feeling or style. Reni's has the fluidity, *sfumato* and linear elegance typical of him, whereas Domenichino's forms are tougher and more austere (notice the strong hand of the saint as he grasps the crucifix). What is especially interesting about Domenichino's *Saint Jerome* is that it shows exactly the kind of control and formal compactness that Agucchi, in whose house the artist was then living, would later praise to Guercino. Foreshortenings are minimised, the figures are clearly separated from one another, the contours are well defined, and the lighting is relatively even.

As the above examples show, the core of Sir Denis's collection consists of works by the great Bolognese masters of the first half of the seventeenth century. Besides ten (originally eleven) paintings by Guercino, there are two (originally three) by Annibale Carracci, and four each by Domenichino and Guido Reni. Mahon also owns a *Holy Family* (cat.72) by Lo Scarsellino, who influenced the young Guercino, and three pictures (cats.15, 16, 17) by the much later Bolognese artist, Giuseppe Maria Crespi, who was influenced *by* Guercino. But this School is very far from constituting the whole of the collection.[49] Most conspicuously, there are ten large paintings of mythological subjects (cats.29–38) by the hugely productive, exuberantly Baroque painter of the second half of the seventeenth century, who was born in Naples but worked all over Italy, Luca Giordano. These paintings, acquired in 1950 and 1952, are *modelli*, or elaborated oil studies, for the artist's masterpiece, the enormous ceiling fresco in the galleria of the Palazzo Medici Riccardi in Florence, which Giordano executed for the Marchese Francesco Riccardi in 1682–5. Several of Giordano's eighteenth-century successors, too, are represented in Mahon's collection: Francesco Solimena, Antonio Pellegrini and Corrado Giaquinto.

Reverting to the seventeenth century, we find a small group of paintings by Genoese artists – an early Bernardo Strozzi (cat.78), a Gioacchino Assereto (cat.3) and a *Madonna and Child with the Infant Saint John* (cat.11) by Valerio Castello, a picture which Mahon bought as early as 1945. Giovanni Battista Gaulli (cat.25), the religious counterpart, as it were, to Luca Giordano, was also born and trained in Genoa, but made his career chiefly in Rome. The Roman School proper is represented by a beautiful Andrea Sacchi, *Saint Anthony of Padua reviving a Dead Man* (cat.70), a very early Pietro da Cortona, *The Oath of Semiramis* (cat.14), and paintings by two of Cortona's followers, Giovanni Francesco Romanelli and Ciro Ferri. Northern artists active in Italy are also well represented: Paul Bril, Pieter van Laer, Sébastien Bourdon, Gaspard Dughet, Johann Liss (whose *Fall of Phaeton*, cat.52, is a particular favourite of Mahon's), and the eighteenth-century French painter who settled early in Rome, Pierre Subleyras. In 1964, Sir Denis bought the early *Rebekah quenching the Thirst of Eliezer at the Well* (cat.60)[50] painted by Nicolas Poussin for Cassiano dal Pozzo, though this picture left the collection in 1977.

Two of the Northern artists just mentioned – Bril and Dughet – were full-time landscapists, and Sir Denis also owns landscape paintings by three Italians: Pier Francesco Mola, Salvator Rosa and Andrea Locatelli. The works by Mola and Rosa have all the power, breadth of handling and depth of tone of the Italian High Baroque. The Mola *Landscape with Saint Bruno in Ecstasy* (cat.56), which was probably painted in Venice, is especially romantic and bold, Rosa's *Landscape with Travellers asking the Way* (cat.66) shows the insertion of figures derived from the Dutch tradition into a purely Italianate landscape, and his two late, 'desolate' landscapes (cats.68 and 69) exemplify Rosa at his blackest and most menacing. Taken in conjunction with Sir Denis's preference for the early over the late Guercino and his ownership of ten spectacular *modelli* by Giordano, these landscapes may serve as a reminder that his tastes, while highly sophisticated and well informed, are pretty robust.

The Mahon collection as it exists today (with the addition of the three pictures that have been sold) was virtually completed by the mid-1960s. Until the late 1950s, the prices of these works were by modern standards very low, and, in the few years after the war, Seicento paintings which would now cost over a million pounds could sometimes be had for a few hundred. Sir Denis stopped buying when he did because, as he has explained,[51] of the huge rise in prices which began in the early 1960s and has never abated since. Although, like any collection, his contains some minor works and even one or two questionable attributions, what is astonishing is how few examples there are in either category. This is a collection not only of outstanding quality but also of exceptional coherence, from which one can learn as well as derive immense pleasure. In 1960, more than half of it, including almost all the most important pictures, was exhibited for the first time at the Royal Academy (*Italian Art and Britain*), with catalogue entries by Denis Mahon himself.[52]

Sir Denis may have practically given up collecting in the early 1970s; he did not give up art history. Indeed, even today, when he is well into his eighties, it is not too late to expect another meticulously argued article, memorandum or letter to come from his typewriter (one doesn't, somehow, see him using a computer). Since 1950, most of his work as an art historian has been connected with exhibitions, either as lender, as selector and cataloguer, or as commentator after the event. In writing after the event, as he frankly acknowledges, he enjoys advantages which the organiser of the exhibition, having had to prepare his catalogue entries without the pictures in front of him, was denied.

More important, Sir Denis regards the scholarly single-artist exhibition, in which as many as possible of that artist's paintings and drawings are brought together in one place, as the ideal forum in which to practise his kind of art history. To compare the works *in the original* side by side, to re-arrange them either mentally or, better still, literally,[53] in the order in which they might have been painted, is, in Denis Mahon's view, the best way to understand both individual paintings and the artist's creative personality: 'individual paintings', because, since visual qualities are of their nature relative, it is only by means of comparative analysis that they can be apprehended; 'the artist's creative personality', because this is best understood as the product of a succession of (usually small) steps, each one related to, yet different from, the last. This is the reason for the importance which Sir Denis attaches to reconstructing an artist's chronology; like making attributions, it is not an end in itself (as such it can be merely pedantic) but a

Fig.5 Caravaggio, *The Calling of Saint Mathew*, 1599–1600. Oil on canvas, 322 x 340 cm. Rome, San Luigi dei Francesi.

means to aesthetic understanding. As he put it in the first of his post-exhibition commentaries, or 'afterthoughts', an article centred on the dating of the *Scenes from the Life of Saint Matthew* (fig.5) by Caravaggio in the Contarelli Chapel, shown in the Caravaggio exhibition at Milan in 1951:

In the writer's view it is necessary (particularly when dealing with some special problem) to see the painter in question as a whole, and there is no better discipline to that end than seriously setting to work to devise a complete chronology.[54]

The chronology for Caravaggio that Sir Denis produced, particularly for the first half of the artist's career, differed markedly from that proposed in the exhibition catalogue by Roberto Longhi, who, he thought, had misinterpreted the available documentary evidence. Then, in a second article[55] written a few weeks later after studying the pictures again, this time in close-up and in a good light when the exhibition had ended, he revised his earlier chronology slightly and, very satisfactorily (though he did not then know it), arrived on stylistic grounds at a dating for the *Saint Matthew* series that was subsequently confirmed by the discovery in the early 1960s of the complete documentation for Caravaggio's work in the Chapel.[56]

Caravaggio, for Denis Mahon, was only a prelude, though an important one. What mainly preoccupied him for the next two decades was the great series of exhibitions of Bolognese painting held in alternate years at the Palazzo dell'Archiginnasio, Bologna, beginning in 1954 with Guido Reni. Of international importance and drawing specialist visitors from all over the Western world, these exhibitions finally set the seal on the rehabilitation of Seicento painting, making it popular with art historians and the general public alike. The principal organiser was the Soprintendente

for Emilia Romagna, Cesare Gnudi, and he was assisted by a loyal permanent team. Denis Mahon was very soon invited to join this team and became its most active member after Gnudi himself, with whom he formed a close professional and personal friendship. In 1956, Mahon wrote the separate volume devoted to the drawings for the catalogue of the Carracci exhibition, and in the following year published two more 'afterthoughts', doing for the chronology of Reni and the Carracci what he had previously done for that of Caravaggio.[57]

In 1962, he selected and catalogued the largest section, that devoted to Nicolas Poussin, in the next-but-one seventeenth-century exhibition to be held in Bologna, *L'Ideale Classico del Seicento in Italia e la Pittura di Paesaggio*.[58] His purpose here was partly to correct by demonstration the errors he had perceived in the cataloguing of the artist's work in the large Poussin exhibition at the Louvre in 1960. The present writer, who was invited to catalogue the Claude section of the *Ideale Classico* exhibition, may perhaps be forgiven for introducing at this point some reminiscences of Sir Denis at work. He and I arrived in Bologna about six weeks before the exhibition was due to open, having travelled together in the very old, unheated, propeller-driven cargo plane that carried the pictures lent from Britain. Sir Denis had brought with him the partly written drafts of his catalogue entries and he completed these, working long hours every day in the heat of a Bolognese August, with Poussin's pictures all around him – in the closest contact, in other words, with the actual works of art. Formally dressed as always, he took off his jacket as a concession to the prevailing temperature but did not, I think, remove his tie. His entries were ready about three weeks, or perhaps less, before the exhibition was due to begin. I remember the young Andrea Emiliani, three days before the opening, walking through the rooms carrying sheafs of proofs and calling out 'ultime bozze! ultime bozze!', as though the Bologna Pinacoteca had temporarily become a newspaper office. A sufficient number of bound copies of the catalogue, perhaps only a hundred, was, however, ready on the day.

In 1968, after more than thirty years of research by Sir Denis into the life and work of Guercino, his labours came to a triumphant climax (though still not yet a conclusion) in the comprehensive exhibition devoted to that artist in Bologna – the last in the series to be held at the Palazzo dell'Archiginnasio. Though benefiting from the organisational support provided by Cesari Gnudi and his colleagues at the Soprintendenza, *Guercino* was in every sense Denis Mahon's exhibition. The selection was largely his, and the contents of the two volumes of the catalogue – *Paintings* and *Drawings* – were his entirely.[59] Here for the first time he was able to deploy his thoughts across the entire range of Guercino's development. He divided the artist's work before the visit to Rome into no fewer than three phases: 'Early' (to 1617), 'Early Maturity' (1617–18), and 'Full Maturity' (1619–21). Then came the 'Roman Period' (1621–3), after that the 'Transitional Period' (to 1634), and finally the 'Late Period' (1634–66). To anyone who understands the rapid development normal to an artist in the first ten years of his career, followed by a gradual diminution in pace afterwards, it is no accident that the divisions Mahon chose become progressively longer. The exhibition contained over a hundred paintings, including all eleven from Mahon's own collec-

Fig.6 Nicolas Poussin, *Landscape with Diogenes throwing down his Drinking Bowl*, late 1650s. Oil on canvas, 160 x 221 cm. Paris, Musée du Louvre.

tion, and some 250 drawings, of which 35 were also lent by him. 'Transitional' and 'Late' works were exhibited to a degree unknown before, and it was generally agreed that Guercino after 1630 was often (though not always) a much finer artist than had previously been thought; indeed Sir Denis, too, had abandoned his former reservations about them.

The 1968 exhibition, however, was by no means the end of Denis Mahon's career as a Guercino scholar; it reached a new peak twenty years later, first with his *catalogue raisonné*, written in conjunction with Nicholas Turner and published in 1989, of the artist's drawings in the Royal Collection at Windsor Castle,[60] and secondly with a still larger exhibition, divided between the Museo Civico Archeologico in Bologna and two locations in Cento, which was held in 1991 to celebrate the quatercentenary of Guercino's birth. A good many more works by the artist had been identified since 1968, mostly by Mahon himself, and there was an even greater emphasis on the late work. Sir Denis took the opportunity in the catalogue to refine his earlier invaluable introductions to each of the six chronological periods into which he has divided Guercino's development, and he also, of course, added new catalogue entries. Reduced versions of this exhibition afterwards travelled to Frankfurt and Washington, and English-speaking readers will be glad to know that the catalogue for the latter (*Guercino: Master Painter of the Baroque*, 1992) contains the original texts, previously published only in Italian, of Mahon's introductions and of Diane De Grazia's essay on 'Guercino as a Decorator', as well as English translations of the essays by Andrea Emiliani and Sybille Ebert-Schifferer.[61]

Perhaps one of the hardest and most vexatious problems Sir Denis has ever tackled arose in connection with the Nicolas Poussin exhibition at the Louvre in 1960. Here he had a formidable opponent in Anthony Blunt, then at the height of his reputation as the leading international authority on the artist. Denis Mahon published no fewer than five separate 'afterthoughts',[62] in addition to the catalogue of the Poussin section of the *Ideale Classico* exhibition, which in a sense also served the same purpose, as has already been said. His disagreement with Blunt, who had catalogued the Louvre exhibition, was over Poussin's chronology, and it was focused mainly, though not exclusively, on the first half of the artist's career, before his visit to Paris in 1640. Whereas Blunt relied for the scaffolding of his chronology on the few securely dated pictures in this period and fitted the others around them on a more or less intuitive basis, Mahon took the argument a stage further by seeking a context for Poussin's stylistic development in the *colore* v. *disegno* and 'Baroque v. classical' debates taking place in Italian art and theory in the late 1620s and early 1630s. Although in a few individual cases Anthony Blunt may have been right, there is no doubt that on balance Denis Mahon had much the better of the argument, and his account of Poussin's development has generally been accepted by more recent scholars.[63]

In some instances, such as the dating of the well-known *Arcadian Shepherds* in the Louvre, he returned the picture to where it had usually been situated, that is, shortly before the artist's visit to Paris, instead of in the first half of the 1650s which Blunt had suggested. But in one case, that of the *Landscape with Diogenes throwing down his Drinking Bowl* (fig.6), also in the Louvre, Sir Denis was bolder, because he insisted on moving it at least ten years forward, from 1648 (the date apparently cited by Poussin's biographer, Félibien) to the late 1650s, which no one had thought of before. The passages in 'Réflexions sur les paysages de Poussin' and 'A Plea for Poussin as a Painter'[64] in which he argues this point of view are moving, meticulously detailed and, I believe, ultimately convincing.[65] To my mind, the second of these two articles is one of the finest things Sir Denis has ever written. It is so not least because it goes beyond questions of chronology and the bearing these have on our understanding of an artist's work and takes into account all those other factors which art historians have to consider, such as the artist's religious or philosophical beliefs, his attitude towards idealisation, his subject matter, the part played by his patrons, down to such mundane considerations as the present condition of his pictures and the consequences of cleaning. Sir Denis assesses all these factors according to how much light they throw on an artist's individual style, or personal contribution. Take subject matter, for instance. This can be of great interest in itself and it may also help to determine the mood of a picture; but it is not enough to study these things in isolation. What makes the work of art valuable is the gifts the artist brings to interpreting that subject matter and that mood; and these gifts can only be those of a painter – in Poussin's case a very great painter. Hence Sir Denis Mahon's plea. For a long time it seemed to fall on deaf ears. But it was surely answered in the Poussin exhibitions in Paris and London in 1994–5. Both through the manner in which those exhibitions were organised (especially the one in London) and in the way the public responded, the claims of Poussin as a painter were at last heard.

A final footnote: although Denis Mahon's collection has never included a painting by Francesco Guardi, he became interested in that artist in the mid-1960s, inspired by two exhibitions in Venice. In 1967, he published 'The Brothers at the Mostra dei Guardi: Some Impressions of a Neophyte',[66] and in 1968, 'When did Francesco Guardi become a *Vedutista*?'[67] The titles of these two articles speak for themselves, and the answer to the question asked in the second was 'in the early 1750s'.

As was said at the beginning of this essay, Sir Denis is not only a great art historian and art collector; he is also a zealous guardian of the public interest. He has a deep love especially of the National Gallery, of which he has twice been a Trustee (1957–64 and 1966–73), of the Ashmolean Museum and of the National Gallery of Ireland, to all three of which he intends to bequeath parts of his collection. At the same time, he has a well-founded suspicion of the good faith, so far as policy towards the visual arts is concerned, both of Government ministers (of whichever political party) and of Treasury officials; nothing is 'safe', he feels, unless it is protected by legislation. To achieve this objective he does not make public speeches or organise petitions; his means of communication are one-to-one conversation and the written word, either in the form of memoranda for submission to parliamentary committees and civil servants or of letters to *The Times*. Crucially, he knows his way around Whitehall and how to speak the language of politicians and civil servants; he knows at least as much about the financial aspects of the subject in hand as they do, and often more; and he never gives up.

He began in the mid-1950s with a campaign to defeat a Government Bill to empower the National Gallery to sell ('de-accession') paintings in its collection – a disastrous procedure if it had been implemented. Next, with Hugh Leggatt, he spearheaded a campaign, which engaged the whole art world, against an attempt by the Conservative Government in 1973 to compel museums and galleries to charge visitors for entry. Here the objection was that, since the contents of public collections were the property of the nation, people should not be charged for going to see what they already owned; moreover, to insist on charges would be at once a breach of faith with past donors and testators and a deterrent to future ones (as, indeed, would be the power to sell).

Perhaps even more exhausting were Sir Denis's repeated fights with the Treasury during the 1970s and early 1980s, under Governments of both parties, to safeguard the national heritage from the danger of a flood of enforced sales abroad of works of art in private collections. The practice of the Treasury of taking away with one hand what it gave with the other – as with the restrictive controls placed on the 'acceptance-in-lieu' provision, whereby works of art could be surrendered to the nation in part settlement of estate duty – was a constant bone of contention. The defeat of these and other measures, the effect of which had been to encourage sales abroad and to discourage sales to public collections in Britain, was largely due to Denis Mahon's courage and persistence. In such cases he often acted in the interests of the National Art Collections Fund, of whose Advisory Panel he has been a member since 1975. But perhaps his greatest triumph – greatest in its consequences at any rate – was the part he played, in conformity with the policy of the NACF, in persuading a Parliamentary Select Committee to recommend the conversion of the Land Fund (which had been set up in 1946 as a memorial to those who had given their lives for their country and which had been conveniently 'forgotten' by the Treasury ever since) into a National Heritage Memorial Fund with independent trustees. When this Fund was established by Act of Parliament in 1980, it was the most generous official support preferred to the heritage until the cascade of lottery money began in 1995.

It says something for the decencies of public life in this country, of which pockets do remain despite present rumours to the contrary, that Whitehall gave its blessing in 1986 to a Knighthood for Denis Mahon, who has often, let it be admitted, made life difficult for politicians and civil servants during the past forty years. But he has always been an honourable foe, and no one would doubt that the accolade is richly deserved. And if Whitehall has been an occasional sufferer, the art world and the British public have, in a much wider sense, been the beneficiary. The National Gallery thanks him through this exhibition for his scholarship, his collection, his championing of a once despised school of art, and for all he has done to preserve and enhance the artistic heritage of this country.

NOTES

1 For Winckelmann's principal writings see Winckelmann 1755 and Winckelmann 1764.
2 On this see Mahon 1947, pp.212ff.
3 Royal Academy Lecture XI, 1806; see Knowles 1831, p.36.
4 Mahon 1947, pp.212ff.
5 *Aphorism* No.104; Knowles 1831, p.100. Fuseli's *Aphorisms* appear to have been written over a longish period, from about 1788 to about 1818.
6 Ruskin 1903–12. In order of citation: Vol.IV, p.213; Vol.III, p.184; Vol.IV, p.203f.
7 Haskell 1976, pp.95–6. Haskell gives a fascinating account of the cross-currents in English taste in the middle decades of the nineteenth century.
8 'We now come to works representative of the decay of the various schools which we have already surveyed – exhibited not, as is the case in many continental galleries, side by side with works of the golden age of Italian art, but hung together in a room devoted to its decadence.' Cook 1897, p.33.
9 For a detailed survey of the ups and downs of Guercino's reputation in England, which may be taken as representative of the changing fortunes of Bolognese painting as a whole in this country, see F. Russell, 'Guercino in England', in London (National Gallery) 1991, pp.4–10.
10 See the concluding section to Riegl 1908. This book was put together by colleagues from Riegl's notes for his lectures given at Vienna in the 1890s, and published after his early death.
11 Wölfflin 1915. Probably the most important translations published during the 1950s and 1960s are the following: (1) *Mannerism and Anti-Mannerism in Italian Painting*, by W. Friedlaender, New York, 1957 (paperback edn., with a good introduction by D. Posner, New York 1965) – originally published in German as two separate articles in 1925 and 1930; (2) three articles by N. Pevsner – 'The Counter-Reformation and Mannerism', 'Early

and High Baroque', and 'The Crisis of 1650 in Italian Painting' – published in German periodicals between 1925 and 1932 and included in the author's volume of essays, *Studies in Art, Architecture and Design*, Vol.I, New York, 1968; (3) E. Panofsky, *Idea*, Leipzig, 1924; in English published by University of South Carolina Press 1968.

12 There have been many critiques of the theoretical basis of Wölfflin's system, of which two in English may be mentioned here: an essay by E. Gombrich, 'Norm and Form', in his book of the same title, London 1966, and chapters VI and VII in M. Podro, *The Critical Historians of Art*, New Haven and London, 1982.

13 See Sutton 1978.

14 Longhi 1951; Longhi 1952, reviewed by Denis Mahon in *The Burlington Magazine*, 95 (1953), pp.212–20.

15 Florence 1922.

16 There has also, of course, been a long tradition of Old Master exhibitions in Britain. But until the 1950s they rarely had the same sense of cultural or scholarly purpose; they were more an *omnium gatherum*, where the aim was to bring together whatever could be borrowed within the limits of the exhibition's theme.

17 However, some art history courses were already being given in Scottish universities.

18 London (Royal Academy) 1930, p.xiv. As early as 1922, Witt had bought, in a single lot and no doubt very cheaply, 68 out of the large collection of drawings by Guercino and members of his studio sold at auction that year by the Earl of Gainsborough. Although he was a voracious rather than a discriminating collector, Witt would hardly have acquired these Guercinos if he had actively disliked them. About half of them, including some very fine examples, were bequeathed to the Courtauld Institute in 1952.

19 Briggs 1914. (This article is not as long as the page references suggest, as about half of it is taken up by illustrations.)

20 Fry 1921. The review by H.D. Waley of the English translation of Wölfflin when it came out (*The Burlington Magazine*, 62 (1933), pp.246–7) was much shorter and weaker.

21 Fry 1926, pp. 95–124.

22 Gamba 1922. Even more than Briggs on Bernini, this article is largely illustrations.

23 Mahon 1937.

24 Mention may also be made here of Jacob Hess, the editor of *Die Künstlerbiographien von Giovanni Battista Passeri*, Leipzig/Vienna 1934, and a leading Seicento scholar from the 1920s to the 1960s. Exiled from Germany like so many others in 1933, he moved to Rome and was only in London from 1939 to 1948, where, however, Mahon learnt much from him in 'innumerable casual conversations', as he acknowledges in a footnote to *Studies in Seicento Art and Theory* (Mahon 1947), p.1.

25 Waterhouse 1937. Published as an 'occasional volume' annexed to the papers of the British School in Rome, 1937; revised and enlarged edition, published as *Roman Baroque Painting*, Oxford 1976 (Waterhouse 1976).

26 This interview, with Umberto Allemandi, was originally published in Italian in *Il Giornale dell'Arte* in September 1985, and afterwards in English translation in the National Art Collections Fund Magazine, *Art Quarterly*, Autumn, 1986.

27 Clark has recalled in his autobiography, *Another Part of the Wood* (London 1974, pp.105, 123–4), how he came to 'rather like it'. His predecessor at the Ashmolean, C.F. Bell, was a man whose taste 'stopped short soon after 1810', and, when he accompanied Clark on the latter's first visit to Italy in 1925, insisted that they stay first in Bologna before going on to Florence – something which Clark always recalled with gratitude.

28 In 1933, Pevsner had already published the volume on Mannerism and Baroque in the *Handbuch der Kunstwissenschaft* series, in addition to the three articles whose English titles are cited here in note 11. These articles give a vivid idea of the flavour of Pevsner's early writings.

29 Respectively (apart from Longhi on Caravaggio, for whom see note 14): Tietze 1906; Bodmer 1939; Kurz 1937; Posse 1919.

30 Serra 1909.

31 Marangoni: 'Il vero Guercino' was first published in *Dedalo*, 1 (1920), pp.17–40 and 133–42; re-written in 'Il Guercino' (*Piccola Collezione d'Arte*), 1920, and *Arte Barocca*, 1927, pp.69–83. Voss: Thieme-Becker *Künstlerlexikon*, Leipzig, 1922, vol. 15, pp.216–22.

32 Respectively, Longhi 1934, and Longhi 1935.

33 Gombrich 1984, pp.234–49.

34 See Kurz 1937.

35 Mahon 1937.

36 London (Royal Academy) 1938.

37 Gregory XV was of Bolognese origin, and it was as a result of his election in 1621 that Guercino was summoned to Rome; his unexpected death two years later destroyed the artist's hopes of further employment in the city, hence his return to Cento. Agucchi was also a member of a noble Bolognese family.

38 Since 1947 Sir Denis's appreciation of Guercino's later works has enormously increased. This is explained in his catalogue of the 1968 Guercino exhibition (Mahon (Dipinti) 1968, pp. 63–4), in which he points out that in the 1930s, when he began to study Guercino's paintings, not one of them was in clean state; and in the case of the late paintings this meant that the delicate colour harmonies which are so essential a feature of them had become completely obscured.

39 For further particulars of this book, see Mahon 1947, p.113.

40 For example, Roger Fry in the essay on 'The Seicento' in *Transformations* (1926), p.110: 'The Carracci,... intensely self-conscious and theoretical as they were...'. Or Lionello Venturi, *History of Art Criticism*, New York, 1936: 'Their mode of reaction to Mannerism was therefore indirect, born of the need to know the values of art rather than to create them, so that they allowed their personalities to develop on the basis of their doctrine rather than on their mode of feeling' (p.110 in paperback edition, New York 1964).

41 Lee 1951. His fundamental article, '*Ut Pictura Poesis*: The Humanistic Theory of Painting', had appeared in the *Art Bulletin*, 22, 1940, pp.197–269, and was reprinted with the same title as a separate paperback, New York 1967.

42 Mahon 1953.

43 Mahon 1953, p.308.

44 Dempsey 1977.

45 Bodmer 1935. In this article the informal and entrepreneurial character of the Academy is stressed, distinguishing it from the official academies of Florence and Rome, with their rules and hierarchy of officers.

46 Mahon 1947, p.228, note 86.

47 Pope-Hennessy 1948. See also Wittkower 1952; Kurz 1955; and, the largest of them all, Mahon/Turner 1989.

48 The complete Mahon collection of Guercino drawings was first exhibited at Cento in 1967 (see Mahon (Collezione) 1967), and then again at the Ashmolean Museum and at Hazlitt, Gooden & Fox, London, in 1986 (Mahon/Ekserdjian 1986); in both cases, the catalogue was written by Sir Denis himself, though in the latter instance with modifications by Helen Davies, to which he added revisions. The 1986 catalogue was originally published as a supplement to the March issue of the *Burlington Magazine* for that year (Vol.128) and then again as a *separatum*.

49 This is perhaps the moment to refer to the article by Giuliano Briganti (Briganti 1953) which was published when the collection was already almost two-thirds complete and which remains useful especially for paintings other than those by Bolognese artists.

50 Published by Denis Mahon: Mahon 1965b.

51 In the interview cited in note 26.

52 London 1960.

53 He usually takes the trouble to persuade the organisers to let him view the exhibition, aided by a lamp and step-ladder, out of normal opening hours, and physically to move the pictures around, propping them against the wall, after the exhibition has closed.

54 Mahon 1951a.

55 Mahon 1951b.

56 Röttgen 1964 and 1965. Among the various documents published in these articles were the crucial ones showing that Caravaggio received the contract for the *Calling* and *Martyrdom of Saint Matthew* on 23 July 1599 and was paid for these two paintings on 4 July 1600. It also emerged that both the first, rejected altarpiece representing *Saint Matthew and the Angel* and the second one, now *in situ*, were probably painted in quick succession in 1602–3. (Mahon's proposal on this score was less accurate.)

57 Respectively, Mahon 1956, Mahon 1957a and Mahon 1957b.

58 Bologna 1962.

59 Respectively Mahon (Dipinti) 1968 and Mahon (Disegni) 1969.

60 Mahon/Turner 1989.

61 Washington 1992. Diane de Grazia, 'Guercino as a Decorator', pp.41–73; Andrea Emiliani, 'Guercino: From Natural Talent to the Romanticism of Reality?', pp.11–40; Sybille Ebert-Schifferer, '"Ma c'hanno da fare i precetti dell'oratore con quelli della pittura?" Reflections on Guercino's Narrative Structure', pp. 75–110.

62 These were Mahon 1960a; Mahon 1960b; Mahon 1961; Mahon 1962; Mahon 1965.

63 In dealing with Poussin's first half-dozen years in Rome, more recent scholars have, it is true, tended to shift most paintings backwards by a year or two, to fill up the period 1624–6, directly after the artist's arrival in the city, which Mahon had left rather empty. However, his present view is that since those distant days around 1960, it has become reasonable to deduce, though largely by inference, what Poussin could have been painting up to 1627. He found most useful in this regard the assemblage of early work by Poussin (including some discovered since 1960) which was exhibited in the Kimbell Museum at Fort Worth in 1988 (Oberhuber 1988). His conclusions, which do not coincide with the sequence suggested in the catalogue, have not, however, been published. Nevertheless the broad pattern of Poussin's development up to 1640 as proposed by Denis Mahon has been retained. It may be noted in passing that his analysis of that development by reference to contemporary Italian painting has not been welcomed by French scholars who, ever since the mid-nineteenth century, have been uncomfortable with the idea that Poussin was part of the Roman art world, as distinct from being a French artist living in Rome (which he also was, of course).

64 For the references see note 62.

65 Here I must introduce another personal reminiscence. When I originally read these articles not long after they were published, I was persuaded by them that Mahon's revisions of Blunt's chronology, including the later dating of the *Diogenes*, were mostly correct. However, in the catalogue of the Poussin exhibition in Paris in 1994, the traditional date for this picture was reaffirmed, and the picture itself was hung close to other landscapes of 1648–51, a long way distant from the late landscapes by the master. After some hesitation I came to the conclusion that '1648' was right after all, and said so in my review of the exhibition in the *Burlington Magazine*, 137 (January 1995), pp.28–34, to which Sir Denis replied in March (pp.176–82). By then, the corresponding exhibition at the Royal Academy in London was in progress, and, a few days before it ended in April, I had the privilege of two hour-long 'tutorials' from Sir Denis in front of the landscapes, which were now all hung in the same large gallery and in a much better light than they had been in Paris. In the course of these discussions, which I enjoyed immensely, he convinced me that 1658–60 *was* correct for the *Diogenes*, as he had maintained for the past thirty years. In point of fact, I found the clinching argument to reside in the treatment of the figures, which are remarkably similar to that of Orion in the picture of that title of the same date (New York, Metropolitan Museum) and of those in the *Baptism of Christ* in Philadelphia, also of about 1658. The interpretation of the landscape (of the *Diogenes*), on the other hand, may have become a touch more problematic from the point of view of style than it appeared in the 1960s, owing to the discovery of new paintings and some other factors; but that is another story and doesn't alter the late dating of this picture. I wish to put this episode on record, partly as a confession of a double change of mind and partly as a tribute to the fascination of Sir Denis's conversation, his powers of persuasion, and the acuteness of his eye.

66 Mahon 1967.

67 Mahon 1968.

Francesco Albani 1578–1660

1 *The Trinity with the Virgin Mary and Musician Angels*

Oil on copper, 41.9 x 31.4 cm

The Virgin Mary kneels before the Holy Trinity in heaven. God the Father raises his hand in blessing and Christ points to the wound on his side; the dove of the Holy Spirit is just discernible between them, surrounded by divine radiance. The instruments played by the angels are, clockwise from lower left: a *viola da gamba*, a tambourine and a *cornetto*; in the centre is a small organ, a sacbut, and a *viola a mano* (or early violin).

The painting is on copper, a support which was particularly favoured by artists from Bologna in the later sixteenth century (see cat. 61). Denys Calvaert, the Flemish-born painter who settled in Bologna and was the teacher of both Reni and Albani, frequently painted on copper and transmitted this practice to his pupils.[1] These panels, which were sometimes worn-out engraving plates, tended to be used for small-scale figure compositions of particularly delicate execution, like the present picture.

Albani left Calvaert's workshop in about 1595 and went to study in the Academy of the Carracci. There under Ludovico (who took charge of the Academy after the departure for Rome of his younger cousins Agostino and Annibale) he practised drawing from the model and assisted in the execution of large painting projects.[2] Through Ludovico, Albani obtained his first public commissions: the altarpiece for the Bolognese church of San Fabiano e San Sebastiano showing the *Virgin and Child enthroned with Saints Catherine and Mary Magdalene* (Bologna, Pinacoteca Nazionale), which is dated 1599, and the *Risen Christ appearing to the Virgin* in the Oratorio di San Colombano of 1599–1600. However, both works tend towards the classicising manner of Annibale Carracci rather than the stern and more ponderous style of Ludovico. In 1601 Albani went to Rome with Guido Reni, and there joined Annibale, becoming his most trusted assistant. He enjoyed considerable success in Rome and subsequently in Bologna, where he returned in 1617. He received numerous commissions for altarpieces, but above all he painted cabinet pictures of great charm showing religious and mythological subjects; these were especially admired in France.[3]

The painting was attributed to Albani by Giuliano Briganti in an article in *Connoisseur* in 1953 describing the Mahon collection. He considered that the work showed the influence of both Ludovico and Annibale and dated it to 1598–9.[4] Subsequently, similarities have been identified between the typologies of the Virgin and angels, and certain figures in the frescoes showing scenes from the *Aeneid* that Albani painted in Palazzo Fava in these years.[5] It has also been suggested that the picture might be identified with a work by Albani which the eighteenth-century connoisseur-collector, Marcello Oretti, saw in the collection of Petronio Landi in Bologna: 'Copper, in which one may see the Holy Trinity in a glory of Angels, and one of his [Albani's] finest works.'[6]

TECHNICAL NOTE
The copper panel is quite thin. There are scattered retouchings throughout the picture but it is generally in good condition. Examination by infra-red reflectography revealed that there is a considerable amount of brush underdrawing. It is visible to the naked eye in the area of the wings of the angel on the right playing the sacbut. There are some pentimenti, notably the left hand of the tambourine-playing angel was in a different position, as was the right hand of Christ. The robe of Christ has been reduced in size on the right-hand side.

PROVENANCE
Acquired by the present owner at Christie's, London, 17 October 1952, lot 130 ('Domenichino, The Trinity').

EXHIBITIONS
Not previously exhibited.

1 Malvasia records that Reni and Albani painted works on copper which were then signed by Calvaert (1841, I, p.200).
2 There is no up-to-date monograph on Albani; but see Boschetto 1948, two unpublished doctoral dissertations by Van Schaak (1970) and Puglisi (1983), and the following articles: Puglisi 1981 and Benati 1981.
3 See Paris 1988–9, pp.106–9, and Brejon de Lavergnée and Volle 1988, pp.34–41.
4 Briganti 1953, pp.5 and 16, no.1.
5 Puglisi 1981, p.35.
6 'Rame, sul quale vedesi pinta la SS.ma Trinità in gloria d'Angioli, e delle migliori sue opere' (Bologna, Biblioteca Comunale, manuscript B.27, f.451), quoted in Puglisi 1981, p.45, note 34.

Studio of Francesco Albani 1578–1660
2 Faith, Hope and Charity

Oil on canvas, 41.7 x 56.2 cm

The three women represent the Theological Virtues, so-called because these virtues relate immediately to God, in contrast to the Cardinal Virtues (Prudence, Justice, Fortitude and Temperance) which relate to the earthly realm. The figure of Faith on the left holds the chalice and host of the sacrament. Charity, fruitful and generous, provides sustenance for her three children; the pomegranates which appear on the tree above are commonly a symbol of charity.[1] Hope is represented with an anchor and column base, signifying security and steadfastness. There was a well-established iconographical tradition for the representation of the Virtues.[2] Here the subject matter is invested with considerable charm by the graceful poses and gestures, the bright colours, and by the landscape beyond the elegant stone dais on which the figures sit.

The painting would appear to be a studio copy of a lost picture by Albani which was bequeathed in 1676, with the rest of his collection, to the church of Madonna di Galliera in Bologna by Conte Ettore Ghisilieri.[3] Three paintings by Albani from the bequest were removed by the French in 1796 and taken to Paris and from the descriptions made at the time we know that they were on copper.[4] In addition to the 'Vertus théologales' there was a *Christ served by Angels* (now Grenoble, Musée des Peinture et Sculpture) and a *Christ appearing to the Virgin*, an oval painting now untraced, probably a version of the painting in Palazzo Pitti in Florence.[5] In 1811 Albani's 'Vertus théologales' was apparently destined for the church of Saint-Roch in Paris, but there is no evidence of it ever having been sent. Given the similarity in composition and style between the Mahon copy and the *Christ served by Angels*, it is likely that the original and the Grenoble picture were painted as pendants and that they date from the 1650s.[6]

Following his return to Bologna from Rome in 1617, Albani established a large studio to assist him in the execution of the numerous public commissions he received for altarpieces and to satisfy the great international demand for small easel pictures by him. These usually show mythological subjects with graceful and elegant figures set in a landscape with frolicking putti. The studio also functioned as a school for painters, and through it Albani, as the principal artistic heir of Annibale Carracci, was able to transmit the classical ideals of his master and to

exert a great influence on the next two generations of both Bolognese and Roman painters. Among his pupils were Andrea Sacchi (who was the teacher of Maratti), Carlo Cignani (who was the teacher of Marcantonio Franceschini) and Pier Francesco Mola.

Albani seems to have painted several independent paintings of Charity. In Sudeley Castle there is a very fine autograph painting of *An Allegory of Charity* (fig.7), perhaps dating from the 1620s, of slightly different composition from the group in the present picture.[7] In Folkestone there is a squared drawing of a Charity group[8] made in preparation for a lost painting known from copies.[9] A third painting of *Charity* by Albani (now untraced) was engraved in 1722 by Jacob Frey when it was in the collection of Cavaliere Ferdinando Bolognetti, Rome.

TECHNICAL NOTE
The support is a fine plain-weave canvas. The painting

has been lined on at least two occasions; the present wax lining was probably carried out in the last 50 years. The painting is in generally good condition. There is retouching on all four edges. The area of retouching above the head of the figure on the left representing Faith masks a tear. The area of her right eye is a reconstruction. There is a repaired tear through the foremost child in the centre of the composition. The ground layer appears to be pale brown in colour. The artist seems to have painted a light blue sky and painted the trees and leaves over it; he then painted a slightly darker blue over the area of sky up to the foliage, leaving areas of the lighter blue visible adjacent to the foliage. The contour of the green drapery of the figure on the right representing Hope has been modified on the left side just above the white undergarment.

PROVENANCE
Christie's, London, 13 November 1959, lot 133 ('RAPHAEL, Faith, Hope and Charity'), where acquired by the present owner.

EXHIBITIONS
Not previously exhibited.

Fig.7 Francesco Albani, *An Allegory of Charity*, 1620s. Oil on canvas, 71 x 97 cm. Gloucestershire, Basildon Pictures Settlement at Sudeley Castle.

1 Levi d'Ancona 1977, p.317.

2 See, for example, the prescriptions of Ripa in his *Iconologia*. The page references cited here are from a late edition: Ripa 1645, pp.84–5 ('Carità'); p.201 ('Fede Cattolica'); pp.589–90 ('Speranza'). The colours worn by the personifications in this picture are canonic: white for Faith, red for Charity, and Green for Hope.

3 Ghisilieri's inventory has been made available to the present writer by Dssa Raffaella Morselli; see also Puglisi 1983 (unpublished) and Paris 1988–9, p.108. Madonna di Galliera is an Oratorian church and Ghisilieri joined the order there as a priest in 1652.

4 Blumer 1936, p.249, nos.1–3. The original Albani of which the Mahon painting is probably a copy (the dimensions are quite close) is described by Blumer as follows, 'ALBANI, 2. Les Vertus théologales. H.0,38; L.0,52. Cuivre. Bologne, Madonna di Galliera, 2 juillet 1796; Paris 8 novembre 1796. Destiné en 1811 à l'église de Saint Roch, à Paris. (Ne s'y trouve pas.).'

5 For the *Christ served by Angels*, see Paris 1988–9, no.3. In that entry, by Nathalie Volle, the painting of *Christ appearing to the Virgin* is said to be identical with the painting now in Palazzo Pitti (apparently following Puglisi), but that picture was actually taken by the French in 1796 from Palazzo Pitti, and not from Madonna di Galliera, and is no.14 in Blumer's list.

6 Van Schaak 1970 (unpublished) suggests a date in the early 1650s for the *Christ served by Angels* while Puglisi 1983 (unpublished) simply places it in the 1650s. These views are recorded in Paris 1988–9, under no.3, pp.108–9. Apparently Puglisi considers that the Mahon painting is identical with the one taken to Paris, despite the fact that it is on canvas.

7 It was exhibited in London (Harari and Johns) 1987, no.14.

8 Folkestone, Public Library, Museum and Art Gallery, Inv.114, black chalk, pen and brown ink and wash on blue paper, squared, 10 3/4 x 8 1/4 inches (approximately 273 x 210 mm). The drawing was brought to my attention by Aidan Weston-Lewis, who believes it may be a copy.

9 For example, Berlin, Mandelbaum & Kronthal, 8 April 1936, lot 396 ('Kreis des Francesco Albani'), 67 x 55 cm (photograph in Witt Library, Courtauld Institute of Art); Sotheby's, New York, 2 April 1996, lot 54 ('French School, 17th century').

Gioacchino Assereto 1600–1650
3 The Angel appears to Hagar and Ishmael

Oil on canvas, 118.5 x 167.1 cm
On long-term loan to the National Gallery since 1992

The story of Hagar and Ishmael is recounted in the Book of Genesis. Hagar was the Egyptian maidservant of Sara, the wife of Abraham. Being old and barren, Sara gave Hagar to Abraham as a concubine so that he might have a child by her. She bore him Ishmael. Some years later Sara gave birth to Isaac and subsequently she demanded that Abraham banish Hagar and Ishmael. This he reluctantly did and Hagar and Ishmael wandered into the wilderness. Their supplies soon ran out, but as they prepared to die Hagar was visited by an angel who instructed her to pick up the child for he was to become the progenitor of a great nation (the Ishmaelites). She was shown a source of water where they were able to drink (21:17–19). Two paintings of this subject by Assereto survive, the present picture and another, probably dating from some years earlier (fig.8).[1]

According to the biography of Assereto published by Rafaele Soprani in his *Vite de' Pittori, Scultori e Architetti Genovesi* of 1674, the artist was born in Genoa in 1600 and was a pupil first of Luciano Borzone and then of Giovanni Andrea Ansaldo, both Genoese painters. He was precocious and the celebrated patron of art Prince Gian Carlo Doria admired and encouraged his talent. On completing his training Assereto produced pictures for the churches of Genoa and the towns of the Ligurian Riviera. In 1639 he was briefly in Rome. Soprani says he painted frescoes in the palaces of Genoa and that some of his pictures were exported to Spain, where he was much admired, especially in Seville. He died in 1650.[2]

Very little has been added to Soprani's skeletal biography in the intervening centuries and since the artist almost never dated his pictures there are very few fixed points on which to base a chronology of his works. However, it is clear that Assereto's work is strongly influenced by the Lombard artists Cerano and Giulio Cesare Procaccini, and also by the Genoese Bernardo Strozzi. The tendency towards a more naturalistic style which is apparent in Assereto's later works may have been reinforced by his trip to Rome where he would have been exposed to, among other things, much Caravaggesque painting. His subject pictures are characterised by dramatic compositional and lighting effects and an eloquent use of gesture.[3]

In this work, one of three Genoese paintings in the Mahon collection (see cats.11 and 78), Assereto lends drama to the biblical narrative by tilting the whole composition along the diagonal and boldly cropping the figure of

Hagar and the wings of the angel. The sense of a sudden encounter is expressed in Hagar's startled pose and impulsive gesture: her right thumb unintentionally catches her veil. The angel's hand gestures conform to the text: 'Fear not; for God hath heard the voice of the lad where he is.' Ishmael lies against a tree in the distance, his empty water gourd cast on the ground beside him. Hagar wears a gypsy's hat in accordance with the long-established tradition of identifying Egyptians with gypsies. The sombre palette and flickering light effects, the broad application of liquid paint, and the subtlety of the facial expressions, indicate that the work dates from the later part of Assereto's career, after his trip to Rome.[4]

The composition of Assereto's earlier treatment of the subject is also aligned along the diagonal, the figures are similarly compressed into the picture space and the gestures are equally elegant, but the greater distortion of form and the stronger colours and contrasts, reveal a greater dependence on Lombard painting. The painting probably dates from the early 1630s. A comparison of these two renditions of the subject with those by his successful Genoese contemporary Giovanni Andrea de Ferrari shows how inventive and dramatic an artist Assereto was.[5]

Fig.8 Gioacchino Assereto, *The Angel appears to Hagar and Ishmael*, early 1630s. Oil on canvas, 124 x 146 cm. Genoa, Civica Galleria di Palazzo Rosso.

1 The latter painting was published in Marcenaro 1947, pp.141–2, fig.4.

2 Soprani 1674, pp.167–73. He gives the date of death as 1649, but it has recently been established as 1650, see Ausserhofer 1991.

3 On Assereto, see Longhi 1926; Marcenaro 1947; Pesenti 1986, pp.371–432; Castelnovi 1987, pp.85–9 and 133–5.

4 Newcome Schleier dates the work to about 1640 in Frankfurt 1992, p.84.

5 For De Ferrari's paintings, see Castelnovi 1971, fig.88 (Genoa, Private collection, 1640s), and Newcome 1972, fig.41a (Genoa, SS Annunziata, c.1650). A drawing associated with the latter picture is in the Palazzo Rosso (Newcome 1972, no.41). Interestingly all of these, and Assereto's two paintings, show a gourd for carrying water.

Pompeo Batoni 1708–1787

4 Portrait of a Lady of the Milltown Family as a Shepherdess

Oil on canvas, 49.9 x 39.5 cm (painted surface 47.2 x 36.2 cm)
Signed and dated on the rock on the left: *P.B./1751.*

Joseph Leeson (1701–83), a wealthy Irish brewing heir and collector, and 1st Earl of Milltown from 1763, visited Rome twice.[1] In 1744–5, he was the first in a long line of Grand Tourist sitters from Ireland and Britain to be painted by Batoni (Dublin, National Gallery of Ireland).[2] On his second visit, in 1750–1, he was accompanied by his son, also called Joseph (1730–1801), later the 2nd Earl of Milltown, whom Batoni painted on a slightly smaller scale and wearing a similar fur-lined costume (Dublin, National Gallery).[3] It was on this second visit that the small full-length portrait of a *Lady of the Milltown Family as a Shepherdess* and its pendant (fig.9) must have been commissioned from the artist.[4] All four of these pictures are listed in J.P. Neale's 1826 description of Russborough, the country house built by the elder Leeson near Blessington, County Wicklow, although the two pictures of women are identified only as a 'Sheperdess' and 'Diana' and not described as portraits.[5] The present picture had left the Russborough collection before 1902 when the Countess of Milltown, widow of the 6th Earl, presented the contents of the house to the National Gallery of Ireland.

The two small full-length female portraits were thought by Wynne to represent the same sitter, Anne Preston (1720/1–76), who became the second of Joseph Leeson's three wives in 1738.[6] However, the two paintings actually seem to show different sitters and the poses and compositions suggest that they were conceived as complementary.[7] A close comparison of the two heads reveals differences in the form and curvature of the eyebrows, in the shape of the eyes and nose, and in the contours of the face. None of the female members of the family seems to have accompanied the Leesons, *père et fils*, when they went to Rome in 1750–1 and it has been suggested that Batoni must have copied the faces from contemporary miniatures (although drawings would have sufficed) which the Leesons brought with them from Ireland.[8] Anthony Lee (fl. 1724–67), who painted two portraits of Joseph Leeson, one of them signed and dated 1735 (Dublin, National Gallery of Ireland) and another in the collection of Sir Roy Strong, is the obvious candidate for the execution of these miniatures or drawings.[9]

As there is no certain portrait of Anne Preston Leeson, 1st Countess Milltown, it is not possible to say which of the two paintings by Batoni shows her.[10] Neither seems to show Joseph's first wife, Cecilia Leigh (who died in 1737), of whom there is a portrait in the National Gallery of Ireland.[11] The pendant portrait may represent another family member, for example Mary Leeson, daughter of Joseph Leeson and Cecilia Leigh, who was born in the early 1730s.[12]

TECHNICAL NOTE

The support is a fine plain-weave canvas. The painting is lined (the lining appears to date from before 1900) and the original tacking edges have been spread open on to the lining canvas. A yellow border has been painted around the image to mask the join between the open tacking edges and the lining canvas. The same has happened to the pendant in the National Gallery of Ireland (fig.1). There is some abrasion on the surface and drying cracks are apparent on the left forearm of the sitter. A stretcher-bar mark running horizontally through the middle of the picture was caused by an earlier stretcher or strainer. The painting is generally in very good condition, however. The ground is reddish in colour.

PROVENANCE

Presumably commissioned by Joseph Leeson in Rome in 1751; by descent in the Leeson Milltown family, Russborough, County Wicklow; Sotheby's, London, 1 June 1960, lot 41 (bought by Julius Weitzner); acquired from Weitzner by the present owner in 1960.

Fig.9 Pompeo Batoni, *Portrait of a Lady of the Milltown Family as Diana*, signed with initials and dated 1751. Oil on canvas, 50 x 39.5 cm (painted surface 47 x 36 cm). Dublin, National Gallery of Ireland.

EXHIBITIONS
London (Agnew) 1965, no.47; Lucca 1967, no.31.

1 On Leeson as an art collector, see Wynne 1974; see also Wynne 1986, p.6.
2 The portrait (137 x 101.9 cm) is signed and dated 1744, see Clark-Bowron 1985, cat.87, fig.86.
3 The portrait (99 x 61 cm) is signed and dated *P.B.1751*, see Clark-Bowron 1985, cat.146, fig.138.
4 It was not uncommon in the eighteenth century for sitters to be painted in the guise of saints or mythological figures. In the same year he painted these pendant portraits, Batoni portrayed Sarah, Lady Featherstonhaugh, as Diana, see Clark-Bowron 1985, cat.155, fig.144.
5 'A Sheperdess – Pompeo Battoni' and 'Diana – Pompeo Battoni' (they hung in the same room), see Neale 1826, unpaginated, second page of the account of Russborough.
6 Wynne 1974, p.106. Anne's birth date is deduced here from Doubleday and Howard de Walden 1910–40, VIII, p.708. For the Leeson family, see Wynne 1974 and Leeson 1963 (unpublished).
7 Clark-Bowron 1985, p.250. Wynne seems to have conceded in 1986 that they are not the same sitter (p.8).
8 The suggestion was made by Anthony Clark in a letter to Denis Mahon. Mahon has pointed out that the face of the 'Sheperdess' is 'strikingly similar to reperesentations of female charm as conventionalized in the English School at this precise moment, the most celebrated example being Gainsborough's early *Mrs. Andrews*' (*Mr and Mrs Andrews*, London, National Gallery), London (Agnew) 1965, p.33.
9 On Lee see Dublin/London/Belfast 1969–70, p.39.
10 A small Leeson family portrait by an unknown artist in the National Gallery of Ireland shows the elder Joseph Leeson (copied from Batoni's 1744 portrait) with a woman holding an infant girl in her arms, and an older boy in seventeenth-century costume (Inv.1697). The date '1757' is inscribed on the stretcher (information provided by Sergio Benedetti). If this is the date of the execution of the picture then it is likely that the woman is Anne Preston Leeson. Her face is more similar to that of the woman in the Mahon picture than to that of the *Lady of the Milltown Family as Diana*.
11 Inv.699.
12 A portrait of a lady said to be of the Milltown family, and stated to have come from the collection of the Earls of Milltown at Russborough, was sold at Christie's in London on 3 July 1953 (lot 66) with an ascription to Batoni: 'Portrait of a Lady (said to be Lady Milltown), in yellow, red and blue dress with a peacock' (17 1/2 x 12 inches). It was bought by Ryan for 48 guineas. It reappeared at Sotheby's, London, on 21 October 1953 (lot 36) as 'Lady Milltown as Juno' (bought by Athens, a dealer?). Unfortunately it is not reproduced in either catalogue. This painting may be identical with the picture described as 'A Juno' by Neale in his 1826 description of Russborough, but there it has no attribution.

Sébastien Bourdon 1616–1671

5 Abraham's Sacrifice near Bethel (?)

Oil on canvas, 85.5 x 118.2 cm

The painting has at various times been called *The Sacrifice of Abraham*,[1] *The Sacrifice of Noah*,[2] and *Abraham's Journey into Egypt*. The Sacrifice of Noah (Genesis 8:20) can be excluded as the subject because the number of figures in the painting is too great.[3] An episode from the story of Abraham is more likely. When Abraham (or Abram as he was called before the covenant of circumcision) journeyed to Egypt with his wife Sara, his nephew Lot 'and all their substance that they had gathered, and the souls that they had gotten in Haran', he built an altar to the Lord between Bethel and Hai (Genesis 12:4–8). This may be the scene shown, but it may just as well be (as Denis Mahon has proposed) Abraham's sacrifice at the same altar on his return from Egypt (Genesis 13:1–4). The title 'The Sacrifice of Abraham' could apply to either episode.

It has also been suggested that the subject is the sacrifice of Jacob following his reconciliation with Laban (Genesis 31:54),[4] but the heap of stones and pillar which they called upon to witness their mutual promises are absent. Other possible candidates for the scene depicted are the sacrifice of Jacob after his reconciliation with Esau (Genesis 33:20), or that at El-bethel (Genesis 35:6–7), or that at Beersheba (Genesis 46: 1).

Of all these possibilities one of the sacrifices by Abraham in the company of his nephew Lot seems the most likely, because of the prominence given to the older of the two men approaching the altar.[5] However, the precise identity of the figures is of secondary importance in what is essentially a biblical genre scene in which animals and cooking utensils are more prominent than patriarchal or other figures. Such scenes were a known speciality of Bourdon's Genoese contemporary Giovanni Benedetto Castiglione (1616–70), who was in Rome during the years 1632–5 and again in the later 1630s,[6] and to whom this painting was for a period attributed.[7] Bourdon, who was in Rome from 1634 to 1637, made his living at the time from pastiches of works of his contemporaries,[8] but while the concept of this painting owes much to Castiglione, its figures are too gentle in expression to have been executed by him. Furthermore, its silvery tonality is quite unlike Castiglione's ruddy colouring and suggests a painting made in the manner of Castiglione but for the Paris art market around 1640, when Bourdon executed many genre works. Indeed,

the painting's soft colouring and its cursive quality may explain its apparent popularity with a number of distinguished French eighteenth-century collectors, perhaps starting with La Roque (see Provenance), editor of the *Mercure de France* and subject of the only certain portrait by Watteau.

If this painting can be identified with that in the La Roque collection, its attribution to Bourdon has a far longer pedigree than that to Castiglione. The painting was re-attributed to Bourdon by Mahon.[9] This attribution has not been doubted.[10]

HW

TECHNICAL NOTE

The support is a medium-fine plain-weave canvas and shows the marks of earlier stretcher bars. The painting was relined possibly in the early twentieth century. The ground is a pinky red. Pentimenti are visible around the outlines of the heads of the cow at right and the camel in the centre. There are areas of overpainting, for example in the blue robe at bottom left.

PROVENANCE

Possibly the Chevalier de La Roque, his sale, Paris, April 1745, lot 86 (421 livres);[11] possibly Monsieur Deuet of Paris, his sale, London, Prestage, 21 January 1764, lot 8;[12] possibly the Prince de Conti, his sale, Rémy, Paris, 8 April– 6 June 1777, lot 564,[13] in which case in the collection of the Comte de Merle, his sale, Paris, Paillet & Julliot, 1–4 March 1784, lot 11 (1,800 livres);[14] possibly in Christie's, London, 30 April 1785, said to include pictures 'from the celebrated Cabinet of Monsieur le Compte de Merle, sold last year in Paris', and there described as 'Bourdon...Noah with his family sacrificing after the flood, a very singular fine picture from the cabinet of le Comte De Merle', lot 56 (£99 15s.0d. to Baillie); possibly the painting by Bourdon called 'The Departure of Jacob from Laban' in the collection of Harenc de Presle at 24 rue du Sentier, Paris, by 1787;[15] possibly in the Harenc de Presle sale, Paris, Lebrun, 30 April 1795 and days following, where said to be described as 33 x 45 *pouces* and as from the collections of the Prince de Conti and the Comte de Merle;[16] possibly in the sale of Lafontaine et al., Paris, Coquille et Lacoste, 10–11 January 1816, where described as 'Un sacrifice', 80 x 120 cm;[17] possibly in the Moret sale, Paris, Paillet et al., 4 December 1843, where described as 'Départ de Jacob pour l'Egypte', 88 x 121 cm;[18] acquired by Professor Thomas Bodkin (later Director of the National Gallery of Ireland and then of the Barber Institute, Birmingham) by October 1925;[19] his sale, Sotheby's, London, 11 November 1959, lot 25 (as by Giovanni Benedetto Castiglione), where acquired by the present owner through Patch.

EXHIBITIONS
London (Agnew) 1925, no.8 (as by G.B. Castiglione).

1 London (Agnew) 1925, no.8.
2 Bodkin 1926, and so called in the Bodkin sale, 1959, and with a query in Chamoux et al. 1973, p.18.
3 As noted by Fowle 1970, p.81.
4 Fowle 1970, p.86.
5 As pointed out in Fowle 1970, p.88, n.5.
6 Standring 1990, pp.13–28.
7 By Thomas Bodkin in Bodkin 1926.
8 Guillet de Saint-Georges 1854, I, pp.88–9.
9 Sitwell 1964, p.385, fig.7. The attribution to Bourdon was agreed in Chamoux et al. 1973, p.18.
10 Fowle 1970, p.85.
11 'Un très-beau Tableau peint sur toile par le Bourdon... dans le goût de Benedete. Il...réprésente Jacob offrant un Sacrifice; il est fort riche d'ouvrage & orné de quantité de Figures & d'Animaux...[33 x 44 pouces].'
12 'Seb. Bourdon. Noah's Sacrifice.'
13 As by Bourdon. '564 Le Départ de Jacob. Ce tableau richement composé, dans le goût de Benedette, est argentin, & touché en grand Maître; il est peint sur une toile de 2 pieds 9 pouces de haut, sur 3 pieds 9 pouces de large.' The metric equivalent of these measurements is 89.2 x 121 cm.
14 'SÉBASTIEN BOURDON. Le départ de Jacob. Ce tableau, d'une riche ordonnance, est composé dans le genre de Bénedette... Il étoit un des morceaux distingués du Cabinet de Monseigneur le Prince de Conti, No. 564 de son Catalogue: hauteur 33 pouces, largeur 45 pouces. T[oile].'
15 Thiéry 1787, I, p.444, where Thiéry describes it as 'sur les côtés de la porte d'entrée [du] cabinet'. Bonnaffé 1873 (p.109 note 2) identifies the painting as that bought by Harenc de Presle at the de Merle Sale of 1784 for 1,800 livres.
16 So said by Fowle 1970, p.6.
17 Mireur 1911–12, I, p.425; F. Lugt, no.8794.
18 Mireur 1911–12, I, p.425; F.Lugt, no.17170. There should also be noted lot 32 of Thomas Holcroft's sale, Christie's, London, 30 April 1803, described as a 'Return from Egypt. From the sale of Martin at Paris' (presumably Martin's sale of 5 April 1802, *Lugt 6396, B.N.Impr.*).
19 The painting was owned by Bodkin at the time of the Magnasco Society exhibition, London (Agnew) 1925, no.8. It was further published by him in Bodkin 1926, where the illustration was captioned 'Private Collection'.

Paul Bril 1554–1626

6 Mythological Landscape with Nymphs and Satyrs

Oil on canvas, 70.6 x 92.8 cm
Signed and dated lower right: *P. BRiLLi / 1621*

This painting shows a mythological scene set in an imaginary landscape which is based on that of the Roman Campagna. The circular classical building in the distance on the left may be intended to suggest the Temple of the Sibyl at Tivoli, of which Bril had made drawings. The subject is not a particular mythological event: it represents nymphs and satyrs dancing, music-making and garlanding one another with flowers. In the middle ground satyrs are carrying off nymphs on their shoulders.

Paul Bril was born and trained in Antwerp.[1] He travelled to Rome to join his brother Matthijs there in about 1575. Paul's earliest works after his arrival in Rome were small, highly finished forest scenes very much in the Flemish tradition, painted on oak or copper panels. However, his style was transformed by his study of contemporary Italian landscape painting and in particular by the broadly brushed classical landscapes of Annibale Carracci. Bril's frescoes in the Vatican and Lateran palaces, carried out in the 1580s and 1590s, already show his study of Annibale's landscapes. In his easel paintings Bril began to work on a larger scale, usually on canvas, creating an elegant marriage between what the Italian biographer Giovanni Baglione, writing in 1642, was to call his 'prima maniera Fiamenga' and the 'buona maniera Italiana'.[2]

Bril's mature style, seen to great effect in this painting of 1621, shows well-ordered and calm landscapes which are ideal yet based on close observation of nature and a confident handling of aerial perspective. It proved immensely successful with Roman patrons and was to be profoundly influential on both Italian and Netherlandish landscape painting. In the year in which this picture was painted Bril was working with Domenichino in the Casino Ludovisi, where both artists painted a landscape fresco. Bril was widely acknowledged to be the leading landscape painter in Rome: in 1621 Mancini called him the best in the city.[3] Flemish merchants and pilgrims visiting Rome bought his work, which was also engraved, and in these ways knowledge of his new 'composite' style was circulated north of the Alps.

Bril collaborated with Rubens, whom he met during the latter's stay in Rome, on *Landscape with Psyche* (Madrid, Prado).[4] Bril painted the rocky, forested landscape with its dramatic waterfall in 1610 and presumably sent it to Rubens in Antwerp, where – some years later – he painted the figure of Psyche, and the eagle and dragon. He repainted sections of the landscape to accommodate these figures. Rubens

kept the painting in his collection until his death in 1640.

There is a painting in the National Gallery's permanent collection which is strikingly similar in style and composition to the Mahon landscape. *Diana and Callisto* (fig.10) has been attributed to Agostino Tassi (*c*.1580–1644)[5] but close comparison reveals that it is in fact by Bril. The figures in these works, however, are not by Bril but by the same collaborator, who is probably Pietro Paolo Bonzi, known as 'Il Gobbo dei Carracci' (*c*.1576–1636).[6]

There is an early copy of the Mahon painting showing the landscape slightly extended on the left. It was with Agnews in 1969[7] and it is now in a private collection in the United Kingdom. It is possibly by Johann König (1586–1642).

CB

TECHNICAL NOTE
The support is a plain-weave medium-fine canvas. The canvas has been lined and the vertical crossbar stretcher is of an English type. The tacking edges left and right have been cut off but those at top and bottom are partially preserved; the painted area has been slightly extended by incorporating these edges on the surface of the lining canvas. There is some discoloration in the foliage of the trees on the left of the picture. Some lining abrasion is apparent in the lighter areas but the painting is in good condition. The circular classical temple in the background appears to have been painted over finished trees. The figures are mostly painted over the landscape but on the right it is evident that the green paint of the landscape was applied around the figures in that area after their completion.

PROVENANCE
Collection of the Ducs d'Orléans, Palais Royal, Paris, before 1727;[8] with Wilson, for sale in London 1793 (no.27); subsequently appeared at the sale of the late Lucy Copeman of Long Stratton, Norfolk, Christie's, London, 13 June 1898, lot 16; acquired by the present owner in 1957 from the Heim Gallery, Paris.

EXHIBITIONS
Cardiff 1960, no.19; Bologna 1962, no.125; London 1965 (Agnew), no.6;[9] London (National Gallery) 1996, no.8.

Fig.10 Paul Bril, *Diana and Callisto*, *c*.1620. Oil on wood, 49.5 x 72.4 cm. London, The National Gallery.

1 There is no satisfactory modern monograph on Bril. A. Mayer's *Das Leben und die Werke der Brüder Matthäus und Paul Bril* (Leipzig 1910) is still useful and A. Berger's *Die Tafelgemälde Paul Brils* (Münster/Hamburg 1991) provides a valuable chronology but a full catalogue raisonné is sorely needed and this is currently being prepared by Luuk Pijl (University of Utrecht).

2 Baglione 1642, p.297.

3 '... qual da molti anni in qua in simil sorte di pittura par che habbia tenuto il primo luogo et invero meritamente', Mancini 1956–7, I, pp.260–1.

4 Oil on canvas, 93 x 128 cm. The painting has recently been cleaned. It was lent to the exhibition *Rubens's Landscapes* held at the National Gallery, London, in 1996. Examination of the painting while it was in London revealed that

Rubens's participation was in fact far greater than had previously been thought. He not only painted Psyche and the eagle but extensively repainted the landscape in this area and added the rainbows and the dragon and retouched the waterfall and other passages. It appears that the painting was completed by Bril in 1610, sent to Antwerp and then repainted by Rubens in about 1616. It is probably to be identified with no.26 in the *Specification*, the list of the artist's paintings made at the time of his death in 1640: 'Un paysage de Paul Bril avec l'histoire de Psyche', see Muller 1989, p.100.

5 Levey 1971, pp.212–13, as Tassi(?). A painting in the Galleria Nazionale, Rome, contained a false monogram *AT* which led Levey and many others to believe that the group of paintings to which it belongs was the work of

Tassi. In fact, as has been demonstrated by Teresa Pugliatti (1975, especially p. 16), they are by Bonzi.

6 As was first pointed out by Salerno 1977–80, III, p.994, note 28, and p.1005.

7 London (Agnew) 1969, no.19, oil on panel, 27½ x 41½ inches.

8 Dubois de Saint Gelais 1727, p.360, and Dezallier d'Argenville 1749, p.81. While in the Palais Royal, the painting was engraved in reverse by Pillement, late in the eighteenth century (Galerie du Palais Royal 1786/1808, II, fourth painting by Bril, with incorrect dimensions).

9 Where the following literature is cited: Denys Sutton, *Arte Figurativa*, 8 (1960), no.2, p.20, and *Goya*, Jan.–Feb. 1961, p.250; F.W. Hawcroft, *The Burlington Magazine*, 102 (1960), pp.127 and 129 (fig.38).

Annibale Carracci 1560–1609

7 Saint John the Baptist in a Landscape

Oil on canvas, 129.3 x 98 cm

Saint John the Baptist withdrew into the wilderness of Judaea to preach repentance and to baptise in the waters of the Jordan. During the course of the sixteenth century, with the increased interest in landscape painting, representations of the Baptist in a landscape became quite common. The scene shown here does not correspond with any particular episode in the Gospels, although the motif of the fallen tree which bridges the brook on the right may have been inspired by the saint's own words: 'And now also the axe is laid unto the root of the trees: therefore every tree which bringeth not forth good fruit is hewn down' (Matthew 3:10). He wears a garment of camel hair and carries the reed cross which is traditional.

When the painting was in the Camuccini collection in Rome it was considered to be a collaborative effort between Domenichino and Ludovico Carracci, who was thought to have painted the glory of angels.[1] Shortly after it entered the collection of the Duke of Northumberland at Alnwick, Waagen proposed the attribution to Annibale which has found general acceptance.[2] Opinions have differed as to whether the painting was executed shortly before or shortly after the artist's removal to Rome in 1595. Cavalli and Mahon have argued the former;[3] Posner has sustained the latter on the basis that a 'Romanized' version of the composition given to Albani in the Ringling Museum, Sarasota, which he dates to about 1602/3, must have been painted in Rome from Annibale's original.[4] The similarity in the typology of the angels in the Mahon painting and those in the *Coronation of the Virgin* (cat.8), which is certainly an early Roman painting, is striking, but the handling, colour and organisation of the picture are even more closely related to Annibale's Bolognese works. Mahon has spoken of this work as foreshadowing the early years in Rome and so it seems appropriate to date the painting about 1594–5.[5]

At this date the artistic conventions for an historiated landscape were still being formulated but Annibale's example was to prove very influential. The three-tier arrangement in which the foreground is composed of predominantly brown tones, the middle ground of greens, and the distant mountains of a crystalline blue, became standard in seventeenth-century landscape painting, as may be seen in several pictures in this exhibition (see cats.19, 22 and 23, for example). Annibale, however, also builds in a diagonal recession: the figure kneels on a rocky dais in the left foreground but immediately to the right the landscape plunges down to the brook in the middle distance. Although the figure is wholly enveloped by the landscape it stands out through colour contrast and through the strong illumination from upper left which invests the whole scene with a limpid clarity. The frothing waterfall with its trailing water and bouncing droplets is an impressive piece of natural observation.

Technical note

The support is an open plain-weave canvas. It was lined before 1853 (the date is established by the three seals on the lining canvas which were applied at the time of the export of the work from Italy in that year)[6] and attached to a smaller stretcher. The tacking edge on the left – the only one it is possible to see since there are strips of wood nailed all the way round the stretcher – appears to have some original paint on it. There is pronounced craquelure which is probably due to the application of a thick ground layer. The painting has suffered some abrasion in the sky, and the foliage, painted in a green copper pigment, has discoloured. The painting is generally in good condition, however. The ground appears to be pale brown. The work is freely painted and some parts were probably not carefully planned in advance: the hand of the left-hand angel is painted over completed clouds, for example, and the tree on the left is painted over the completed blue hill and sky. The left hand of Saint John has undergone some modifications.

Provenance

Apparently brought from Bologna to Rome before entering the Lante collection, Rome;[7] in the collection of the painter Vincenzo Camuccini (1771–1844), before 1842, Rome;[8] his son, Giovanni Battista, by whom sold, together with the entire Camuccini collection of 74 paintings, to Algernon, 4th Duke of Northumberland in 1853; by descent at Alnwick Castle; bought by Agnew's in 1953, and acquired in the same year by the present owner.

Exhibitions

London 1858, no.50 (as Domenichino); on loan to the Kunsthistorisches Museum, Vienna, from May to July 1955; Birmingham 1955, no.31; Bologna 1956, no.73; London 1960, p.149, no.383; London (Agnew) 1973, no.16.

1 In Tito Barberi's manuscript catalogue of the Camuccini collection (*Catalogo ragionato della Galleria Camuccini in Roma*, c.1851) in the Alnwick Castle Archives, the picture is described as follows: '... S.Giovanni nel deserto. Quadro del Zampieri, dipinto però nella gloria dal Carracci suo maestro. Era dei Sig.ri Lante, presso i quali esisteva memoria essere stato mandato in Roma da Bologna. Nella gloria vi si riconosce la maestra mano di Lodovico Carracci, come nel restante del quadro, e specialmente nel paese l'impronta di quella invincibile timidezza del Domenichino... scendiamo a dedurre avere avuto in animo il Carracci d'incoraggiare il valoroso giovane, quando per esso lui la gloria di questo quadro dipinse mentre la trepidazione che scorgesi nel restante, attribuirsi dee alla giovanissima età in cui Domenichino era, quando a tal lavoro s'accinse', I am grateful to Nicholas Penny for providing this reference. See also Platner 1830–42, III, 3, p.270.

2 Waagen 1854/7, supplement, p.470. The exceptions are Clovis Whitfield, whose attribution of the work to Agostino Carracci has not met with support (Whitfield 1986 (1988), pp.89–90), and Alessandro Brogi, who has argued that the old attribution to Domenichino is correct (Brogi 1990, pp.56–8 and 60, note 23), but this is difficult to reconcile with what is now known about the handling of Domenichino's early landscapes. Indeed, if the picture was in Rome when Domenichino arrived there it is not impossible that he could have seen and admired it.

3 Cavalli in Bologna 1956, no.63; Mahon 1957, pp.283–4, and London 1960, no.383; see also Boschloo 1974, I, p.36.

4 Posner 1971, I, p.176, note 15, and II, p.38; for the Sarasota painting, Inv. SN 115, oil on copper, 49.2 x 37.1 cm, see Tomory 1976, cat.127, pp.123–4.

5 Mahon 1957, pp.283–4.

6 One shows the Colosseum and is that of the 'Commissario delle Antichità', another has a shield with a helmet surmounted by an eagle, and the third has a shield with a crown above it. These three seals appear on all the Camuccini pictures (see Provenance). The remains of another seal on the stretcher are illegible.

7 See note 1 above. This is the collection of the Duchi Lante, an eminent Roman family.

8 The picture is mentioned in Platner 1830–42, III, 3, p.270, where it is stated that it carried an unconvincing attribution to Domenichino.

Annibale Carracci 1560–1609
8 The Coronation of the Virgin

Oil on canvas, 117.8 x 141.3 cm
Inscribed lower left corner: *244 D CARCCI*
New York, The Metropolitan Museum of Art (Inv.1971.155)

The *Coronation of the Virgin* is one of Annibale Carracci's most serene and classical paintings. It was almost certainly painted for Cardinal Pietro Aldobrandini (1572–1621), the nephew of the ruling pope, Clement VIII, shortly after the painter's arrival in Rome in 1595, and is listed under item 244, the number which is inscribed on the painting, in the 1603 inventory of the Cardinal's collection.[1]

Annibale had been called to Rome by Cardinal Odoardo Farnese, great-great-grandson of Pope Paul III, in order to execute frescoes in the Palazzo Farnese. In 1595–6 he decorated the Camerino, the Cardinal's study, with scenes from the stories of Hercules and Ulysses, and from 1597 to 1600 he painted the ceiling of the Galleria Farnese, which is his masterpiece. There was a uneasy relationship between the Farnese and Aldobrandini cardinals but an important dynastic marriage in 1600 brought them into a closer alliance. Annibale's friendship with Monsignor Giovanni Battista Agucchi, who was secretary and later *maggiordomo* to Cardinal Aldobrandini, may have facilitated Aldobrandini's acquisition of works by him. By 1603, in addition to the *Coronation of the Virgin*, the Cardinal owned the *Christ appearing to Saint Peter on the Appian Way* (*'Domine, Quo Vadis?'*) in the National Gallery,[2] and four other works by Annibale.[3] It is arguable that his commission for a series of lunettes with religious scenes in landscape settings for the chapel in his newly acquired palace on the Corso (now in the Galleria Doria Pamphilj, Rome, see fig.21) could have taken place as early as 1602.[4]

The subject of the present painting, the Coronation of the Virgin as Queen of Heaven by the Holy Trinity, is not described in the New Testament but it corresponds with the fifth Glorious Mystery of the Rosary, the culminating devotion in the sequence of Marian meditations. On banks of cloud to the left and right of the main group are musician angels, and beneath them are figures who invoke the Virgin's intercession. Particularly impressive is the vision of the angelic choir set in serried ranks in a heavenly arena illuminated by the divine radiance of the Godhead. The Coronation of the Virgin often graced the central panel of fourteenth- and fifteenth-century altarpieces but the subject was less frequently treated in the sixteenth century and only rarely appears in easel pictures on this scale. Annibale's painting must have been intended for the private devotion of the Cardinal.[5]

A large drawing by the artist in the Museum in Dijon shows the same scene although the composition is more loosely structured and more vertical.[6] On stylistic grounds it has been argued that the drawing was made by Annibale in Bologna in about 1593 and that he brought it with him to Rome. The clarity of the forms in the painting, the compact design, and the elegant classicism of the figures of God the Father and Christ, illustrate how rapidly Annibale responded to the canonic art of Antiquity and Renaissance Rome.[7] He effected a synthesis of elements drawn from ancient sculpture and Raphael, whose fresco of the *Disputa* in the Stanza della Segnatura seems to have served as a model for the compositional clarity of this work,[8] and from Correggio, particularly the types and poses of the angels and the warm unifying light. Mahon has highlighted how the work exemplifies the artist's key position at the source of both Baroque and Classical tendencies in later Seicento painting.[9]

PROVENANCE
Cardinal Pietro Aldobrandini, Rome, 1603; Cardinal Ippolito Aldobrandini, 1626;[10] Olimpia Aldobrandini-Pamphilj, inventories of before 1665,[11] and 1682;[12] inherited by the Pamphilj before 1710;[13] recorded in the apartments of Cardinal Benedetto Pamphilj in the Palazzo Pamphilj al Corso (formerly Palazzo Aldobrandini); his inventory, 1725; after his death in 1730 the painting apparently went to Villa Aldobrandini; with the extinction of the male line it passed to the Borghese family and is listed in the apartments of Prince Aldobrandini in Palazzo Borghese; acquired from there, in about 1799–1800, by Alexander Day; his sale, Christie's, London, 21 June 1833, lot 37; acquired by Samuel Rogers; his sale, Christie's, London, 3 May 1856, lot 730; 5th Duke of Newcastle, Clumber House; by descent until sold by the Earl of Lincoln, Christie's, London, 4 June 1937, lot 18 (bought by Bloch); acquired by Denis Mahon in 1939; acquired from him by the Metropolitan Museum of Art, New York, in 1971.

EXHIBITIONS
London 1819, no.46; London 1835, no.32; Manchester 1857, no.335; London (Wildenstein) 1955, no.20; Birmingham 1955, no.30; Bologna 1956, no.92; Manchester 1957, no.128; London 1960, no.400; Newcastle-upon-Tyne 1961, no.203; New York/Naples 1985, no.26; Bologna/Washington/New York 1986–7, no.95.

1 '244. La coronazione della Madonna del Caraccio', D'Onofrio 1964, p.207.
2 D'Onofrio 1964, no.174, p.203. The painting was commissioned by him in the spring of 1601, see Zapperi 1981.
3 D'Onofrio 1964, nos.315–18, pp.207–8.
4 For the dating of the beginning of this project to about 1602, see the essay by Silvia Ginzburg Carignani, 'Domenichino e Giovanni Battista Agucchi' in Rome 1996, especially pp.131–2.
5 In an inventory of Villa Aldobrandini of 1611, associated with the Cardinal's sister Olimpia, there is a reference to a 'Coronation of the Virgin' on the altar of the small chapel ('cappilluccia'). Although the painter's name is not given, it has been suggested that this is Annibale's picture, see Della Pergola 1960, pp.426–7, no.14. The identification is improbable, however.
6 The drawing is in brown ink with pen and wash, sanguine and heightening with white gouache, 462 x 476 mm, see Jaffé 1960, who accurately notes that in the drawing 'the emphasis ... is on the mystery of apotheosis rather than on the ritual of coronation' (p.28).
7 Mahon dated the picture to about 1596 in London 1960, no.400, p.161; Briganti (1953, p.5) and Posner (1971, II, no.94, p.41) date it 1596–7.
8 Annibale's admiration for the fresco is also apparent in the altarpiece of *Christ in Glory with Saints* (Florence, Palazzo Pitti) which he painted for Cardinal Odoardo Farnese in about 1597.
9 Mahon 1947, pp.40–1, and London 1960, p.161; see also Briganti 1953, p.5.
10 Della Pergola 1960, pp.432 and 442, no.119. The Cardinal died in 1638.
11 'Un quadro d'una Coronatione della Madonna in tela d'imperatore, mano del Caraccioli, alto p. quattro e tre quarti, largo sei incirca, con sua cornice dorata, segnato n.244', D'Onofrio 1964, p.207.
12 Della Pergola 1962–3, pp.426–7, no.14.
13 Recorded in the collection of Prince Giovanni Battista Pamphilj immediately after his death in 1710, see Bologna 1956, p.215.

Attributed to Annibale Carracci 1560–1609
9 *Saint Mary Magdalene at Prayer in a Landscape*

Oil on canvas, 73.6 x 90.5 cm (painted surface 67.7 x 84.5 cm)

The Magdalen is reputed to have become a hermit after the Resurrection of Christ and here she is shown at prayer in a wild rocky place, within sight of a small town. Before her are an open book which rests on a skull, and the jar of ointment with which she anointed Christ, her traditional attribute (see cat.21). A crucifix is attached to a broken branch of the tree on the right.

The painting was first published in the catalogue of the Royal Academy exhibition of 1960, 'Italian Art and Britain', with a catalogue entry by Denis Mahon.[1] The attribution of the painting to Annibale had been proposed by its previous owner, Thomas Bodkin, sometime Director of the National Gallery of Ireland, with the endorsement of the distinguished art historian and connoisseur Tancred Borenius. It was exhibited as by Annibale and dated between 1585 and 1588. The relationship with a drawing by Annibale in the Louvre, which shows the Magdalen similarly posed but in reverse (fig.11), and with a signed and dated (1591) print of *Mary Magdalene in the Wilderness* was noted.[2] It was proposed that the drawing was made in preparation for the painting and then later served as the basis for the print. In his published comments on the exhibition – made only on the basis of photographs – Roberto Longhi cast doubt on the attribution to Annibale and made the unlikely suggestion that the painting was by Giovanni Antonio Burrini (1656–1727).[3] Roseline Bacou wrote the entry on the Louvre drawing in the catalogue of the Carracci drawings exhibition held in Paris in 1961 and adopted the argument outlined by Mahon the previous year.[4]

Following the picture's exhibition under the name of Annibale in Detroit in 1965, the attribution was again contested in a review by Hibbard and Lewine who stated that in their view the painting was based on the print of 1591 and was by a later hand.[5] Posner listed it among the rejected attributions in his 1971 monograph on Annibale Carracci on the grounds that it was stylistically incompatible with his works. He argued that the Louvre drawing was made in preparation for the print and had no direct connection with the Mahon painting.[6] A more cautious assessment was made by Diane De Grazia (1979) who drew attention to the similarity between the pose of the Magdalen and that of Pax in Tintoretto's *Mars driven from Peace and Abundance by Minerva* (Venice, Palazzo Ducale).[7] In 1984 the painting was exhibited in Bologna together with the drawing and print and

it was stated in the catalogue entry (edited by Andrea Emiliani) that the painting should be dated 1585/6, just after the Parma *Pietà*, with whose figures the Magdalen is said to have great affinity.[8] Luigi Salerno, in his review of the exhibition, reaffirmed the position set out by Mahon in 1960, adding only that the dating of the painting to *c*.1585–6 was supported by the presence of 'Baroccesque and Bassanesque elements'.[9]

While the traditional attribution to Annibale is retained here, there are several features in the painting which give pause for some reflection. The rather energetic brushwork, particularly apparent in the beautiful landscape, seems a little undisciplined for Annibale; the anatomy of the figure is awkward as the upper half of the body seems larger than the lower half and they do not join convincingly; the modelling of the striped drapery on which she rests is too summarily rendered. However, there are also some very fine passages of painting. The head of the Magdalen is sensitively rendered, her feelings of loss and regret mingled with love are beautifully conveyed, and the reflected highlight of the red robe on her left elbow is especially well observed. Given the close association of the picture with Annibale's conception and the problems which must arise from suggesting a

Fig.11 Annibale Carracci, *The Penitent Magdalen*, 1580s. Red chalk, 216 x 163 mm. Paris, Musée du Louvre.

date after the mid-1590s for its execution, it is difficult to propose an alternative attribution.

A painting by Ludovico Gimignani (1640–1697) of the *Penitent Magdalen*, in a private collection in Rome, has been said to perhaps be based on this picture. In spite of its horizontal format, however, the figure is actually closer to the print of 1591 and more probably adapted from that.[10]

TECHNICAL NOTE
The support is a plain-weave canvas; a seam runs horizontally about 9 cm from the lower stretcher edge. The painting has been lined and attached to a larger stretcher. Parts of the original tacking edges survive and have been splayed out on to the lining canvas; canvas inserts have been used to fill in the gaps up to the stretcher edge. The painting now has a border 3 cm wide all the way round, painted brown, although this is hidden by the frame. A thick black line has been painted around the image inside the splayed-out tacking edges. The robe of the Magdalen, painted in red lake, has faded a little and there may be some discoloration of the copper green of the blanket on which she rests. The ground layer is a pale terracotta colour. There are minor modifications in the contour of the Magdalen's hair, to left and right, and in her right leg.

PROVENANCE
Acquired in Dublin in about 1924 by Thomas Bodkin (1887–1961);[11] acquired by the present owner through Colnaghi at Sotheby's, London, 11 November 1959 (Bodkin sale), lot 23.

EXHIBITIONS
London 1960, no.401; Detroit 1965, no.71; Bologna 1984, no.113.

1 London 1960, no.401, pp.161–2.
2 For the print (etching and engraving, 223 x 160 mm) see De Grazia Bohlin 1979, Annibale no.12*, pp.440–2.
3 Longhi 1960, p.61.
4 Paris 1961, no.26, pp.26–7.
5 Hibbard and Lewine 1965, p.371, no.71.
6 Posner 1971, II, no.194[R], pp.80–1.
7 De Grazia Bohlin 1979, p.442, note 9. Annibale's older brother, Agostino, made an engraving (in the same sense) after Tintoretto's painting in 1589 (ibid., Agostino no.148, pp.258–9), but De Grazia observes that if the Mahon painting is by Annibale and dates from *c*.1586/7, the figure of the Magdalen would have been based directly on the Tintoretto.
8 Bologna 1984, no.113, p.170.
9 Salerno 1985, p.189.
10 De Grazia Bohlin 1979, p.442, note 11; for a reproduction of the painting, see Cortese 1963, fig.13.
11 London 1960, p.161. A paper label on the reverse states 'W.Bodkin/ no frame'.

Ludovico Carracci 1555–1619

10 The Agony in the Garden

Oil on canvas, 100.8 x 114.5 cm (original canvas 98 x 111.3 cm)
On long-term loan to the National Gallery since 1993

After sharing the Passover meal with the Apostles and knowing that his Passion would soon begin, Christ took Peter, James and John with him to the Mount of Olives. There he prayed: 'Father, if thou be willing, remove this cup from me: nevertheless not my will, but thine, be done' (Luke 22:42). The Apostles fell asleep but an angel appeared from heaven to comfort him. In the painting the angel is shown bringing the cup from which Christ will indeed have to drink, but he also points to the glorious apparition of the instruments of the Passion – the cross and crown of thorns, the column of the flagellation, the sponge and reed, and the shaft of the spear with which Christ was pierced. This iconography in scenes of the Agony in the Garden was traditional. In the distance to the right Judas leads a detachment of guards to arrest Christ. The Apostle in the left foreground who holds a sword is Peter, who cut off the ear of the high priest's servant, and the sleeping figure with the red cloak is Saint James. Saint John lies behind him to the right.

Ludovico was the eldest of the Carracci, and with his cousins Agostino and Annibale was jointly responsible for a profound renewal of Italian painting at the end of the sixteenth century. They established an Academy in their native city of Bologna in 1582 in which young artists were taught to draw from the model and to adopt nature as their guide. The early style of the Carracci was modelled on sixteenth-century Emilian painting, especially that of Correggio and Parmigianino, and on Venetian art. In the mid-1590s Annibale and Agostino left for Rome, where their painting acquired the paradigmatic character for which it was so admired in successive centuries, but Ludovico remained in Bologna where he continued his teaching activity. In his later works Ludovico's style became more mannered and inward-looking; the artist consciously developed a non-classicising manner which placed less emphasis on natural observation and painterly virtuosity and more on meaning and solemn presentation.[1]

Painted in the late 1580s, this is the earliest surviving painting of this subject by Ludovico and was almost certainly a private commission.[2] Ludovico's probable point of departure was the small painting of the same subject by Correggio (fig.12),[3] which appears to have been in the col-lection of Francesco Maria Signoretti in nearby Reggio Emilia until at least 1584.[4] Christ is dressed in blue and white, as in that picture, and the angel is a similarly elegant and artistically accomplished figure. Ludovico, however, has placed more emphasis on the narrative elements and his composition is less tightly structured. He employs a greater variety of light sources: the soldiers bear a torch and lantern, the moon peers above a gloomy cloud generating a silvery glimmer on the horizon, and the figure of Christ and the other foreground figures are illuminated by the aura surrounding the instruments of the Passion. The restless composition and artificial lighting, combined with the compressed sense of space and the elongated proportions of the figure of Saint Peter, are an indication of Ludovico's Mannerist tendencies and illustrate how his artistic development was often at odds with that of Annibale even at this early date.

In a recent analysis of the chronological development of Ludovico, made possible by the direct examination of a large number of works by the artist on the occasion of the exhibition held in Bologna in 1993, Mahon has convincingly proposed that the painting should be situated between the documented *Conversion of Saint Paul* of 1587–8 and the *Pala di Cento* of 1591, and in close proximity to the *Madonna dei Bargellini* of 1588; he suggests a date of 1588–9.[5]

Fig.12 Correggio, *The Agony in the Garden*, mid-1520s. Oil on panel, 37 x 40 cm. London, Apsley House, The Wellington Museum.

TECHNICAL NOTE

The support is a medium-weight plain-weave canvas. The painting is lined and the original tacking edges have been cut off. The stretcher is stamped 'G.MORILL/LINER'. The presence of cusping at the top and bottom edges indicates that on these sides at least the painting appears not to have been reduced. The edges of the original canvas on all four sides are heavily retouched. There are scattered local retouchings but the painting is in very good condition. The ground is a warm brown in colour. There are no obvious pentimenti.

PROVENANCE[6]

Robert Napier (1791–1876), West Shandon, Dumbartonshire, before 1865;[7] his sale, Christie's, London, 13 April 1877, lot 387 (as 'A.Carracci'); Christie's, London, 20 March 1959, lot 34 (as Sisto Badalocchio), where bought by Colnaghi; acquired by the present owner from Colnaghi in 1960.

EXHIBITIONS

London (Colnaghi) 1960, no.1; Detroit 1965, no.66; London (Agnew) 1973, no.19; Rio de Janeiro/São Paulo 1989, no. 18; Oxford/London 1990–1; Bologna/Fort Worth 1993–4, no.27.

1 For Ludovico, see, most recently, Feigenbaum 1984 (unpublished), Bologna/Fort Worth 1993–4, and Pepper 1994.

2 See Bologna/Fort Worth 1993–4, no.27. A slightly later treatment is the painting in the Prado, which belonged to Maratti, ibid., no.45. Another painting of the subject is recorded in the collection of the 7th Marqués del Carpio in 1687 but it is untraced, see Burke 1984 (unpublished), II, p.336.

3 As pointed out by Whitfield in London (Agnew) 1973, no.19.

4 For the provenance of this work, see Kauffmann 1982, pp.46–8.

5 See Pepper 1994, pp.53 and 60.

6 In Gail Feigenbaum's entry for this picture in Bologna/Fort Worth 1993–4, no. 27, it is erroneously stated that it was sold at Sotheby's, London, December 1947. A 'Christ on the Mount of Olives' by Ludovico Carracci was sold at Sotheby's, London, 17 December 1947, lot 92, but it was on metal and much smaller than the Mahon picture (18 1/4 x 14 1/2 inches).

7 See Robinson 1865, p.17, no.346 (as Annibale Carracci).

Valerio Castello 1625–1659

11 The Virgin and Child with Saint John the Baptist

Oil on canvas, 99 x 73.9 cm
Inscribed: ECCE [AGNU]S DEI on the scroll

Castello was born in Genoa, the son of the painter Bernardo Castello (1557–1629). After training with Domenico Fiasella and Giovanni Andrea de' Ferrari, he travelled to Milan and to Parma, probably in the first half of the 1640s. The pictures that seem to date from this decade are a stylistic synthesis of the charged emotional intensity of Milanese painting with the elegance and refinement of Correggio and Parmigianino. Castello spent the rest of his brief career in Genoa where he paid special attention to the numerous works of Van Dyck, which led to his adoption of scintillating chromatic effects. He painted frescoes in the palaces and churches in the city and enjoyed enormous success, which was cut short by his early death.[1] The chronology of his works is speculative since there are very few dated or datable works.

The composition of the *Virgin and Child with Saint John the Baptist* is based on a series of diagonal lines which cross in the dynamically posed figure of Christ. The sense of movement, the flickering light and the lively brushwork create a sense of visual exhilaration, which is a notable characteristic of Castello's pictures. The setting, with the column base to the left, is reminiscent of Van Dyck's portraits, while the long-necked Madonna with her graceful profile and elegant hands calls to mind the feminine ideal of Parmigianino. The colouring is rich and intense and the juxtaposition of the cold dark blue and the hot red of the Virgin's draperies, and the dense network of white impastoed strokes that make up the cloth underneath the child, sustain the spirited theatricality of the image. Castello makes use of tiny accents of scarlet on the lips, hands and feet to keep the surface of the painting vibrant. The painting has been dated to about 1650 by Manzitti.[2]

Another version of the painting of almost identical dimensions is in the Musée des Beaux-Arts in Nantes.[3] There are small formal differences: the position of the Virgin's left hand and Christ's left foot is altered, the heads of the children are brought closer together, and the column base is not included; but the most significant differences lie in the use of light and in the handling. The figures in the Nantes painting are set against a stormy, threatening sky in which a flash of light surrounds the Virgin's head. As in the present work, her neck is strongly lit, but in contrast, her face is almost completely in shadow. The handling of the Nantes painting is looser and the picture generally less worked up. This might suggest that its execution precedes the more finished painting exhibited here.[4]

Castello painted the subject of the Virgin and Child with Saint John the Baptist on two other occasions, although the compositions of those works are quite different.[5]

TECHNICAL NOTE
The support is a dense medium-weight canvas. The painting has an old lining and is attached to an oak strainer probably dating from the eighteenth century. There are wooden strips about 1 cm wide attached to the top, left and right sides of the strainer. There is some surface abrasion due to the lining process, on the Virgin's left and right hands, and in other places, but in general the condition is good. The painting has a reddish ground. The blues in the picture have probably darkened.

PROVENANCE
Lord Gwydir, Grimesthorpe Castle, Lincs, by 1812;[6] Christie's, London, 9 May 1829 (Lord Gwydir sale), lot 77; Neeld collection, Grittleton House, Chippenham, Wilts; sold by L.W. Neeld at Christie's, London, 13 July 1945, lot 8; acquired there by the present owner.

EXHIBITIONS
London 1960, no.363; Dayton/Sarasota/Hartford 1962–3, no.20.

1 For Castello's life, see Soprani 1674, pp.231–6, and Soprani/Ratti 1768, I, pp.339–50; see also Manzitti 1972, and Gavazza 1987, pp.187–200.
2 Manzitti 1972, cat.59, p.137.
3 Inv.41, oil on canvas, 98 x 74.5 cm, see Manzitti 1972, cat.58, p.136, and Sarrazin 1994, no.128, pp.180–1. The painting went to the museum in 1804 and apparently came from the royal collection at Versailles. Briganti described it as 'rather coarser in quality' than the Mahon picture (1953, p.13).
4 See the comments in Briganti 1953, p.13, and those of Robert and Bertina Suida Manning in Dayton/Sarasota/Hartford 1962–3, under no.20.
5 Manzitti 1972, cats.124 and 150, pp.215 and 242.
6 According to the *Inventory of the Household Furniture at Grimesthorpe Castle in the County of Lincoln the Property of the Right Honorable Lord Gwydir, corrected to 1812* (typescript copy in the National Gallery Library of an inventory marked BR805, lent by the British Records Association): 'Chinese Room, Paintings, No.7 Virgin and Child with St John Valerio Castelli'.

Pietro da Cortona 1596–1669

14 The Oath of Semiramis

Oil on copper, 51.2 x 70.7 cm

Semiramis was the legendary Queen of Babylon who founded the Assyrian empire; she conquered much of Egypt and Ethiopia and built great cities and monuments. After a long and successful reign she abdicated in favour of her son and was said to have been taken to heaven in the form of a dove. The source of the scene depicted in this painting is an anecdote recounted by the first-century writer Valerius Maximus in his *Facta et Dicta Memorabilia*.[1] While Queen Semiramis was dressing her hair, a messenger arrived to tell her that Babylon had revolted; she abandoned her toilette precipitately and refused to complete her coiffure until the rising was quelled and peace restored. The painting shows her raising her right hand and eyes towards heaven to solemnise her vow. Having laid aside her comb she prepares to don a helmet. The moral import of the episode was considered to be significant, but its precise meaning remains obscure.

Although Tuscan by birth, Cortona became the leading painter of the Roman Baroque. He painted highly impressive frescoes in the Barberini and Pamphilj palaces in Rome and in Palazzo Pitti in Florence, as well as altarpieces and frescoes for the churches of Rome, and large history pictures.[2] In the early 1620s, before he was taken up by the Barberini, Cortona was in contact with the antiquarian Cassiano Dal Pozzo who became his intellectual mentor and friend, and (according to Mancini, writing before 1626) commissioned several works from him, none of which has yet been identified.[3] Dal Pozzo encouraged Cortona to study the architecture and sculpture of Imperial Rome and several of his drawings of the reliefs of Trajan's column and other antique sculptures survive.[4] The results of this programme of study are apparent in the frescoes in Palazzo Mattei (1623) and especially in those in the Roman church of Santa Bibbiana (1624–6) showing scenes of her trial and martyrdom.[5] In them one sees a profusion of classical architecture, costume, furniture, sculpture and militaria, integrated into compositions of potent human drama. It is among Dal Pozzo's circle, made up of learned civil servants, bibliophiles, poets and collectors, that the patron of this small collector's picture with its recondite subject matter and emphatic antiquarian character should be sought.

The painting, executed with a fluid stroke and warm palette, is very close in style to the frescoes Cortona painted in Palazzo Mattei. Briganti has highlighted the analogies with the two 'quadri riportati', or fictive easel pictures in fresco, on the ceiling of the Galleria in Palazzo Mattei showing *Solomon and the Queen of Sheba* and the *Idolatry of Solomon*.[6] The figure types and costumes are very close but the similarity lies above all in the use of a shallow foreground area with the figures arranged as in a frieze against a scenographic backdrop. This feature reflects the contemporary classic trend in painting, of which the prime exponent was Domenichino; his frescoes in the Polet Chapel in San Luigi dei Francesi provided the canonic example. In Cortona's two fresco scenes in Palazzo Mattei the pictorial formula of the *Oath of Semiramis* is transposed to a larger scale and performed with full orchestra.

There is a preparatory compositional drawing in the Uffizi which shows that Cortona originally planned a more complex figure arrangement.[7] In the drawing the woman who here hands the sword to Semiramis is shown bending forward with her head inclined, investing the group at the right with greater depth and movement. The woman who carries a lance was originally gesticulating dismissively to two attendant women, one of whom carries a mirror, who do not appear in the painting. Another kneeling figure, a companion of the messenger, was also excluded from the painting.

TECHNICAL NOTE

The support is a quite thick copper panel. The reverse is heavily scored, presumably to provide purchase for attaching the panel to some form of support, which no longer survives. Residues of animal glue are visible. The letters 'I.H' are scratched on the reverse, followed by several other letters which are difficult to read, the last two may be 'us'. The painting is in very good condition but there are scattered small losses. There are small pentimenti: the blue cloak of the kneeling messenger once stretched further to the right, whereas his left leg was further to the left. The changes suggest that he was originally begun further to the left, as in the drawing.

PROVENANCE

Possibly the painting recorded in the collection of Gerrit Uylenburg in Amsterdam in 1675;[8] with an artist/restorer in Poissy, near Paris, before 1956;[9] Galerie Heim, Paris; acquired by the present owner in 1957.

EXHIBITIONS

Paris (Heim) 1956, no.22; London 1960, no.406; Detroit 1965, no.32.

1 Book IX, chapter 3, part 4. The Latin passage is quoted in Mahon 1949, p.217, note 2.
2 For Cortona, see Briganti 1982 and Merz 1991.
3 '…alchune altre cose ch'à il signor cavalier del Pozzo', Mancini 1956–7, I, p.263.
4 Briganti 1982, figs.2–4; pl.286, fig.26; Merz 1991, pp.35–41, figs.8–13 and 52–4.
5 Briganti 1982, figs.36–40.
6 Briganti 1982, cat.6, pp.162–3; see also Merz 1991, pp.132, 134 and 144. For the frescoes, see Briganti 1982, figs.15 and 16.
7 Inv.11771, pen and wash with white heightening, 240 x 170 mm; reproduced in Briganti 1982, fig.21.
8 'Semiramis van Peter de Cortone 400:—:—', Dudok van Heel 1982, p.85. The subject was quite rare and no other reference to a painting of this subject by the artist is known. The valuation of 400 *guilders* is quite high. Uylenburgh (*c*.1626–*c*.1690) was a wealthy Amsterdam collector who owned a significant number of Italian paintings by 1675, the date in which the inventory of his collection was taken.
9 Information from Monsieur François Heim (1996).

Giuseppe Maria Crespi 1665–1747

15 *Noli Me Tangere*

Oil on canvas, 52.8 x 41.3 cm

Crespi was born in Bologna and trained with the leading history painters active in the city in the late seventeenth century, Canuti, Cignani and Burrini. Crespi was very conscious of the rich inheritance of Bolognese and Emilian painting, and his early works in particular betray a greater debt to artists like Ludovico Carracci, Guercino and even Giovanni Lanfranco, than to his own teachers. Later on Crespi would encourage his pupils to steep themselves in the manner of these great artists in order to have their example in mind when they painted their own works.[1] The *Noli Me Tangere* shares the heightened emotional intensity of the paintings of Ludovico Carracci and the dramatic flickering light of Guercino.[2] The work forms part of a group which is dated to the late 1680s, when Crespi was in contact with Burrini, and includes the *Saint John the Baptist Preaching* (Bologna, San Salvatore, painted as a pendant to Burrini's *David*), in which the pose of the saint is very close indeed to that of Christ in the *Noli Me Tangere*, and the *Resurrection* (Raleigh, North Carolina Museum of Art), which dynamically posed figures similar to the Magdalen.[3]

The risen Christ in this picture, draped in blue, assumes an elegant classical contrapposto as he greets the grieving Magdalen. He points to himself to indicate that he is the one she is looking for: 'Jesus saith unto her, "Mary". She turned herself, and saith unto him, "Rabboni"; which is to say, Master' (John 20:16). The flowers at Christ's feet and the staff leaning against the tree situate the encounter in a garden as the Gospel narrative demands. Crespi treats the scene as a nocturne with the moon setting over the distant hills. The light plays over the forms, throwing the head and torso of Christ into relief and picking out the right side of the Magdalen's face and her right arm, heightening the drama of the encounter. The eighteenth-century writer Marcello Oretti described a 'Magdalen before the Redeemer' in the house of Crespi's early Bolognese patron Giovanni Ricci which is probably identifiable with this work.[4]

Ricci was a wealthy merchant and the patron of Crespi's early *Wedding at Cana* now in the Art Institute of Chicago. According to Crespi's biographer Giampietro Zanotti (1739), they were introduced by Burrini, and Crespi came to an arrangement with Ricci whereby when the painter had no other commissions he would paint pictures for Ricci who committed himself to buy them for a good price. If Ricci sold these paintings the profit would go to the artist. This arrangement worked in both of the men's favour: Crespi never wanted for money and Ricci came to own a fine group of paintings and drawings by the artist.[5] According to Luigi Crespi, the artist's son, writing in 1769, Ricci also paid for the artist's trips to Venice, Parma and Umbria.[6] At his death Ricci's paintings and drawings passed to his nephew, Antonio Marchesini.[7]

TECHNICAL NOTE

The support is a very fine, plain-weave, canvas. A glue-paste lining was applied when the painting was still in the Grassi collection, probably in the first half of this century. The original tacking edges do not survive, but the evidence of cusping on all four sides of the canvas indicates that it retains its original dimensions. The surface has suffered slight abrasion, apparent mostly in the light areas, but the painting is generally in good condition. There are small retouchings around the edges and in Christ's blue robe. The ground is brown in colour.

PROVENANCE

Possibly the work painted for Crespi's early patron, Giovanni Ricci, Bologna; Luigi Grassi, Florence, in the second quarter of this century;[8] acquired from Colnaghi by the present owner in 1958.

EXHIBITIONS

London (Colnaghi) 1958, no.10; Bologna 1959, no.101; London 1960, no.371; Rio de Janeiro/São Paulo 1989, no. 24; Bologna 1990, no.4.

1 '...ecco il perchè esortasse egli di continuo i suoi scolari ad imbeverarsi delle maniere de grandi uomini, per averle poi presenti alla fantasia, allorchè operassero...', Crespi 1769, p.204.
2 Crespi made copies of Guercino's *Ecstasy of Saint Francis* in the Louvre, see Pajes Merriman 1980, nos.116 and 117, and shows a version of it on the rear wall of *The Artist in his Studio* (Hartford, Wadsworth Atheneum), no.222. A copy of Guercino's *Investiture of Saint William* in the Dusmet collection is claimed to be by Crespi, ibid., no.125.
3 Pajes Merriman 1980, nos.46 and 64.
4 'Maddalena avanti al Redentore', M. Oretti, *Notizie de' Professori del disegno cioè pittori scultori ed architetti bolognesi e de forestieri di sua scuola raccolte ed in più tomi divise...*, Bologna, Biblioteca Comunale, manuscript B.131, *c*.1760, vol.IX, ff.358–9. The connection was proposed by Maurizio Calvesi in Bologna 1959, p.201.
5 Zanotti 1739, II, p.36, quoted in Fort Worth 1986, pp.15–16; see also Crespi 1769, pp.204–5.
6 Crespi 1769, pp.204–5.
7 Zanotti 1739, II, p.36, quoted in Fort Worth 1986, p.16.
8 A red wax seal on the stretcher bears the letters 'AG'.

Giuseppe Maria Crespi 1665–1747

16 Musicians

Oil on canvas, 100.8 x 50.1 cm

17 Peasants with Donkeys

Oil on canvas, 94.1 x 53.8 cm

Although he was trained with artists who worked in the academic tradition of Bolognese painting, Crespi chose to make himself the direct heir of the Carracci as a painter of everyday life. Thanks to the patronage of important figures like the Grand Prince Ferdinando de' Medici and Cardinal Pietro Ottoboni, and to taking on Giambattista Piazzetta and Pietro Longhi as his pupils, Crespi played a significant role in developing the taste among his contemporaries for genre scenes of the kind represented by these two paintings.

Peasants with Donkeys is in the Bolognese tradition of street-vendor subjects.[1] The principal figure is lifting a basket of bread rolls from the donkey's side and a bearded man on the right raises his hand to purchase three of them. In *Musicians* three peasants play an assortment of instruments: a large triangle with rings, a recorder and, curiously, a lyre. Two of them wear fur hats perhaps identifying them as shepherds. Behind them is a man pulling a horse by the bridle and to the left are soldiers with riders beyond. None of the figures looks out at the viewer and two actually turn away. The nocturnal setting allows for more dramatic scenes and stark highlit details, like the thrust-out forearm holding the bridle in *Musicians*, or the white sleeve of the bread vendor, but it also makes the figures look a little sinister.

The triangle player looks towards the left as though observing something outside the picture; in *Peasants with Donkeys* the man carrying a sack on his shoulders strides forward but meets abruptly with the edge of the canvas. Both paintings have in fact been cut down on the left side. *Musicians* is clearly the right side of a larger canvas and the same is true of *Peasants with Donkeys*. It has often been stated that the two canvases are fragments of a single larger painting, possibly a narrative subject drawn from the Old Testament,[2] but technical evidence indicates that they were always two separate works. Both canvases are also cut at the top and it is consequently impossible to know how large they originally were. The two paintings are now slightly different sizes but the similarity in figure scale, palette and brushstroke, as well as the identical canvas type, suggests that they must always have been intended as pendants. They are in all likelihood fragments of larger pure genre compositions of the kind represented by Crespi's *Fair with a Dentist* (Milan, Pinacoteca di Brera) or the *Scene at the Wall of a Cathedral* (present location unknown).[3]

Crespi's interest in peasant subjects seems to date from his exposure to works by the Bamboccianti during his stay in Florence in 1709. While he was there he painted his masterly *Fair at Poggio a Caiano* (Florence, Uffizi) which contains a large number of popular types. The present pictures must date from shortly after the trip to Florence. The stylistic similarities with the series of *Seven Sacraments* (Dresden, Staatliche Kunstsammlungen), commissioned by Cardinal Ottoboni in about 1712 (in which religious subject matter is treated as genre), suggest that they should be dated between 1710 and 1715.

Several figures from these two works were copied by Giuseppe Gambarini (1680–1725), a minor Bolognese painter of genre subjects.[4] He is not recorded as a pupil of Crespi but must have had access to his studio in the 1710s. In his *Dance in the Country* in Stuttgart (fig.13), Gambarini includes two musicians which are closely based on Crespi's, although the unlikely lyre is replaced with a rustic tambourine. In the pendant, *Friars receiving Alms* (fig.14), Gambarini quotes, in reverse, the donkey and bread vendor from Crespi's *Peasants with Donkeys*, transforming the tradesman into a mendicant friar. Crespi's triangle player in *Musicians* reappears as a ribbon seller in Gambarini's *Women Embroidering* (New York, Alan E.Salz collection) and as a languid peasant in his allegory of *Summer* in the Uffizi.[5] The chronology of Gambarini's oeuvre is not established but his genre pictures are thought to date from after his visit to Rome of 1712–13.[6] The smooth surfaces and clearly outlined forms of

Fig.13 Giuseppe Gambarini, *A Dance in the Country*, c.1715–20. Oil on canvas, 61.5 x 76.5 cm. Stuttgart, Staatsgalerie.

Fig.14 Giuseppe Gambarini, *Friars receiving Alms*, c.1715–20. Oil on canvas, 62 x 76.5 cm. Stuttgart, Staatsgalerie.

his works stand in stark contrast to Crespi's fragmented lighting and broken contours. Gambarini did not copy whole compositions by Crespi, preferring to adopt single figure motifs, but his charming rococo peasants have none of the grimy realism of Crespi's.

The seated woman in Gambarini's *Friars receiving Alms* and the seated woman on the right of *Women Embroidering* are based on another painting by Crespi, *Study of a Seated Woman* (fig.15).[7] This is a fragment of a larger composition and in handling, tonality and size of figure it is very similar to the two Mahon pictures; it has been dated to the same period.[8] It is possible (and Gambarini's borrowings might suggest) that this fragment may originally have been part of either *Musicians* or *Peasants and Donkeys* when these were in their integral state. This brings us to the question of when the Mahon pictures were cut down.

It has been argued that the canvases were already in their mutilated state when Gambarini painted the two Stuttgart paintings, since his figures are cropped in the same way as Crespi's pair. If this is so then it is unlikely that anyone but Crespi would have cut the pictures to their present configuration.[9] However, we now know that the right edges of both Crespis are original and that the crop of the recorder player in Gambarini's *Dance in the Country* corresponds with the complete right edge of Crespi's *Musicians*. The crop of Gambarini's reversed donkey actually differs from that on the incomplete left side of Crespi's *Peasants and Donkeys*. This would seem to indicate that Crespi's canvases had not necessarily been reduced by the time Gambarini painted his pictures. Gambarini's use of Crespi's *Seated Woman* (which, as has been suggested, may have been part of one of the Mahon paintings) in his *Friars receiving Alms* strengthens this probability. It has been acutely observed that Crespi's paintings are particularly susceptible to mutilation because of the artist's distinctive way of isolating figures in darkness.[10] The reduction of the Mahon canvases may have taken place long after the artist's death.

TECHNICAL NOTE
Both paintings are on plain-weave, fairly coarse canvas. They have a glue-paste lining, applied by G.Morrill (stamp on both stretchers) shortly before they were acquired by the present owner. There are no remnants of tacking edges on either painting. X-radiographs made at the National Gallery show that none of the forms of either painting crosses over into the other. They also show cusping on the right and bottom margins of both paintings, indicating that these edges have not been sig-

nificantly reduced from when the canvases were stretched on their first stretchers. No cusping is visible on the other two sides of either picture. This technical evidence disposes of the idea that the two pieces of canvas were ever part of the same painting.

The ground in both paintings is a warm reddish brown and of gritty consistency. It is more apparent today because of the abrasion of the paint surface and the increased transparency of the paint itself. In *Peasants with Donkeys* the ground is particularly evident in the area of the foremost donkey's head. The blue on the horizon in *Musicians* has blanched. There are pentimenti in both paintings. In *Musicians* the right arm of the triangle player was originally higher. In *Peasants and Donkeys* the figure carrying a sack was originally posed differently: the head was lower down and both arms were raised well above the head as though he were lifting something over it. When Crespi altered the figure he painted the left arm reaching horizontally across his chest, but he then changed it to its present position.

PROVENANCE
Reputed to have belonged to the physician Dr Pelham Warren (1778–1835), Worting House, Basingstoke;[11] by descent to Mrs Warren-Codrington, Worting House; her sale, Christie's, London, 27 May 1949, lot 3 (bought by Cooper); acquired by the present owner from the Leger Gallery, London, in 1949.

EXHIBITIONS
Birmingham 1955, nos.37a and b; London 1960, no.379; Bologna 1970, nos.73 and 74; Fort Worth 1986, nos.10 and 11; Bologna 1990, nos.46 and 47.

Fig.15 Giuseppe Maria Crespi, *Study of a Seated Woman, c.*1710–15. Oil on canvas, 43.5 x 29 cm. Private collection.

1 Annibale Carracci made drawings for a series of *Arti di Bologna* which were engraved by Simon Guillain and published in Rome in 1646, see Posner 1971, I, pp.17 and 155, note 29; Marabottini 1979.
2 London 1960, pp.147–8; Pajes Merriman (1980, p.310) doubts whether the paintings can have been part of an Old Testament subject.
3 See Pajes Merriman 1980, nos.265 and 275. J.T. Spike showed that the painting of *Musicians* (Pajes Merriman 1980, no.263) in the collection of Pamela Askew, Millbrook, New York, is a fragment of *Scene at the Wall of a Cathedral* (Fort Worth 1986, no.16, pp.138–40).
4 This was first pointed out by Roli (1977, pp.185 and 187).
5 For *Women Embroidering*, see Fort Worth 1986, no.33. *Summer* is one of a set of *Four Seasons*, see Florence 1993 (nos.27–30), no.28. In the scene showing *Autumn*, Gambarini repeats Crespi's lyre-player from *Musicians* but has him play a guitar-like instrument, ibid., no.29.
6 Fort Worth 1986, p.173.
7 Bologna 1990, no.41. Spike, who published the picture in 1986, states that there is a basket at lower left, in the same position as it appears in Gambarini's *Friars receiving Alms*, but that this had been painted over in a recent restoration, Fort Worth 1986, fig.32.1, pp.174–5.
8 Giordano Viroli in Bologna 1990, p.78.
9 Spike in Fort Worth 1986, p.128.
10 Spike in Fort Worth 1986, p.128. An example of this is mentioned in note 3 above.
11 See London 1960, p.147, under no.379. Dr Pelham Warren was the son of Richard Warren (1731–97), physician to George III.

16

17

Donato Creti 1671–1749

18 Artemisia drinking the Ashes of Mausolus

Oil on canvas, 62.7 x 49.9 cm

Donato Creti was an academic painter whose art is rich in allusions to the great tradition of Bolognese painting. His compositions are highly elegant in style and refined in execution. He was born in Cremona but moved with his family to Bologna in 1673. According to his early biographers he was extremely precocious and there are, in the Uffizi, two drawings dated 1685, when Creti was only fourteen.[1] He seems to have spent some time making life drawings in the 'accademia del nudo' of Lorenzo Pasinelli (1629–1700), the leading painter in Bologna in the last decade and a half of the seventeenth century. The young Creti was taken under the wing of Count Alessandro Fava, who offered him hospitality in his palazzo and numerous commissions.[2] In 1709 Creti was one of the founder members of the Accademia Clementina in Bologna and thereafter he was several times one of its directors and in 1728 its *Principe*. In 1729–30 he participated (together with Canaletto, Piazzetta and Sebastiano Ricci among others) in the commission from the Irishman Owen McSwiney for a series of paintings of allegorical tombs intended for the 2nd Duke of Richmond at Goodwood. Creti painted decorative frescoes and, in his later years, some altarpieces but most of his activity was undertaken for private patrons.

This painting has always been called 'Sophonisba taking Poison', as it was thought to represent the suicide of Sophonisba, spouse of the Numidian king Massinissa, recounted by Livy. The identification of the subject as Artemisia drinking the ashes of Mausolus by the present author is dependent upon the comparison with a painting by Giovan Gioseffo dal Sole (1654–1719), on which Creti based his composition (fig.16).[3] Dal Sole's painting was made for Senatore Bovio of Bologna and is usually dated to shortly after 1700.[4] It is larger than Creti's picture and has an elaborate architectural setting which includes, on the left, the great funerary monument (mausoleum) built by Artemisia at Halicarnassus in memory of her husband, which became one of the wonders of the ancient world. The similarities between the paintings are

Fig.16 Giovan Gioseffo dal Sole, *Artemisia drinking the Ashes of Mausolus*, c.1700–10. Oil on canvas, 157 x 190 cm. Rome, Galleria Corsini.

numerous, and range from poses and gestures to the colour of the fabric draped over the dais. Creti, who admired Dal Sole,[5] reduced the scale and increased the intimacy of the scene, investing it with a refined delicacy.

The subtle colouring and the precise calligraphic brushstroke employed in this painting are typical of Creti. Stylistically the work is very close to the series of four paintings of the life of Achilles made for Marcantonio Collina Sbaraglia of Bologna in about 1713–14 (Bologna, Collezioni Comunali d'Arte).[6] The figure of the female attendant is repeated exactly in the *Achilles entrusted to Chiron* where, however, instead of proffering a dish she hands over the infant Achilles. Furthermore, her graceful profile and intricate hair-style (reminiscent of Parmigianino) is found again in the figure at the left of the *Achilles immersed in the Styx*. The present picture clearly dates from the same time. Roli has identified it with a work listed in the inventory of paintings – drawn up by Creti himself – in Palazzo Fava in 1745: 'Cleopatra che beve il veleno presentatole da un paggio, con cornice dorata, del Creti, L.100'.[7] However, the description does not correspond very closely with the subject matter of this painting.

TECHNICAL NOTE

The support is a fine plain-weave canvas and the original tacking edges survive. The painting is lined and wooden strips have been attached to the left, right and bottom edges. Stretcher-bar marks visible on the surface of the picture on all four sides are those of an earlier stretcher/strainer that was about 3 cm wide. The ground is a warm brown and the flesh areas appear to have been underpainted in a grey-brown colour. There are no obvious pentimenti. The patterned green cloth on the right was painted over the sleeve of Artemisia and over the red drape on the floor. The painting is in excellent condition.

PROVENANCE

The painting was acquired by the present owner from Colnaghi in 1963.

EXHIBITIONS

London (Colnaghi) 1963, no.3; London (Agnew) 1965, no.9; Bologna 1979, no.100.[8]

1 Roli 1967, figs.102–3.
2 The inventory of the paintings and drawings in Palazzo Fava, Bologna, drawn up by Creti himself in 1745 lists a large number of works by him, see Campori 1870, pp.602–15.
3 The story is recounted by Diodorus (XVI, 45).
4 See Thiem 1990, cat.Q27, p.110 (colour plate on p.41); see also Rome 1984, no. 8, and Rome 1993, no.12 (entries by Sivigliano Aloisi). Roli, however, dated the work to about 1692, see Roli 1985, p.38. Dal Sole's oil sketch for this work is in the collection of Brian Sewell, London (see Thiem 1990, cat.Ch18). Dal Sole had been a pupil of Pasinelli a generation earlier than Creti. Marcello Oretti actually lists Creti among the pupils of Dal Sole, although there is no corroborating evidence for this statement, see Thiem 1990, p.66.
5 Creti mentions him in passing in a letter of 26 December 1700, Roli 1967, p.80.
6 Roli 1967, cats.15–18, figs.40–3. The frames for what are almost certainly these pictures were paid for in 1714–15, see Marcon 1990, p.129, and Roli 1990, p.52.
7 Roli 1967, cat.74, p.94, and reiterated by him in Bologna 1979, cat.100, p.60.
8 With bibliography.

Domenichino (Domenico Zampieri) 1581–1641
19 Landscape with Boating Parties

Oil on canvas, 36.6 x 56.3 cm (original canvas 35 x 55 cm)

The motifs of the boat with several figures to the left of centre and the small boat in the distance, as well as the pollarded tree on the left, are freely derived from a drawing by Annibale Carracci, *River Landscape with a Boating Party*, now in the Cleveland Museum of Art.[1] This association led to the picture being catalogued as by Annibale when it was first exhibited in 1960 (see Exhibitions). Another drawing associated with Annibale in the Louvre reflects the source for the motif of the boat with an oarsman and lute-player.[2] The painting was attributed to Domenichino in 1962, and this view found wide acceptance.[3] An alternative attribution to Domenichino's collaborator and imitator, the Bolognese landscape specialist Giovanni Battista Viola (1576–1622), has recently been proposed.[4]

During the course of preparation for this exhibition the pendant to this work, *Wooded Landscape with a Hunting Party*, was identified (fig.17).[5] The canvas type, lining and stretchers of the two pictures are identical. More importantly, the handling, the figure types and the use of the same soft light in both landscapes indicate that they are by the same hand. The existence in the National Gallery of a pair of paintings of larger format which repeat the compositions, with some variations (fig.18), provides further evidence that the two pictures are pendants.[6]

The composition of *Landscape with Boating Parties* illustrates considerable organisational skill: the river meanders convincingly into the distance with the cool light playing over the glassy surface and creating alternating patches of silvery reflection and grey shadow. The hills rise up gradually from the distant bank and on the right the snowy peaks are dramatically highlit through the trees. Around the central motif of the river are arranged the figure groups engaged in genteel recreation or unstrenuous labour. Washerwomen and fishermen perform their tasks in pastoral tranquillity. The river landscape in this work is complemented by the valley view in *Wooded Landscape with a Hunting Party*. Elegantly dressed riders begin their day's hunting while members of their retinue water the dogs and sound the horn. Some of the figures are painted with a delicacy and sensitivity to light effects – notably the foremost rider in this work and the couple on the left in *Landscape with Boating Parties* – that seem beyond the ability of Viola in his few relatively certain works. The luxuriant character of the vegetation and the tiny figures in the middle ground reflected in the water recall the example of Elsheimer, who had settled in Rome in 1600.

Although Domenichino at the beginning of his career would have considered his landscape painting activity a pleasurable sideline, it played an important role in establishing the taste for small-scale landscapes of this kind. His works were very influential from the start on Pietro Paolo Bonzi, Viola and possibly Antonio Carracci. The sequence of Domenichino's early landscapes is a matter of opinion since there are only two documented works which survive: the Kimbell Art Museum's *Landscape with the Sacrifice of Isaac*, which is listed in the inventory of the collection of Cardinal Pietro Aldobrandini (January 1603), and the Louvre *Washerwomen in a Landscape* which belonged to Annibale Carracci and therefore dates from before 1609 when he died.[7] Domenichino's concern with hunting and boating subjects is apparent in several works which are usually dated to the first decade of the century, notably the *Landscape with Figures fording a River* (Rome, Galleria Doria Pamphilj), the lost *Landscape with a Poling Boatman and a Woman with a Basket of Crabs* (known from a copy) and the Christ Church *Fisherman, Hunters and Washerwomen*.[8] The heavy dependence of the *Landscape with Boating Parties* on drawings by and associated with Annibale, and the similarity between the figures in the two works under discussion here and the figures in the Kimbell *Sacrifice of Isaac*, indicate that they are early works perhaps dating from around 1602–3.

TECHNICAL NOTE
The support is a medium-weight plain-weave canvas. The painting was glue-lined probably in England in the nineteenth century and the original tacking edges have been cut off. The ground appears to be a warm brown-grey in colour. The painting is in generally good condition, although at some point it has suffered some cleaning damage and the glazes on the water appear broken up. There is some ultramarine blanching in the two figures in blue on the boat just to the left of centre. There is some retouching in the group of trees to the left of centre.

PROVENANCE
Possibly Christie's, London, 12 June 1811, lot 50 (as Annibale Carracci, offered with companion picture, lot 49);[9] acquired by the present owner at Appleby's, London, in 1957.

EXHIBITIONS
London 1960, no.394 (as Annibale Carracci); Newcastle-upon-Tyne 1961, no.201 (as Annibale Carracci); Bologna 1962, no.13 (as Domenichino); Utrecht 1965, no.174 (as Domenichino); Frankfurt 1966, no.67; London (Agnew) 1973, no.23; Rome 1996, no. Ia.

1 Inv.72.101, pen and brown ink, 224 x 405 mm, see Rome 1996, p.522, fig.1. The drawing was the source of a print by M. Corneille in the Recueil Jabach 1754, no.11B.
2 Probably after Annibale, *Two Men in a Boat*, pen and brown ink, 165 x 219 mm, Paris, Musée du Louvre (Inv.7213), see Rome 1996, p.522, fig. 2. This drawing was the source of a print by M. Corneille in the Recueil Jabach 1754, no.16B.
3 Cavalli in Bologna 1962, pp.85–7; Jaffé 1962, p.413; Utrecht 1965, p.252; Frankfurt 1966, p.57; London (Agnew) 1973, no.23; Salerno 1976, I, p.80, no.19.2; Whitfield 1988, p.90. It was questioned only by Schaar 1963, p.54, Borea 1965, p.195, and Spear 1974, p.224.
4 Spear 1980, pp.302 and 305; see also Spear 1982, I, p.316.
5 Sotheby's, London, 17 November 1982, lot 47 (as Viola). It is not known when the two pictures were separated, but it was certainly before 1957; see Rome 1996, no Ib.
6 *Landscape with a River and Boats* (NG56) and Landscape with a Hunting Party (NG63). These have recently been attributed to Viola, see Rome 1996, nos. IIa–IIb, with bibliography. Two drawings in the Devonshire collection (attributed by Jaffé to Grimaldi, Jaffé 1994, IV, no.552, p.136) on the *recto* and *verso* of the same sheet record the National Gallery compositions and provide further evidence that these two paintings are pendants, as pointed out by Van Tuyll (1996, p.698). Thus the proposal advanced by Spear (1980, p.305) that the pendant to the Mahon painting is the Louvre's *Concert on the Water* (40 x 52 cm), which he also attributes to Viola, is not acceptable.
7 Spear 1982, I, no.3, pp.126–7, and Whitfield 1988, pp.68–72, fig.2, respectively; see also Rome 1996, nos.2 and 9.
8 Spear 1982, I, nos.16–18, pp.138–40.
9 '49. A.Carracci: A landscape with a road at the foot of a mountainous range, and Figures in Pastoral Employment – a masterly production worthy of the great mind of Carracci, and apparently executed a l'improviso. For variety and distinctness of objects and freshness of tone this landscape has no equal.' (Bought in, Higgins, at 225 guineas); '50. Carracci: The debouchement of a river with figures in a boat; the front ground occupied by a sketch of trees through which appears a picturesque scene – painted with a masterly hand and a sweet tone.' (Bought in, Higgins, at 250 guineas.)

Fig.17 Domenichino, *Wooded Landscape with a Hunting Party*, *c*.1602–3. Oil on canvas, 37 x 56 cm (original canvas 35.1 x 55.8 cm). Private collection.

Fig.18 Attributed to Giovanni Battista Viola, *Landscape with a River and Boats*, after 1603. Oil on canvas, 95.3 x 132.1 cm. London, National Gallery.

Domenichino (Domenico Zampieri) 1581–1641

20 The Vision of Saint Jerome

Oil on copper, 49.4 x 37.2 cm

The iconography of the painting does not correspond with a specific incident in the life of Saint Jerome but his upward glance and the angel's heavenward gesture clearly allude to the divine inspiration which was understood to mark his life and his writings. Jerome (c.331–420), a scholar, polemicist, hermit and ascetic, was revered as the founder of western monasticism and several religious orders have him as their patron saint. His greatest achievement was the Latin translation of the Bible, known as the *Vulgate*, which, in revised form, is still in use today. When the Council of Trent (1545–63) reaffirmed the authority of Jerome's text in one of its decrees it gave new impetus to the imagery of the saint. Indeed, he is sometimes represented almost as a fifth Evangelist, as in Domenichino's painting of the saint in the National Gallery.

Domenichino made several paintings of Saint Jerome during his first period in Rome (1602–10). The earliest is the National Gallery picture painted in 1602 and recorded in the inventory of Cardinal Pietro Aldobrandini the following year.[1] Aldobrandini was the cardinal-nephew of Pope Clement VIII who in 1592 had issued the definitive edition of the *Vulgate*, known as the Clementine. In both size and iconography the present work is similar to the Gallery picture, although they are stylistically divergent. In 1604–5 Domenichino painted three frescoes showing scenes from the life of Saint Jerome on the portico of the church of Sant'Onofrio.[2] This was a commission from Cardinal Girolamo Agucchi, whose younger brother was the art theorist Monsignor Giovanni Battista Agucchi, in whose house the artist lived from 1603/4 until 1608. The Glasgow *Landscape with Saint Jerome* would appear to date from about 1610.[3]

In his Life of the artist of 1672, Giovan Pietro Bellori describes a painting on copper which Domenichino executed when he was living in the Agucchi household. It showed 'Saint Jerome kneeling at a rock with the Crucifix in his hand'. Bellori noted that it had been sent to France together with a 'Saint Francis kneeling before the Crucifix'.[4] The support of the Mahon painting, the subject, and the French provenance, enabled Briganti to identify it as this work, although he dated it 1608–10, which is just after Domenichino had left the Agucchi household.[5] Spear has proposed a date of about 1606–8, which is preferable.[6]

The lion in the painting is closely based on a drawing by Agostino Carracci at Windsor made in preparation for his celebrated engraving of *Saint Jerome*, which was finished after his death by Francesco Brizio and published in Rome, probably in 1604.[7] The angel is derived from Annibale Carracci's *Saint Gregory in Prayer* (fig.19), a painting that was in the church of San Gregorio al Celio, Rome, and the lower half of the saint is similar to Domenichino's own fresco of the *Vision of Saint Jerome* at Sant'Onofrio. The borrowings and the self-quotation are successfully integrated into a composition of considerable grace and elegance. The sternness of the National Gallery painting and its '*gigantismo*', which is indebted to Ludovico Carracci, have been abandoned in favour of harmonious proportions, even lighting, and a warm and intense palette. The measured classicism of the work bears witness to how at this time Domenichino was firmly committed to the ideals embodied in Annibale Carracci's ceiling frescoes in the Galleria Farnese.

TECHNICAL NOTE

The copper plate is glued to a fixed wooden cradle with a wax resin adhesive. The reverse of the copper has been extensively scratched, presumably to provide some purchase for the adhesive used to attach the cradle. An inscription in pen and ink on the cradle states: *S.Jerome by Domenichino From the Orleans Gallery*. Beneath it, at the centre of the bottom edge, are the remains of a red wax seal (?). There is fine craquelure in many of the darker passages but in general the condition is good. There is some retouching in the area of the landscape, on the saint's red robe and on his torso. Two pentimenti are apparent: the angel's right foot was originally painted about 5 mm lower, and what appears to be an alternative position for one of the angel's legs can just be made out.[8]

PROVENANCE

In France before 1672;[9] Monsieur Paillot, Paris;[10] Duc d'Orléans, Paris, and in the Palais Royal until the Revolution in 1789; displayed at Mr Bryan's Gallery, 88 Pall Mall ('A catalogue of the Orléans Italian pictures, which will be exhibited for sale by private contract on Wednesday, the 26th of December, 1798, and following days'), no.86, and bought by Henry Hope for 350 guineas; his sale, Christie's, London, 29 June 1816, lot 78; George Watson Taylor by 1822 (see Exhibitions); his sale, Christie's, London, 13–14 June 1823, lot 56* (bought Kibble); Mrs Whyte of Barron Hill, Rocester, Staffs (about 1830);[11] by descent to her great-nephew Captain Arthur Finch Dawson (1836–1928); his sale, Christie's, 14 December 1928, lot 128; acquired by the present owner in 1952.

EXHIBITIONS

London 1822, no.59; London 1879, no.210 (where incorrectly stated to be on panel); London (Wildenstein) 1955, no.34; London 1960, no.393; Bologna 1962, no.18; Rome 1996, no.14.

Fig.19 Annibale Carracci, *Saint Gregory in Prayer*, *c.*1601–2. Oil on wood, 265 x 152 cm. Formerly Bridgewater House (destroyed).

1 D'Onofrio 1964, p.210; see Levey 1971, pp.95–6, and Spear 1982, no.2, pl.3.

2 Spear 1982, nos.15i–iii, pls.26–8.

3 Spear 1982, no.37, pl.136.

4 Bellori 1672, p.295; for the *Saint Francis*, which is known from copies, see Spear 1982, II, no.28, p.149 (pl.47).

5 Briganti 1953, pp.5–6. Briganti also noted that the engraving after the picture by Pietro del Po was published in Paris in 1663.

6 Spear 1982, I, no.27, p.148; see also Rome 1996, no.14.

7 See De Grazia Bohlin 1979, no.213, pp.346–51; the drawing is fig.213e; see also Wittkower 1952, no.106, p.114.

8 Briganti (1953, p.5) stated that Domenichino initially 'tried a pose for the angel which is related in reverse to that in his own canvas of the same subject in the Prado'. The painting referred to is Prado Inv.130, attributed to Domenichino but actually a Carracci workshop picture, with an old attribution to Lucio Massari, see Pérez Sánchez 1965, pp.131, 166. There is a small reproduction in Prado Inventario 1990, no.630, p.180. Given the difficulty of deciphering the pentimento in the Mahon picture the similarity is doubtful.

9 Bellori 1672, p.295. The painting probably went to France shortly after 1663, see note 5 above.

10 Bonnaffé 1884, p.241.

11 This is stated in the Finch Dawson sale catalogue.

Domenichino (Domenico Zampieri) 1581–1641
21 Saint Mary Magdalene

Oil on canvas, 122.4 x 95.7 cm (painted surface 120 x 92.8 cm)

Saint Mary Magdalene is shown at prayer resting her right arm on a stone slab, probably intended for the tomb of Christ. Her attribute of the jar of ointment is discernible just behind her elbow. Mary Magdalene is named in the Gospels (Mark 16:1; Luke 24:1 and 10) as one of the women who brought spices with which to anoint the body of Christ after his crucifixion. She is also traditionally identified (erroneously, say the exegetes) as the unnamed woman who brought a jar of ointment to anoint Christ's head and feet in the house of Simon (Matthew 26:6–13; Mark 14:3–9; Luke 7:36–50).[1] Domenichino has painted a nocturnal scene in accordance with the Gospel of Matthew (28:1).

Although Domenichino's conception of the figure ultimately derives from Correggio's grieving Magdalen in his *Lamentation over the Dead Christ* (Parma, Galleria Nazionale), the orientation of the figure and the pose of the head recall the anguished mother who wrings her hands in Reni's celebrated *Massacre of the Innocents*, a painting which Domenichino greatly admired.[2] In the mid-1610s Reni painted several saints of this type, three-quarter length raising their eyes to heaven,[3] which Domenichino would have known. Although Domenichino's forms are more solid and weighty, by the mid-1610s both artists were employing a physiognomic type based on Hellenistic sculptures such as the *Dying Alexander* and the *Niobe Group*, then in the Villa Medici in Rome.[4] The 'marmoreal' features of the Magdalen, her large eyes, elegant nose, and slightly swollen throat, correspond with the increasingly classicising and rarefied aesthetic that Domenichino was developing in the 1620s.[5]

Pope-Hennessy, who identified two preparatory drawings at Windsor for the painting, dated it about 1625.[6] The type of the Magdalen is comparable with the frescoed figures of the *Virtues* in the choir of Sant'Andrea della Valle, painted in the mid-1620s, and the handling of the drapery and the use of the corner view of a landscape are very similar to those in the *Saint John the Evangelist* painted in the later 1620s (fig.20).[7] The painting is executed with a quite surprising boldness for the artist. The mantle is laid out in broad strokes of vermilion and the highlights on the yellow lining are executed with great assuredness. In several places the cascading curls are laid over previously painted areas; the hair on the saint's right shoulder, for example, is painted over the white drape which rests on her right arm and comes up over her shoulder.

Fig.20 Domenichino, *Saint John the Evangelist*, late 1620s. Oil on canvas, 259 x 199 cm. Glyndebourne, Sussex, Tapeley 1978 Chattels Trust.

The early history of the painting is not known. The discovery of a full-size copy in Palazzo Pandolfi Elmi in Foligno, evidently executed to replace the original, has enabled the earliest recorded owners (late eighteenth century) to be identified as members of the Roncalli Benedetti family.[8]

TECHNICAL NOTE

The support is a plain-weave, medium-coarse canvas. The painting has been lined, probably in England in the nineteenth century, and placed on a larger stretcher. The original tacking edges on all four sides of the painting are intact but they have not been taken round the stretcher and are instead laid flat on the lining canvas. The stretcher-bar marks apparent on the surface indicate that the original stretcher/strainer had a single horizontal cross bar. The members were about 4 cm wide. There is a large repaired tear running vertically through the landscape, about 19 cm in from the left edge, down to the Magdalen's right sleeve. There are small damages in the lower left corner which have been filled in. In general, the painting is in good condition. The ground is pale brown in colour. There is a pentimento in the saint's left ear.

PROVENANCE[9]

Possibly in Rome in 1780;[10] Canonico Vincenzo and Francesco Roncalli Benedetti, Foligno, by 1796; acquired in that year by John Udny (1727–1800), British Consul at Livorno, for 300 scudi (the uncashed promissory notes are still preserved at Foligno); his brother, Robert Udny (1722–1802), and after his death sold at Christie's, London, 18–19 May 1804, lot 90; Robert Heathcote, his sale, Phillips', London, 5–6 April 1805, lot 100 (bought William Dermer); collection of Sir Simon H. Clarke, Bt; his sale, Christie's, London, 9 May 1840, lot 83, bought by Buchanan for R.S. Holford at Dorchester House; Sir George Lindsay Holford; at Dorchester House until 1927; sold Christie's, London, 12 May 1939, lot 42 (bought by Battery for 14 guineas); acquired by the present owner from Robert Frank, London, in 1946.

EXHIBITIONS

London 1818, no.5; London 1841, no.19; London 1851, no.37; London 1960, no.366; Bologna 1962, no.30; Bologna/Washington/New York 1986–7, no.154; Rome 1996, no.46.

1 She is also sometimes identified with Mary the sister of Lazarus who, in the Gospel of John (12:1–8), anoints the feet of Christ.
2 Pepper 1984, no.34, p.225, fig.49.
3 For example, the *Magdalen* in the Liechtenstein collection and the *Saint Sebastian* in Palazzo Rosso, Genoa, both of 1615–16, Pepper 1984, nos.48–9, figs. 75–6.
4 All these sculptures are now in the Uffizi, see Haskell and Penny 1981, nos.2 and 66. Bellori specifically mentions the *Niobe Group* as a source for Reni's heavenward gazing Magdalens, Lucretias and Madonnas, Bellori 1976, p.529.
5 For other examples of Domenichino's use of this physiognomic type, see Spear 1982, II, figs.297–8, 311–12, 323 and 325.
6 Pope-Hennessy 1948, nos.209–10, pp.44–5. A black chalk drawing on blue paper of *Saint Mary Magdalene* (296 x 221 mm), sold at Sotheby's as 'attributed to Domenichino' (London, 13 July 1972, lot 27), is also preparatory for this painting.
7 See Briganti 1953, p.6; Spear 1982, I, no.92, pp.261–2. Mahon wondered whether the 'corner of twilit landscape background' constituted evidence of Domenichino's study of Guercino's paintings where such details often appear (Mahon 1947, p.104, note 174).
8 See London 1960, pp.137–8.
9 The provenance, with references, is given in London 1960, no.366, pp.137–8. There are a few additional items here.
10 The engraving by Cunego after the painting is inscribed 'Aloisius Cunego del. et sculp. Romae 1780'.

Domenichino (Domenico Zampieri) 1581–1641

22 Landscape with a Fortified Town

Oil on canvas, 113.2 x 197 cm

One of Domenichino's most famous landscapes, this painting was greatly admired by Constable who praised 'the grandeur of the composition, and the urbanity of tone which pervades it'.[1] With the exception of the frescoes painted in the Villa Aldobrandini at Frascati, it is Domenichino's largest landscape painting. Unlike those scenes, there is no narrative subject but the composition is rich in anecdote. Beside the recumbent young woman in the left foreground a fisherman sorts his catch; the flowers she holds and the guitar she has just laid aside suggest amorous dalliance but the playful and untidy child and the older woman who emerges from behind the door of the hut brandishing a frying pan strike a discordant note of domestic realism. The girl's pointing gesture is echoed by that of one of the boatmen. The straining poleman on the right of the vessel is a favourite motif of Domenichino and was much employed by members of the Carracci workshop.[2] A shepherd, whose pose recalls that of the *Borghese Gladiator*, drives his sheep from the bank and just behind the knoll on the right there is a group of figures which resembles the Holy Family on the flight into Egypt.[3] Their inconspicuousness, however, suggests that they are merely incidental staffage.

The composition of the landscape and the fortified town in the centre of the picture are closely based on Annibale Carracci's *Flight into Egypt* (fig.21), the most celebrated of the lunettes painted by Annibale and members of his workshop for the chapel of the Aldobrandini Palace. That work played a formative role in Domenichino's career as a landscape painter and it has sometimes been seen as constituting the fountainhead of a whole vein of classical landscape painting in the seventeenth century and beyond. So similar are the two paintings that one can speak of a respectful adaptation of Annibale's composition by his best-loved pupil Domenichino. With the exception of the domed building, the arrangement of the fortified town is almost identical, even to the point of there being the same number of windows on individual façades.[4] The motif of the flock coming to water is present and the group of the cowherd with ambling cows appears in exactly the same place.

By contrast with Annibale's painting, however, in which the narrative subject unifies the elements of the composition and gives the ferryman and the camels in the distance on the left, for example, their *raison d'être*, Domenichino's painting lacks a narrative focus. The pointing gestures of the girl and boatman

Fig.21 Annibale Carracci, *Landscape with the Flight into Egypt*, c.1604. Oil on canvas, 122 x 230 cm. Rome, Galleria Doria Pamphilj.

may have been deployed to unify the disparate anecdotal elements. The artist's concern with preventing the composition from becoming too fragmented may explain why he painted out the group of the nursing mother in the boat which from the X-radiograph looks as though it was fully worked up. This pentimento is visible to the naked eye.

A compositional drawing at Windsor in black chalk is assumed to be preparatory for the painting but it does not show the nursing mother.[5] Although there are differences, the close relationship between drawing and painting (there is, for example, the same number of forward-facing and rear-facing sheep in the front row at the river bank) suggests it could be the artist's *ricordo*. Also at Windsor is a preparatory black chalk study for the reclining woman, and in the Louvre there is a study for the poleman (fig.22).[6] On the basis of the style of the Windsor compositional drawing, Pope-Hennessy dated the painting to the artist's late years when he was active mostly in Naples. It has been proposed quite convincingly that the painting was executed between the early summer of 1634 and the late spring of 1635 when Domenichino returned to Rome to escape the pressure of his Neapolitan commissions and the antagonism of his rivals there. During this time he was under the protection of the Aldobrandini and would have had the opportunity to see again the lunettes in the Aldobrandini chapel.[7]

A copy of the painting is reproduced in a photograph in the Witt Library but no indication of the size or location is given.[8]

Fig.22 Domenichino, *Study of a Poleman*, 1634–5. Charcoal and white heightening on blue paper, 394 x 240 mm. Paris, Musée du Louvre.

1   Quoted in Spear 1982, I, p.116.
2   Domenichino uses it, for example, in his *Landscape with the Flight into Egypt* (Oberlin, Allen Memorial Art Museum) and in the fresco of the *Calling of Saints Peter and Andrew* (Rome, Sant'Andrea della Valle), Spear 1982, II, figs.36 and 286.
3   Michael Jaffé deemed this to be the subject of the picture, Jaffé 1962, p.417.
4   The motif of a town with a waterfall is to be found in several drawings by Domenichino: a pen study of the *Flight into Egypt* in the Louvre (Inv. R.F.635), see Borea 1966, fig.54, and another in the Prado (Inv.1806), see Spear 1969, as well as in the compositional drawing at Windsor related to the present painting.
5   Pope-Hennessy 1948, no.207, p.44.
6   Ibid, no.208; the Louvre drawing is Inv.7333.
7   Briganti 1953, pp.6–7; Spear 1982, I, pp.20–1 and 302–3. Briganti points out that the reclining girl is a quotation from Titian's *Andrians* (Madrid, Museo del Prado), which at that time was in the Ludovisi collection in Rome.
8   Grimaldi based one of his prints (Bartsch 49) on Domenichino's landscape, see Bologna/Washington/New York 1986–7, p.449, note 2.
9   Dubois de Saint-Gelais 1727, p.125; see also Bonnaffé 1884, p.136.
10 Dubois de Saint-Gelais 1727, p.125; Dézallier d'Argenville 1752, p.70; engraved in reverse by Michel in Galerie du Palais Royal 1786/1808, II (*VIIIe tableau de Dominique Zampieri dit le Dominiquin*).

Ciro Ferri 1634(?)–1689
24 The Adoration of the Shepherds

Oil on copper, 52.5 x 38.8 cm
Signed on the column base: CIRVS.FERRI. Inscribed GLORIA IN [EXCELSIS DEO] on the scroll held by the angels.

Ferri was a pupil of Pietro da Cortona and the faithful propagator of his style, as this picture clearly shows. He joined Cortona's workshop in Rome in about 1650 and quickly became his most trusted collaborator. In 1659 he went to Florence to complete the frescoes in the Sala di Apollo in Palazzo Pitti which Cortona had not been able to finish due to his numerous papal commissions in Rome.[1] The frescoes are painted in the master's grand and airy manner. Ferri worked in Bergamo in 1665–7 and may have gone on to Venice. After Cortona's death in 1669, he returned to Rome to complete other projects left unfinished by his master, such as the mosaics in the right aisle of St Peter's. Ferri was especially active as a designer of sculpture, prints (see fig.26), architecture and ephemera, but he also played a significant role as a teacher, taking charge in 1673 of the newly founded Accademia dei Fiorentini which was established by Cosimo III de' Medici, Grand Duke of Tuscany, to improve the training of young Florentine artists, and then serving as *Principe* of the Academy of Saint Luke from 1681 to 1687.

Despite the prominent signature on the column base, the *Adoration of the Shepherds* was considered a work of Cortona until 1882. Even the German connoisseur Gustav Waagen, who saw the painting when it was in the Hamilton collection, missed the inscription and described the work as a 'pleasing and careful picture' (for Cortona).[2] The composition is in fact a variant of Cortona's paintings of this subject.[3] There are several drawings by Ferri which are associated with the Mahon painting, although none seems to be directly preparatory. A compositional drawing with the same figures but with some small differences, and in reverse, is in the Bowdoin College Museum of Art,[4] and another is in Düsseldorf.[5] A third drawing, perhaps the most elaborate, was formerly in the collection of Lord St Helens and is now untraced; it is known from a print (which presumably shows it in reverse) by Conrad Metz, published in his *Imitations of Drawings* of 1798.[6]

The kneeling shepherd in the foreground of the Bowdoin College and the ex-St Helens drawings was the model for one of the shepherds in the earliest sculpted relief of Giovanni Battista Foggini (1652–1725), the *Adoration of the Shepherds* (St Petersburg, Hermitage).[7] As a young man Foggini was sent to study sculpture in the Florentine Academy in Rome and his teachers were Ercole Ferrata, a sculptor who had worked with both Bernini and Algardi, and Ferri himself, who also practised sculpture. Ferri may have suggested his shepherd figure as a model for the young Foggini. The relief is known to have been sent to the Grand Duke in Florence in 1675.[8] The Mahon painting may be assumed, therefore, to date from no later than the early 1670s.

TECHNICAL NOTE
The support is a thin copper panel. There are scattered small retouched losses around the edge of the picture. A small retouched loss is apparent on the Christ Child's left brow. The blues of the Virgin's robe have darkened and have been somewhat repainted. The ground is a warm ochre. The painting is in very good condition.

PROVENANCE
Jean-Baptist-Joseph Damazit de Sahaguet, Baron d'Espagnac (1713–83), Paris; Colonel John Trumbull (1756–1843), the American painter; his sale, Christie's, London, 17 February 1797, lot 40 (as 'Pietro da Cortona', with the d'Espagnac provenance given), where bought by Bryan; Dukes of Hamilton; Christie's, London, 24 June 1882 (12th Duke of Hamilton sale), lot 384 (as Ciro Ferri), bought by Agnew's; 1st Earl of Plymouth (1857–1923), Hewell, Worcs; his daughter, Lady Phyllis Benton; her sale, Sotheby's, London, 26 April 1950, lot 129, where acquired by the present owner.

EXHIBITIONS
Not previously exhibited.

1 See Campbell 1977, pp.215–18, 250–1, 274–9, figs.42–88.
2 'PIETRO DA CORTONA. – 1. The Adoration of the Shepherds. A pleasing and careful picture for him' (1854/7, III, p.299). The picture, which was in the possession of the 10th Duke of Hamilton, must have been obscured by a heavily discoloured varnish.
3 The fresco altarpiece in the Cappella Sacchetti at Castelfusano, 1626–9; the altarpiece in San Salvatore in Lauro, Rome, 1628–30; and another in San Francesco, Aversa, c.1650, see Briganti 1982, nos.23, 59 and 116, respectively (figs.69 and 59; the last is not reproduced). Several of Cortona's pupils painted pictures which are essentially variants of these compositions.
4 Inv.1811.65, black chalk, touches of red chalk, with pen and brown ink, 396 x 248 mm, see Bowdoin College 1985–6, no.67. A close version of this drawing is in Berlin (Inv.KdZ 16643, see Dreyer 1969, no.5, pl.2) and a copy in reverse is in Düsseldorf (Inv.FP1588).
5 Inv.FP11910, pen and brown ink, 89 x 100 mm.
6 Reproduced in Montagu 1973, p.334, fig.4.
7 Montagu 1973. The marble sculpture is in high relief and measures 138 x 86 cm.
8 Montagu 1973, pp.331–2.

Giovanni Battista Gaulli, called Baciccio 1639–1709

25 The Virgin with the Child piercing the Head of the Serpent ('Madonna della Serpe')

Oil on canvas, 142.7 x 99.6 cm

Gaulli, also known as 'Il Baciccio' (the Genoese version of Giovanni Battista), was blessed with a dazzling talent, the protection of Gian Lorenzo Bernini, and the opportunity to decorate one of the most important churches in Rome, the Gesù. He was perhaps the most flamboyant painter of the Roman Baroque, acquiring great fame and prosperity and exerting a powerful influence on European decorative painting.[1]

Gaulli was born in Genoa but came to Rome in 1658; by 1662 he was a member of the Accademia di San Luca and in 1673 he was elected its *Principe*. Thanks to Bernini's intervention in 1666 he received the commission to paint the pendentives in the church of Sant'Agnese in Piazza Navona, which was under the protection of the papal Pamphilj family. These show the influence of Correggio, whose works Gaulli had gone to Parma to study by way of preparation in 1669, as well as of Pietro da Cortona. In the Jesuit church of the Gesù he frescoed the dome and pendentives, the semidome of the apse, the nave vault and the vaults above the high altar and the left transept (1672–85). The nave vault with the *Adoration of the Name of Jesus* shows the powers of heaven, earth and the underworld submitting to the divine trigram. It is painted so that the roof of the church appears to have opened up to reveal the heavenly host, and the damned tumble out of the sky and into the physical space of the nave. The illusionism and the control of theatrical effects are masterful: architecture, painting and sculpture are integrated to create 'one of the most radiant and joyous visions of a triumphant Catholicism' (Enggass). Gaulli was also a portrait painter (the National Gallery has the *Portrait of Cardinal Marco Gallo*) and executed several altarpieces and narrative pictures with mythological subjects. In his later years he sought to rein in his pictorial exuberance to conform to the more sober classicising taste exemplified by Carlo Maratti (1625–1713), but the works of this period are less impressive.

The painting was recognised as by Gaulli by Ellis Waterhouse when it was in St Mary's Parish Church, Swanage.[2] Enggass drew attention to the typical character of the Virgin's head and draperies, particularly the use of puffed sleeves with sharp angular folds, and the frosted pink and rose tones.[3] He proposed a date at the very end of the artist's middle phase, that is about 1683–5, although the painting he offers as a specific comparison with the figure of Christ is the *Putto with the Emblem of Ludovico Gaulli* which is dated 1695.[4] The Mahon picture is in

fact more likely to date from the following decade since the closest formal similarities are with the altarpiece of 1697–8, the *Christ and the Virgin with Saint Nicholas of Bari*, made for the Roman church of Santa Maria Maddalena.[5] In the altarpiece the Virgin is in a similar pose and the arrangement of her draperies is close. The pose of the Christ Child in the present work resembles that of the standing putto in the altarpiece and both children have the same stiff curls. The distant view of rolling hills, a town and lakes with boating, testifies to the artist's love of landscape, which is frequently manifested in the background of his altarpieces.[6]

The subject matter of the picture is based on the so-called 'proto-evangelium', the verse in the Book of Genesis which alludes to the destruction of Satan by Christ. God addressed the serpent saying: 'I will put enmity between thee and the woman, and between thy seed and her seed; it shall bruise [some translations have 'crush'] thy head, and thou shalt bruise his heel' (3:15).[7] Christ and the Virgin are shown as the New Adam and the New Eve, a typological comparison which is made explicit by the presence of the apple in Christ's hand and the gesture of the Virgin who points to the serpent. Christ is about to crush the head of the beast with a cross, the sign of his redeeming sacrifice.[8]

A rapidly executed compositional drawing in Düsseldorf presents a few small differences from the painting, notably the Christ Child does not hold an apple and the Virgin is not pointing down at the serpent.[9] A more highly finished drawing in red chalk, also in Düsseldorf, almost certainly by Gaulli himself, is squared for transfer and records the final stage of preparation before the painting was begun.[10]

TECHNICAL NOTE
The support is a dense, plain-weave canvas, fairly coarse in texture. The painting is unlined, which is rare for a work of this date, and it is in very good condition.[11] There are scattered retouchings on the torso of Christ and there is retouching around the Virgin's left eye. Three small tears have been repaired with canvas patches applied to the reverse. The reverse of the canvas has been painted with a brown pigment and bears several inscriptions: *PRESENTED TO/ SWANAGE PARISH CHURCH/ BY/ 1941. REV.H.V.NICOLL-GRIFFITH.RECTOR*; above this in black paint in a different script: *1338*; lower down, in a third hand: *Gio.Agos Geminiano/ 1629*. The stretcher is old but not original. The upper bar bears an inscription which repeats the earlier (?) one on the reverse: *BY - GIO.AGOS.GEMINIANO 1629* and the lower bar has *A.D.1629*. The ground is a warm ochre. There are no obvious pentimenti.

PROVENANCE
The Reverend H.V. Nicoll-Griffith before 1941 and presented by him to Swanage Parish Church in that year (according to the inscription on the reverse); acquired by the present owner (through Oscar & Peter Johnson Ltd) at Sotheby's, London, 21 July 1965, lot 178A.

EXHIBITIONS
Oberlin 1967, no.15.

1 On Gaulli, see Pascoli 1730/6, I, pp.194–209; Soprani/Ratti 1768–9, II, pp.74–90; Enggass 1964a; Oberlin 1967.
2 See Enggass 1964b. Inscriptions on the reverse and on the stretcher give the picture to 'Gio.Agos Geminiano/ 1629'; possibly Giacinto Gimignani (1606–1681) is meant.
3 Enggass 1964b.
4 Reproduced in Enggass 1964a, fig.129.
5 Enggass 1964a, p.144 and fig.122.
6 See Waterhouse's comments on Gaulli's interest in landscape in Oberlin 1967, p.66.
7 For the theological significance of this text, see Journet 1958, pp.31–8; Mâle discusses its importance for painting in the seventeenth century (1984, pp.49–51). Caravaggio's *Madonna dei Palafrenieri*, which is in essence a 'Madonna della Serpe', has provided the focus for a voluminous literature on the iconography of this subject; for a summary, see Cinotti/Dell'Acqua 1983, pp.497–9.
8 Enggass's interpretation of the subject as 'a not too veiled reference to the Madonna and Child destroying the evil serpent of heresy' (1964b) is correct (see the comments in Mâle 1984, p.49) but too narrow.
9 Inv.FP 1973, pen and brown ink and grey wash, over black chalk, 173 x 136 mm, Graf 1976, cat.260.
10 Inv.FP 1924, red chalk over traces of black chalk and squared in black chalk, 405 x 269 mm, Graf 1976, cat.579. Graf describes this as a workshop drawing, although he admits that the quality is so high it could be autograph.
11 The assessment of the picture's condition in Enggass 1964b is unduly harsh.

Benedetto Gennari 1633–1715
26 Portrait of Guercino

Oil on canvas, 63 x 52.2 cm

It is entirely appropriate that the collection of Sir Denis Mahon should have a portrait likeness of the artist to whom, as an art historian and collector, he is most devoted. Mahon's earliest art-historical publication, of 1937, was on Guercino, he has organised and catalogued several exhibitions of his work, and even now, some six decades later, he is at work on the first major volume to be published in English on the artist's paintings.

The portrait shows the artist in the act of painting, holding a rectangular palette and an assortment of brushes. He wears an elegant silk jacket with slashed sleeves and a black lace border. The portrait displays frankly why he was called 'Il Guercino', a nickname which means 'the squint-eyed'. Carlo Cesare Malvasia, who knew the painter, records in his biography that as an infant, while in the care of an inattentive nurse, he had been so startled by a booming voice that when he awoke he had acquired a pronounced squint in his right eye.[1]

In style and handling the portrait is clearly the work of Benedetto Gennari, the painter's nephew, but it is almost certainly based on a lost self portrait by Guercino.[2] The pose and arrangement are similar to Guercino's only certain *Self Portrait* (fig.23),[3] which dates from the mid-1620s, although here he is considerably older and wears a jacket and collar of different design. He is perhaps a little older than in the *Portrait of Guercino with a Picture in the Background*, a copy in the Royal Collection documented as by Gennari after a lost Guercino original which was probably painted about 1645, when the artist was in his mid-fifties.[4] He also appears a little younger than the portrait in the Uffizi, which is assumed to be a copy of the untraced self portrait that Guercino made for Cardinal Leopoldo de' Medici in 1664 for his collection of artists' self portraits.[5] We may assume, therefore, that the original upon which the present picture is based was made in the 1650s.

Benedetto Gennari was the son of Guercino's sister, Lucia Barbieri, and Ercole Gennari.[6] He lived with Guercino in Bologna from the age of eleven and was presumably engaged in making copies of his works. His first independent work is a signed portrait of 1655 but throughout his long career he remained faithful to Guercino's late style. Benedetto was in the employ of Louis XIV at the French court from 1672 to 1674 and then moved to London

where he was court painter to Charles II and James II until January 1689. He painted several large religious paintings for the chapels of St James's Palace and Whitehall, as well as mythologies and portraits. On his return to Bologna he pursued a successful career as a history painter and executed altarpieces for Cesena, Rovigo and Faenza. He was not an artist of the first rank but combined a hard-working and professional disposition with an ability to skilfully exploit the prestige that came from being the nephew and artistic heir of Guercino.

Several versions of the present work are known: one is in the Royal Collection at Hampton Court,[7] another was sold at auction in London in 1954,[8] and a third is in the sacristy of the church of the SS. Rosario in Cento.[9] An apparently 'similar picture' was in the Earl of Darnley's collection at Cobham Hall, Kent.[10]

TECHNICAL NOTE
The support is a plain-weave medium-weight canvas. It retains its original tacking edges on all four sides and it has been lined. The ground is a warm light brown and quite granular. There is a small discoloured retouching on the white sleeve adjacent to the brushes. The painting is in very good condition.

Fig.23 Guercino, *Self Portrait*, c.1624–6. Oil on canvas, 64.1 x 52.1 cm. New York, Richard L.Feigen & Company.

PROVENANCE
Apparently Palazzo Fava, Bologna;[11] acquired from Palazzo Fava by George Hayter (1792–1871) for the Bedford collection before 1834;[12] Dukes of Bedford, Woburn Abbey;[13] acquired by the present owner at Christie's, London, 19 January 1951 (Duke of Bedford sale), lot 102 (as by Guercino).

EXHIBITIONS
Not previously exhibited.

1 Malvasia 1678, II, p.361; Malvasia 1841, II, p.257.
2 See Briganti 1953, pp.11 and 16, and Bagni 1986, cat.27, p.47.
3 See Bologna 1991, no.62, and Frankfurt 1991–2, no.26. There is a copy in the Louvre (see Paris 1990, no.19). Although the painting was recently discovered in Denmark, it has a British provenance and may be the same picture that Waagen saw in the collection of the Earl of Shrewsbury at Alton Towers in 1835, see Waagen 1838, III, p.254. It might also be identical with a painting listed in 'Sr Thomas Sebright's and Mr Bacon's sale of Pictures 1737', 2nd day's sale, lot 94: 'His Ritratto, by Himself Guercino', see Houlditch Manuscript 1711–59, I, p.104.
4 See Mahon 1981a, pp.231 and 234–5, notes 12 and 13; Levey 1990, pp.89–90.
5 Borea 1975, no.142, pp.195–6, fig.85.
6 For Gennari, see Bagni 1986.
7 Levey 1990, cat.498, p.90, plate 121.
8 Christie's, London, 29 January 1954 (Duke of Abercorn sale), lot 134, 23 x 20 inches (58.4 x 50.8 cm).
9 Bagni 1986, p.47.
10 Tavistock and Russell 1890/2, I, part I, p.130; Waagen saw it there (1854/7, III, p.21).
11 An inscription in pen on the crossbar states: 'Rittrato [sic] del Guercino./ da se stesso/ dallo Palzzo [sic] FAVA in Bologne [sic].' It is not recorded in the 1745 inventory of the paintings in Palazzo Fava published in Campori 1870, pp.602–15.
12 Woburn Abbey 1834, no.CLXVII, p.120.
13 See Waagen 1854/7, supplement, p.336; Tavistock and Russell 1890/2, I, part 1, p.130, no.142.

Corrado Giaquinto 1703–1766
27 Madonna and Child in Glory appearing to Four Saints

Oil on canvas, 49.8 x 24 cm (original painted surface 47.8 x 21.2 cm)

According to the eighteenth-century biographer of Neapolitan artists, Bernardo De Dominici, the painters of Naples had a special affection for the oil sketch. In general they did not spend a great deal of time making preparatory drawings; they preferred, instead, to express their ideas on small canvases and then go straight on to the full-size work, often without making cartoons.[1] This painting is a particularly fine example of Giaquinto's mastery of the oil sketch. Small in scale but grand in conception, the sketch is a rapid 'jotting' for the design of a ceiling, or more likely an altarpiece, and the execution is vital, fluid, unerring. There is evidence from the early eighteenth century that artists considered their oil sketches to be the most authentic expression of their artistic intent and that they thought of the finished works for which the sketches were preparatory as 'copies'.[2]

Although the composition is quite fully elaborated and the essential iconographic elements are in place, no altarpiece of this design is known and we are ignorant of the circumstances which led Giaquinto to produce the sketch. The Virgin is seated on a cloud displaying the Christ Child to the saints below. The cloud rests on a large orb, probably intended for the moon, and behind them is a refulgent disk, perhaps the sun, a combination which alludes to the symbolism of the Immaculate Conception. The design of the upper part of the sketch suggests that the planned altarpiece may have been intended to have an arched top. The four saints on a bank of cloud below are, from left to right: an unidentified bishop saint, to whom the playful putti deliver a crozier; Saint Stephen, the protomartyr, who is identified by his deacon's dalmatic, his palm and the pile of stones at his feet; an unidentified virgin martyr; and probably Saint Benedict in his black habit. The entire scene is illuminated by the radiant Child: rays of light break through the clouds creating dense jagged highlights on the vestments of the saints on the left. The figures are grouped around a pool of light so that the foreground figure of Saint Benedict is cast completely in shadow and the background figure of the woman saint is shown in bright light, a theatrical device which gives depth and visual excitement to the composition.

Giaquinto was born at Molfetta near Bari and was a pupil first of Nicola Maria Rossi and then of Solimena (see cat.75) in Naples.[3] In 1727 he went to Rome and collaborated with Sebastiano Conca (1680–1764) there and in Turin. He went to Spain in 1753 at the invitation of King Ferdinand VI and was engaged on the decoration of the new Royal Palace in Madrid.[4] He was made director of the recently established Royal Academy of San Fernando and the Royal Tapestry Factory of Santa Barbara. In 1762 he made his return to Rome and then Naples. His last important commission was the decoration of the sacristy of San Luigi di Palazzo, the royal monastery in front of the Royal Palace of Naples (1764–5).[5] Giaquinto was an artist of extraordinary technical accomplishment whose grand Rococo manner was particularly influential in Spain. With the advent of Neo-classicism his reputation suffered and interest in his work revived only in the second half of this century.

The present work is executed in Giaquinto's late manner and was perhaps painted in Spain, or more likely in Naples after his return to Italy. There is a related drawing in the Museo Nazionale di San Martino in Naples which shows a similar composition but reversed and with variants including the addition of another male saint.[6] A painting by Giaquinto in the Frances Lehman Loeb Art Center at Vassar College, Poughkeepsie (New York), follows this drawing and the additional figure is there identifiable as Saint Peter.[7] It probably precedes the present work.

Technical note
The support is a fairly fine plain-weave canvas. It is lined and the tacking edges have been removed. The canvas has been attached to a larger stretcher and the made-up border is painted orange. The painting is in very good condition. The artist has used the other end of the brush to draw in the wet paint and this is particularly noticeable in the figure of the Virgin.

Provenance
An Italian collection; acquired by the present owner from Colnaghi in 1959.

Exhibitions
London 1960, no.436; Paris 1960–1, no.8; Barnard Castle 1962, no.85.

1 See Vitzthum's discussion of this topic in Vitzthum 1970, pp.4–5.
2 Sebastiano Ricci wrote to Conte Giacomo Tassis in 1731 concerning an altarpiece he had been commissioned to paint for a church in Bergamo: 'sappia S.V.Ill. che vi è differenza da un bozzetto, che porta il nome di modello, e quello che le perverrà ... questo piccolo è l'originale e la tavola d'altare è la copia', quoted in Ferrari 1990, p.5.
3 There is no recent monograph on the artist, but see: D'Orsi 1958, which is useful, if now outdated, Giaquinto Atti 1971 and Giaquinto Atti 1985, and the recent, if not wholly satisfactory catalogue of the Giaquinto exhibition (Bari 1993).
4 On Giaquinto in Spain, see Saseta 1971, and Urrea 1977, pp.116–50; see also Cioffi 1992 (unpublished).
5 For this project, see Cioffi 1980.
6 Inv.20449, pen, black chalk and white heightening, 479 x 322 mm. See Videtta 1962–3, pp.23–4, no.30 (not reproduced). Videtta considers the drawing to date from 1739–42 but draws attention to Giaquinto's practice of frequently reusing earlier designs.
7 Louise Woodroff Johnston Fund 69.9, oil on canvas, 48.7 x 22.7 cm. The painting was with Colnaghi in 1960, see London (Colnaghi) 1960, no.19, and in Giaquinto Atti 1971, it is mistakenly identified by Mario d'Orsi as the painting in the Mahon Collection, see p.105 and fig.61. After entering for the Vassar College collection in 1969 it was exhibited in New Haven 1987, no.46. In the entry, George Hersey proposes that it is a work by a Spanish follower of Giaquinto; he also identifies the bishop saint as Abercius, for no obvious reason.

Luca Giordano 1634–1705

28 Venus, Mars and the Forge of Vulcan

Oil on canvas, 131 x 158 cm

Venus, wife of Vulcan, god of fire, was smitten with love for Mars, the god of war. Apollo witnessed their illicit union and told the wronged husband. Vulcan prepared a net of fine bronze wire in his forge to ensnare the lovers and once they were tightly enmeshed he called in the other gods to ridicule them. Giordano shows the naked Venus, to whom Cupid clings, seated on her bed and turning towards the youthful Mars. She pulls a red velvet curtain around the bed to conceal their tryst. The putti in the left corner are amused by Mars' shield and perhaps by the reflections it gives. In the background Vulcan, the figure with his back turned, is forging one of Jupiter's thunderbolts, and scattered on the floor are sections of armour, cannon and shot. A comparison with Giordano's *Forge of Vulcan* in the Hermitage confirms that the figure on the left is operating bellows.[1] Beyond the forge may be seen the torture of the Giants Ixion and Tityus. Ixion was bound to a revolving wheel for attempting to violate Juno, and Tityus was condemned to have his liver attacked daily by a vulture for trying to rape Latona. They appear again in one of Giordano's *modelli* for the ceiling of the Galleria in Palazzo Medici Riccardi (cat.36).

Giordano was born in Naples and his early training was with the leading painter in the city, the Spaniard Jusepe de Ribera (1591–1652). He was immensely talented, precocious and prolific and earned the sobriquet 'Luca fa presto' on account of the speed with which he worked. From his naturalistic tenebrist origins Giordano's compositions and palette opened up under the influence of sixteenth-century Venetian painting, Pietro da Cortona and Rubens, and he became one of the great Baroque decorators of the seventeenth century, executing fresco projects, large history pictures, altarpieces, as well as small collectors' paintings. He worked in Venice, Florence, Rome, Naples and in Spain, where he resided from 1692 until 1702.

The present work is marked by a virtuoso touch and a tendency to indulge in spectacular effects of light and energetic movement, and this led Briganti to date the picture rather late in Giordano's career, to the first years of the Spanish period.[2] The chronology of Giordano's works is complicated by the fact that he often painted in the style of other artists and late in his career he occasionally reverted to an earlier style, but it now seems clear that the works with which this painting has most in common are clustered together around 1660.[3] In the painting of *Saint Francis Xavier interceding on behalf of the Plague-stricken* dated 1659(?), the seated figure of Christ dissolves into light in a way which is paralleled by the figures in the left background of this picture.[4] The same broken brushwork and silvery tonality are apparent in the two pictures Giordano painted around 1660 for the Charterhouse of San Martino in Naples, the *Calling of Saints Peter and Andrew* and the *Calling of Saint Matthew*.[5] But perhaps the work to which it is closest is the *Rubens painting the Allegory of Peace* in the Prado, which, although considerably larger, has a similar compositional arrangement, palette and tonal range, and a comparable variety of axial directions in the figures. That work is first recorded in the collection of Don Gaspar Méndez de Haro, Marqués del Carpio, Ambassador to the Holy See, in Rome in 1682/3, but was painted some twenty years earlier.[6]

TECHNICAL NOTE
The support is a plain-weave, medium-coarse canvas. There is a vertical seam to left of centre. The canvas has a glue-paste lining. The original tacking edges have been cut off but the cusping which is evident on all four sides indicates that the canvas has not been significantly reduced, if at all. The painting has a pale brown ground which is readily apparent in areas which have suffered abrasion. There are few obvious pentimenti, perhaps the most notable is the small change in the architecture of the steps to the left of Venus' feet. The painting has suffered some surface abrasion and has been retouched in local areas. The figure of Mars is much repainted in the face, neck and left arm. Overcleaning has removed the details of Venus' sandals.

PROVENANCE
Acquired by the present owner from Roderick Thesiger, London, in 1950.

EXHIBITIONS
Zurich 1956, no.120; London 1960, no.361.

1 Ferrari and Scavizzi 1992, II, fig.164. The subject of this picture is not obviously mythological.
2 Briganti 1953, p.15. He noted the influence of Titian's late style which is so well represented in the works by Titian then in the Spanish royal collection. See also the entry by Mahon in London 1960, no.361, and Griseri 1961, p.431.
3 See Ferrari and Scavizzi 1966, II, p.38; Ferrari and Scavizzi 1992, cat.A90, I, p.264. These authors identify specifically Rubensian qualities in the painting.
4 Ferrari and Scavizzi 1992, cat.A76, I, p.262, II, fig.153.
5 Ferrari and Scavizzi 1992, cats.A65.a and b; reproduced in colour in vol.I, p.23I, plates VIII–IX.
6 Ferrari and Scavizzi 1992, cat.A88, I, pp.263–4, colour plate XIV, p.29.

Luca Giordano 1634–1705

29–38 Modelli for the decoration of the Galleria and Library in Palazzo Medici Riccardi, Florence

The group of ten *modelli*, or elaborated oil studies, by Luca Giordano in the Mahon collection is connected with the decorative projects the artist undertook in the Palazzo Medici Riccardi in Florence at the request of Marchese Francesco Riccardi. Nine are associated with the ceiling of the Galleria (fig.24), and one, the *Allegory of Divine Wisdom* (cat.38), with the ceiling of the adjacent Library (fig.30). The Galleria frescoes, begun in 1682 and completed in 1685, are among Giordano's finest achievements. The term 'fresco' is convenient but not strictly accurate since the ceilings appear to have been painted 'a secco', that is, on dry rather than fresh plaster.

The old Medici family palace was sold in 1659 by Grand Duke Ferdinando II to Gabriello Riccardi and his nephew Francesco, after which it became known as the Palazzo Medici Riccardi.[1] The Riccardi were a wealthy Florentine family which had been ennobled at the beginning of the seventeenth century by the ruling Medici, to whom they were very close. In 1669 the Riccardi began the construction of a new wing on the west side of the palace under the direction of the architect Pier Maria Baldi. By 1677 the Galleria on the first floor, which was intended to house a precious collection of antiquities and function as a public reception room, was complete and awaited decoration.[2]

The Galleria has windows on one long side and one short side, an arrangement which allows a large amount of daylight to enter the room. Giordano responded to this circumstance by employing a light palette, with vast areas of the ceiling given over to blue sky, painted in ultramarine, and translucent white clouds.[3] Greens dominate the frieze register directly above the cornice, and occasional accents of lilac, yellow and red in the sky are provided by the billowing draperies of the numerous flying figures. Giordano's treatment of the ceiling as a single unified picture field without any form of *quadratura* or compartmentalisation is indebted to Pietro da Cortona's much-admired frescoes in the Palazzo Pitti, especially the ceiling in the Sala di Marte, and in its turn it anticipates the eighteenth-century ceilings of Giambattista Tiepolo.

Giordano came to Florence at the beginning of 1682 to paint the Corsini Chapel in the Church of the Carmine. He was probably at work on the Galleria frescoes in September when documents show that lodgings were being prepared in the Palazzo for two of his assistants.[4]

Shortly after Christmas, however, work was interrupted due to the artist's departure for Naples. By this time he had probably painted only the central section of the ceiling with the *Apotheosis of the Medici* (fig.29).[5] He did not return to Florence for over two years. In the surviving correspondence between patron and painter, Giordano professes his commitment to the completion of the project but Riccardi had some doubts and considered handing the commission over to another artist.[6] Giordano arrived back in Florence in the first half of April 1685 and immediately set to work. By 21 April he had completed the scene at the west end of the Galleria showing the *Cave of Eternity*,[7] and the entire ceiling was probably finished by late 1685.

The Library ceiling is usually assumed to have been painted after the Galleria, and finished, at the latest, by March 1686 when Giordano, back in Naples, received a payment of 1000 scudi from the Marchese 'as the balance for all the works he has done for us and as a present'.[8] The Swedish architect, Nicodemus Tessin the Younger (1654–1728), who visited Florence in 1687, records that Giordano painted the Library fresco in only five days.[9]

The arrangement of the frescoes in the Galleria is as follows: in the central area is the glorification of the Medici dynasty (fig.29); at the two short ends are emblematic scenes of human life and the arts (*The Cave of Eternity* and *Minerva as Protectress of the Arts and Sciences*, fig.25 and see cats.34 and 35); on the long sides are mythological narratives (see cats.36 and 37); and in the corners are allegories of the four Cardinal Virtues (see cats.30–33). The programme of decoration combines a panegyric on a cosmic scale of the Medici as paragons of virtue, with an allegory of human life, ennobled by Wisdom, together with historiated allegories of the Four Elements. Giordano succeeded in fusing all these parts together into a vast swirling whole, remarkable for its lightness, transparency and sheer visual brilliance.

Giordano's adviser for the iconography was Alessandro Segni, a man of letters who had been Riccardi's tutor and travelling companion.[10] Segni never published a detailed description of the frescoes but in his account of a reception given by the Marchese in the palace in January 1689 he made made some general observations on the Galleria ceiling: 'It represents in a continuous narrative, comprising several hundred figures, all the theology of the Gentile religion …

Left Fig.24 View of the Galleria in Palazzo Medici Riccardi, Florence.

Fig.25 Luca Giordano, *Minerva as Protectress of the Arts and Sciences*. Florence, Palazzo Medici Riccardi, Galleria.

29 Apotheosis of the Medici

Oil on canvas, 139 x 65.2 cm

This *modello* corresponds with the central section of the Galleria ceiling (fig.29). Jupiter is supported on his throne by Glory and Wisdom (or Eternity and Divinity). The male figures in the central group are members of the Medici family. The only one who has recognisable features is the figure in the centre who has the likeness of the aged Cosimo I. In the ceiling Cosimo I takes up a position to the right of Jupiter and behind him stands a pointing figure (the planet Mercury) who does not appear in the *modello*. The figure in the centre of the *modello* corresponds with Ferdinando II in the ceiling and the figure below him with the red cloak corresponds with Ferdinando's son, Cosimo III, the reigning Grand Duke at the time of the fresco's execution. He holds the attributes of Temperance, a pair of tongs with which he dips a molten piece of metal into a bowl of water. The two horsemen correspond with Cosimo III's sons, Ferdinando on the left and Giangastone on the right. The figure to the left of Jupiter holds the *fasces*, the attribute of Justice, another of the Virtues shown in the corners of the ceiling decoration (see cat.31); in the fresco this figure is probably Francesco I (or Cosimo II). Below the Medici group is Apollo as the sun riding his chariot through the sky, accompanied by the Seasons and preceded by Aurora, from whose breasts pours out dew. Above is the chariot of the Moon drawn by bulls and preceded by the figure of Evening. Saturn holds a scythe and devours one of his children and Mars and Venus appear above him. Each of these planetary deities has a shining star above its head. An engraving of this scene, based on the fresco, is in Riccardi Vernaccia 1822, pl.XII.

TECHNICAL NOTE

The support is a medium weight, plain-weave canvas. There is a vertical seam running the entire height of the picture about 6 cm from the right side. There is pronounced craquelure in the paint on the right-hand strip which is not apparent on the rest of the canvas. The canvas has been strip-lined on all four sides. There is a repaired vertical tear about 8 cm in length to the right of the figure of Jupiter. Stretcher-bar marks from the present stretcher (which probably dates from the first half of the nineteenth century) are apparent on the surface. The painting is in excellent condition. The ground is dark brown in colour. There are no obvious pentimenti. On the reverse of the canvas is a figure *7* in red paint. It corresponds with a 7 on the back of the frame. This numbering, which appears on most of the paintings and frames, is old and probably dates from when the fine carved and gilded frames were made in the late 1680s (see cat.33).

The stretchers of the ten paintings are the same in type and each one bears the nineteenth-century printed paper label of Natale Ussi, 'Pittore Restauratore, Piazza Sta Croce, Firenze'. Remains of red wax seals with the Riccardi arms (an upturned key beneath a crown) are to be found on the frames of all the pictures and on some stretchers. Most of the paintings have a red and white ribbon affixed to the stretcher which originally probably had a wax Riccardi seal attached.

EXHIBITIONS

Florence 1705; Manchester 1957, no.82; London 1960, no.362; Detroit/Florence 1974, no.151.

PROVENANCE OF THE SERIES IN THE MAHON COLLECTION

Marchese Francesco Riccardi, Palazzo Medici Riccardi, Florence; acquired by the Earl of Shrewbury after 1822 and then in the Shrewsbury collection at Ingestre, Staffs; the *Allegories of Fortitude, Justice, Prudence* and *Temperance* and the *Mythological Scene with the Rape of Proserpine* were acquired by the present owner in 1950 from Matthiesen, who had acquired them from Lord Shrewsbury; the remaining five pictures were acquired by the present owner in 1952 directly from Lord Shrewsbury.

Fig.29 Luca Giordano, *The Apotheosis of the Medici*. Fresco. Florence, Palazzo Medici Riccardi, Galleria.

30 Allegory of Fortitude

Oil on canvas, 95 x 99.2 cm

The *modello* corresponds to the group in the corner of the ceiling between the entrance and window wall. Fortitude, one of the four Cardinal Virtues, sits upon a lion resting on a column, both of which are her emblems. She is being crowned with a laurel wreath by Honour who bears the palm of victory. To the left is Constancy resting on an anchor and placing her dagger hand in a flaming brazier. The cowering figure wearing a deer skin represents Fear and in the centre foreground is Misery (or Calamity). The heroic figure on the right represents Valour. Victory sits on a globe holding a standard and a pomegranate. Peace, with torch and olive branch, descends to earth. An engraving based on this *modello* is in Riccardi Vernaccia 1822, pl.V.

TECHNICAL NOTE
The support is a medium weight, plain-weave canvas. The painting is lined. There is a repaired diagonal tear (running from top right to lower left) about 18 cm in length through the arm of the figure holding the wreath. There is a small repaired vertical tear just to the right of the male figure on the right. There is some slight abrasion of the paint surface due to lining, but the painting is in good condition. The retouchings along the bottom edge have become quite apparent. The stretcher-bar marks on the edges of the picture indicate that the original stretcher/strainer was about 5 cm wide. The ground is dark brown in colour. There are no obvious pentimenti. On the back of the frame is a figure 5 in red paint, which presumably corresponds with a 5 on the reverse of the original canvas now hidden by the lining.

EXHIBITIONS
Florence 1705; Detroit/Florence 1974, no.155.

31 Allegory of Justice

Oil on canvas, 99.9 x 96 cm

The *modello* corresponds to the group in the right corner of the ceiling opposite the entrance and to the right of the scene of the *Cave of Eternity*. Justice, one of the four Cardinal Virtues, carries the scales and sword which are her attributes and is borne on an ostrich. To the right are Punishment, with his sword turned down, and Recompense, from whose cornucopia rewards pour out. In the left-hand corner is the masked and serpent-tailed figure of Deceit who holds up a bunch of flowers which conceals a poisonous snake. Behind this figure is a net to ensnare the unwary. On the right are Discord, with bellows, and Strife. The flying figures above represent the effects of Justice, from left to right: Order (with a shield and spear), Fame and Security (holding an anchor and carrying a nest on her head which signifies that children may be reared in safety). An engraving after this *modello* is in Riccardi Vernaccia 1822, pl.XI.

TECHNICAL NOTE
The support is a medium weight, plain-weave canvas. The painting is lined. There is a repaired vertical tear about 13 cm in length running through the face of the winged figure of Fame. There is some slight abrasion of the paint surface due to lining, mostly apparent in the sky, but the painting is in good condition. There are some retouchings along the left edge of the picture and a thin wash of retouching is apparent around the flying figure representing Security. The stretcher-bar marks around the edge of the picture indicate that the original stretcher/strainer was about 5 cm wide. The ground is dark brown in colour. There are a few small pentimenti: the spear of the flying figure on the left was originally at a slightly different angle; the branch in the left hand of the conucopia bearer originally had more sprays of leaves but these were painted out by the artist. On the back of the frame is a figure *11* in red paint, which presumably corresponds with an 11 on the reverse of the original canvas now hidden by the lining.

EXHIBITIONS
Florence 1705; Detroit/Florence 1974, no.160.

32 Allegory of Prudence

Oil on canvas, 99.7 x 95.2 cm

The *modello* corresponds to the group in the corner of the ceiling between the entrance and the wall decorated with mirrors. Prudence, one of the four Cardinal Virtues, carries an arrow with a serpent entwined around it. In the fresco she looks to the left instead of the right. The deer is a symbol of prudence because it has to move cautiously, on account of the weight of its antlers, to retain its balance. On the left are two Oriental philosophers with quadrant and compass, perhaps Archimedes and Euclid, who represent Order and Reason (or Experience). The two-faced figure with claws instead of feet is Fraud, and Ignorance carries a donkey's head. In the sky are figures representing, from left to right, Abundance (or Felicity) with a cornucopia and olive branch (in the fresco she has a caduceus), Grace, who holds a key and drops flowers, and Well-being, with a shield (on which there appears a putto with a dolphin) and a cup. An engraving of this scene, based on the fresco, is in Riccardi Vernaccia 1822, pl.VII.

TECHNICAL NOTE
The support is a medium weight, plain-weave canvas. It has been strip-lined on all four edges. There are some very small flake losses and a few tiny holes, probably caused by insects, but the painting is in very good condition. There is pronounced craquelure in the blue drapery of the two-headed female figure in the foreground. The ground is dark brown in colour. There is a small pentimento in the left hand of the female figure carrying a shield and cup (Well-being). On the reverse of the canvas there are some random brush wipings in black paint; there is a figure *8* in red paint which corresponds with an 8 on the back of the frame and there is also a figure *4* in black paint.

EXHIBITIONS
Florence 1705; Detroit/Florence 1974, no.157.

33 Allegory of Temperance

Oil on canvas, 97 x 101.3 cm (frame 135.6 x 139.5 cm)

The *modello* corresponds to the group in the left corner of the ceiling opposite the entrance and to the left of the scene of the Cave of Eternity. Temperance, one of the four Cardinal Virtues, holds a bridle and a clock and stands beside an elephant which was regarded as the most cautious of animals. Sobriety holds a key (the emblem of the Riccardi family) and rests her foot on a dolphin; Meekness (?) receives flowers from two putti and pours oil or honey from a jar. In the lower part of the composition are shown the effects of intemperance: Sloth is solitary and miserable on the left, Envy in the centre bites her knuckles, and Hunger (?) on the right leans on a ravenous wolf. The flying figures from left to right are Voluptuousness, holding a winged sphere and fish-hooks, Youth, who carries an incense vessel and a ring in the form of a serpent biting its tail, symbol of eternity, and Tranquillity, with a cornucopia and a nest with a sea gull. An engraving after this *modello* is in Riccardi Vernaccia 1822, pl.II. The painting is reproduced in the original carved and gilded Florentine frame made in the late 1680s.

TECHNICAL NOTE
The support is a medium weight, plain-weave canvas. The right tacking edge is complete and there are parts of the tacking edges on the other three sides. The painting was strip-lined and loose-lined in 1996. There is a repaired horizontal tear about 13 cm in length in the centre. There are scattered old retouchings on the surface and some quite large retouched losses along the bottom edge, especially in the lower right-hand corner. The ground is dark brown in colour. There are no obvious pentimenti. There are some random brush wipings in black paint on the reverse of the canvas. A figure *2* in red paint on the reverse corresponds with a similar 2 on the back of the frame.

EXHIBITIONS
Florence 1705; Detroit/Florence 1974, no.153.

34 *The Cave of Eternity*

Oil on canvas, 73.1 x 87.5 cm

The *modello* corresponds with the scene opposite the entrance to the Galleria. The serpent that bites its own tail is a symbol of Eternity. The crowned figure of Janus holds the fleece of life from which the three Fates draw out the thread of human life. The winged figure holding a torch is Prometheus. On the left the hooded figure is Demagorgon who receives gifts from Nature, from whose breasts pours forth milk, and Fortune, who is winged and blindfolded. Seated at the entrance to the cave is the winged figure of Chronos, who represents Time. An engraving after this *modello* is in Riccardi Vernaccia 1822, pl.I.

TECHNICAL NOTE
The support is a medium weight, plain-weave canvas. The painting is lined and the original tacking edges have been cut off. A large irregular repaired tear passes through the back of the figure on the right and through the rocks below. A smaller irregular repaired tear passes through the winged blindfolded figure on the left. There is some local abrasion of paint on the raised threads in the area of the sky, presumably caused during lining. The ground is dark brown in colour. There are no obvious pentimenti.

EXHIBITIONS
Florence 1705; Barnard Castle 1962, no.56; Detroit/Florence 1974, no.152.

35 Minerva as Protectress of the Arts and Sciences

Oil on canvas, 73.5 x 88 cm

The *modello* corresponds with the scene above the entrance to the Galleria. Minerva, the godess of wisdom and of intelligence, accompanied by Mercury, entrusts the key of knowledge to Intellect, beside whom is the kneeling and naked figure of Truth. To the left is the she-wolf with Romulus and Remus, the founders of Rome. Minerva gives a hammer to Craftsmanship (*Artificio*) and Industry, at whose feet lie other tools. The wooden box is a hive and alludes to the industry of the bee. Amphion, who represents eloquence, sits on the mound in the background playing the viol, surrounded by flocks of birds. An engraving after this *modello* is in Riccardi Vernaccia 1822, pl.VI. A slightly smaller painting of this composition formerly on the London art market is probably Giordano's preliminary oil sketch, or *macchia*.

TECHNICAL NOTE

The support is a medium weight, plain-weave canvas. It was lined in 1962. There is a repaired complex tear above the flying figure of Mercury. Some surface abrasion is apparent in the clouds on the left. The ground is dark brown in colour and there are no obvious pentimenti. An inscription in pen on the stretcher in the hand of Denis Mahon states that a figure *12* painted in red and a figure 6 in black was visible on the reverse of the original canvas before lining. The figure 12 corresponds with a similar 12 on the back of the frame.

EXHIBITIONS

Florence 1705; Barnard Castle 1962, no.55; Detroit/Florence 1974, no.156.

36 Mythological Scene with the Rape of Proserpine

Oil on canvas, 121.6 x 193 cm

The *modello* corresponds with the left half of the ceiling decoration above the north wall, opposite the window wall.

On the right Pluto, god of the Underworld, carries off Proserpine, daughter of Ceres. To the left of them are the three infernal judges Minos, Ajax and Rhadamanthys, or alternatively the gods Mars, Hercules and Mercury. Excitable Harpies fly above. Further up are Dedalus and Icarus. The three-headed dog Cerberus guards the entrance to Hades and to the left is the boat of Charon waiting to take souls across the River Styx with Death in attendance, holding a scythe. Behind Cerberus is the forge of Vulcan, and in the background to the left the Giants who challenged the gods of Olympus are suffering their eternal tortures: Sisyphus was condemned to carry a great boulder uphill on his shoulders, Ixion is bound to a revolving wheel, and Tityus is attacked by a vulture. Enveloped in a star-studded blue cloak are Night and Sleep and further up to the left is Prometheus. The scene alludes to the elements of Fire and Air which form an important part of the ceiling's iconography. An engraving, based on the fresco and showing the right-hand part of this composition, is in Riccardi Vernaccia 1822, pl.IX; the engraving which corresponds with the left half is pl.X.

TECHNICAL NOTE
The support is a medium weight, plain-weave canvas. The reverse of the canvas is covered with wax and it has been strip-lined on all four sides. Although the right edge of this work and the left edge of the *Mythological Scene of Agriculture* (cat.37) join up to form a single continuous composition they were always two separate paintings. The original unpainted tacking edge on the right side of this canvas proves this to be the case. Giordano seems to have included some foliage at the right edge of this picture, where the two scenes meet, but then painted it out with sky. There are small repaired tears in the upper left-hand corner, in the grey clouds in the centre and in the sky to the right. Canvas patches have been applied to the reverse in these areas. The painting is in excellent condition. The ground is dark brown in colour. A figure *10* painted on the reverse of the canvas corresponds with a similar 10 on the back of the frame.

EXHIBITIONS
Florence 1705; Rome 1956-7, no.119; London 1960, no.357; Detroit/Florence 1974, no.159; Naples 1984, no.2.125b.

37 Mythological Scene of Agriculture

Oil on canvas, 121.4 x 192 cm

The *modello* corresponds with the right half of the ceiling decoration above the north wall, opposite the window wall. Ceres, the goddess of the harvest, sows seeds in a field ploughed by Triptolemus. Flora is seated with her back turned and Zephyr waters the soil. Flora and Ceres also stand for Spring and Summer (see cats.12 and 13). Between them is Vertumnus, protector of gardens and husband of Pomona, who is seen pruning the branches of a pomegranate tree at the left. The nymphs on the left look on in fear at the rape of Proserpine which appears in the adjacent picture (cat.36). The chariot drawn by peacocks bears Juno through the sky. In the right foreground is a river god. These figures allude, respectively, to the elements of Earth, Air and Water. The river god and the fauns in the background do not appear in the fresco. An engraving of this scene, based on the fresco, is in Riccardi Vernaccia 1822, pl.VIII.

TECHNICAL NOTE
The support is a medium weight, plain-weave canvas. This painting and the *Mythological Scene with the Rape of Proserpine* (cat.36) were conceived as a single scene and some of the forms at the left edge of this canvas cross over into the right side of that one. However, it is clear from an examination of the left edge of this painting, where one can see unprimed canvas, that the two scenes were never on a single canvas. The painting is lined and the tacking edges have been cut off on all four sides. There is a repaired T-shaped tear to the left of the flying figure on the left and two roughly parallel horizontal repaired tears about 18 cm in length in the sky abve the trees on the right. Some abrasion is apparent in the grey foreground area. Generally the painting is in very good condition. The ground is dark brown in colour. There are some small pentimenti: the right arm of the seated figure of Flora originally passed in front of the basket of flowers; the left foot of the sowing figure (Ceres) was lower down. The best preserved of all the red wax seals of the Riccardi family is on this stretcher, attached to a red and white ribbon.

EXHIBITIONS
Florence 1705; Rome 1956-7, no.118; London 1960, no.359; Detroit/Florence 1974, no.158; Naples 1984, no.2.125a.

38 *Allegory of Divine Wisdom*

Oil on canvas, 138.5 x 65.2 cm

The *modello* corresponds with the ceiling decoration in the Library adjacent to the Galleria (fig.30). Unlike the *modello*, that fresco has rounded ends at top and bottom. The kneeling youth represents the human intellect which is being released from the bonds of ignorance. He gazes up at the enthroned figure with globe and sceptre who represents Divine Wisdom. Mathematics, who stands on a set square, gives the young man wings and Philosophy a mirror. The winged figure who takes his arm and points upwards is Theology. The naked woman to the right of Divine Wisdom represents Truth, as in *Minerva as Protectress of the Arts and Sciences* (cat.35). In the fresco Giordano omitted the figures at the top and stretched out the composition along the vertical axis. In order to fill the gap between the earthbound group and the figure of Divine Wisdom he introduced a flying putto on the right side of the composition. The subject is based on a line from Petrarch's *Rime* (X, line 9) which appears in the fresco inscribed on the scroll held by putti (slightly misquoted and with a spelling error): *LEVAN DI TERRA A CIEL NOSTRO INTEILETTO* (sic). The subject is described by Segni, who probably devised it (Segni 1688, p.149, quoted in Büttner 1990, p.162).

TECHNICAL NOTE
The support is a medium weight, plain-weave canvas. There is vertical seam running the entire height of the picture about 6 cm from the right side. The canvas has been strip-lined on all four edges. There are some flake losses in the upper right-hand corner; the fingers of the left hand of the figure at upper right are modern restoration. The painting is otherwise in good condition. The ground is dark brown in colour. There are no obvious pentimenti. A curved stroke in light paint above the head of Divine Wisdom corresponds with the curved end of the ceiling decoration as executed. There are some random brush wipings in black paint on the reverse of the canvas. There is also a figure 6 in red paint. It corresponds with a similar 6 on the back of the frame.

EXHIBITIONS
Florence 1705; Manchester 1957, no.87; London 1960, no.367; Detroit/Florence 1974, no.161.

Fig.30 Luca Giordano, *Allegory of Divine Wisdom*. Florence, Palazzo Medici Riccardi, Library.

Guercino (Giovanni Francesco Barbieri) 1591–1666

39 *Madonna of the Sparrow*

Oil on canvas, 78.5 x 58 cm
Inscribed in white paint in the lower left-hand corner: *105*

The closeness of the figures to the picture plane and the soft controlled lighting create a sense of intimacy appropriate to this image of maternal tenderness. Throughout his career Guercino was always sensitive to the mother and child relationship and here he treats the theme with great naturalness. The attention of both Madonna and Child is focused on the sparrow which the Virgin holds on her finger. The infant stares intently at the little bird with a mixture of curiosity and awe; in his left hand he holds the string to which the sparrow is attached, but with his right he clutches the Virgin's veil, seeking maternal reassurance. In representations of the Madonna and Child a bird can serve as a symbolic reference to the Passion of Christ and often the Child reacts to the creature with apprehension, as in Michelangelo's *Taddei Madonna* (London, Royal Academy), perhaps the most famous example.

Guercino's interest in the motif at the time he painted this picture, about 1615–16, is attested by two other treatments of similar subjects. A drawing of the *Madonna and Child* in in the Fondazione Cini in Venice shows the Child holding the string as the bird flies into the air (fig.31). It may represent an early stage in the development of Guercino's ideas for the present picture. In the painting of the *Holy Family* in

Palazzo Pitti in Florence it is Saint Joseph who holds a fluttering bird on a string and the Child turns to his mother as if afraid.[1]

Mahon has noted the relationship between the figure of the Madonna and Ludovico Carracci's Virgin in the altarpiece he painted for the Capuchin Church at Cento signed and dated 1591 (now in the Pinacoteca Civica, Cento),[2] a work for which Guercino is reported on more than one occasion to have expressed admiration. Perhaps Guercino's greatest debt in this work is to the small-scale religious pictures of Bartolomeo Schedoni (1578–1615), which he could have seen in nearby Modena and perhaps in Bologna. Schedoni's close-knit compositions showing the Madonna and Child engaged in humble familial activity (see cat.74) are marked by a similarly profound human sensibility. The soft fall of light on the forms, the smooth finish and the transitions from warm flesh tones to cool sea-green colours in Schedoni's works are also to be seen here. What distinguishes this work from its exemplars, however, is the sense of everyday realism and a certain solidity in the figures.

A copy of the painting is in the Galleria Nazionale di Parma, and another twice recently appeared at auction in New York.[3]

TECHNICAL NOTE
The support is a fine canvas. It is lined and retains parts of the original tacking edges. The lining is a coarser canvas which has imparted some of its texture to the painted canvas. A stretcher-bar mark on the right side indicates that the original stretcher/strainer was about 6 cm wide. There is a small loss at the left edge, below the Virgin's extended finger. The ground is light brown in colour and can be seen just to the left of the Christ Child's right thumb. The present stretcher is inscribed: *Miss Burdett Coutts* and, in the same elegant script, *(93) Guercino*.

PROVENANCE[4]
Borghese collection, Rome, before 1693; listed in the 1693 inventory of pictures belonging to Giovanni Battista Borghese, Principe di Rossano, in Palazzo Borghese, and said there to bear the number 105 (which referred to an earlier, as yet untraced, inventory); still recorded there in a guidebook published in 1798;[5] bought by William Young Ottley in 1799 or 1800 and offered for sale at 118 Pall Mall, London, in January 1801, no.24; Sir Bernard Scrope Morland, 4th Bt; sold by his executors at Phillips', London, 20 May 1820, lot 63; bought there by Samuel Rogers; sold Christie's, London, 2 May 1857 (Samuel Rogers sale), lot 609, bought by Radclyffe for Miss Burdett-Coutts (whose name appears on the stretcher); sold anonymously at Christie's, London, by a member of the family, 3 May 1946, lot 117, where acquired by the present owner.

EXHIBITIONS
London 1821, no.74; London 1835, no.12; Manchester 1857, no.333; London (Hazlitt) 1952, no.4; Rome 1956–7, no.122; Manchester 1957, no.143; London 1960, no.380; Bologna 1968, no.13; London (Agnew) 1973, no.30; London (National Gallery) 1991, no.1; Bologna 1991, no.12; Frankfurt 1991–2, no.7.

Fig.31 Guercino, *Virgin and Child with a Bird*, 1615–16. Black chalk and charcoal, 161 x 127 mm. Venice, Fondazione Giorgio Cini.

1 See Salerno 1988, no.17, p.96.
2 Mahon (Dipinti) 1968, no.13, pp.35–6.
3 Christie's, New York, 18 May 1994, lot 172, and again Christie's, New York, 10 January 1995, lot 83.
4 The provenance is set out in great detail in Mahon (Dipinti) 1968, no.13, pp.35–6; see also Salerno 1988, no.18, p.97, and Mahon (Dipinti) 1991, no.12, p.42.
5 Manazzale 1798, II, p.218.

Guercino (Giovanni Francesco Barbieri) 1591–1666

40 A Sibyl holding a Scroll

Oil on canvas, 72.7 x 61.7 cm

The scroll and the closed book with vellum thongs identify the figure as a sibyl, one of the pagan female seers who were reputed to have foretold the coming of Christ (see cats.48 and 62). The elaborate headdress is also typical of seventeenth-century representations of sibyls and can be compared with Domenichino's approximately contemporary renderings of the subject in the Borghese, Capitoline and Wallace collections.[1] With its fluent handling, rich colouring and velvety shadows, the painting is typical of the works Guercino painted before his removal to Rome in 1621.

The *Sibyl holding a Scroll* is closely related to the figure of Saint Irene in Guercino's *Saint Sebastian Succoured* (fig.32), a painting executed in Ferrara in 1619 for the Papal Legate of the city, Cardinal Jacopo Serra (1570–1623). Serra was one of Guercino's most important patrons and commissioned at least five subject pictures from him, two of which are in the Mahon collection (cats.43–4). Saint Irene is in exactly the same pose as the sibyl; she wears identical dress and is similarly lit from the upper right. In her right hand, however, instead of a scroll she holds a sponge and squeezes it out in a bowl in readiness to tend Saint Sebastian's wounds. The Mahon painting is always said to have been executed as a study for the figure of Saint Irene and subsequently developed to stand as an autonomous work. By substituting the parchment and book for the sponge and bowl Guercino turned the preliminary sketch into an independent painting he could sell.[2]

However, it is also possible (although Mahon believes this is less likely) that the artist may have made the painting after the *Saint Sebastian Succoured*, in which case it would be not a preparatory painting but an autograph repetition adapted to make it an independent work. The close similarity between details such as the folds of the headdress and sleeves, and the position of the highlights on the bodice, is more readily explicable if the Mahon painting is considered an autograph repetition rather than a preliminary study, although it would be a mistake to be categoric on this matter. The X-radiograph made at the National Gallery indicates that there are no pentimenti in the painting.

There exist three compositional drawings made in preparation for the *Saint Sebastian Succoured*, two in the Uffizi and one at Windsor.[3] The figure to which the *Sibyl* corresponds appears only in the Windsor drawing in pen and wash, which on account of its closeness to the finished painting represents an advanced stage in the preparatory process.[4] A seventeenth-century copy of the head of Saint Irene is in the Longhi Foundation in Florence, and another is recorded in the Pinacoteca di Budrio.[5]

TECHNICAL NOTE
The support is a plain-weave medium-weight canvas. The painting is lined and retains all four tacking edges. The stretcher-bar marks apparent on the surface do not correspond with the present stretcher and indicate that the original stretcher/strainer was about 4.5 cm wide. The ground is warm brown and has a granular consistency. It is visible at the right edge of the scroll. There are no pentimenti. There are a few minor retouchings but the painting is in excellent condition.

PROVENANCE[6]
12th Duke of Hamilton, Hamilton Palace, Lanarkshire, by 1882; Christie's, London, 24 June 1882 (Hamilton Palace sale), lot 385; bought by G.J. Howard, later 9th Earl of Carlisle, and hung at Castle Howard; by descent to the Hon. Geoffrey W.A. Howard; his sale, Christie's, London, 18 February 1944, lot 36 (bought Hills); Christie's, London, 7 March 1952, lot 76 (bought Ryce); acquired in 1952 by the present owner.

EXHIBITIONS
Zurich 1956, no.19; London 1960, no.368; Bologna 1968, no.34; London (National Gallery) 1991, no.5.

1 Spear 1980, cats.51 (fig.171), 80 (fig.255) and 85 (colour plate 6).
2 Briganti 1953, no.28, p.17; Mahon (Dipinti) 1968, no.34, pp.82–3; Helston and Henry in London (National Gallery) 1991, no.5, p.19; Mahon (Dipinti) 1991, under no.39, p.110.
3 Mahon (Disegni) 1969, nos.41–3.
4 See Mahon/Turner 1989, no.9.
5 See Longhi 1968, p.66 and fig.51; Gregori et al. 1980, no.75, p.269, fig.88.
6 The provenance is set out in detail in Mahon (Dipinti) 1968, no.34, pp.81–2.

Fig.32 Guercino, *Saint Sebastian Succoured*, 1619. Oil on canvas, 179 x 255 cm. Bologna, Pinacoteca Nazionale.

Guercino (Giovanni Francesco Barbieri) 1591–1666

41 Head of an Old Man

Oil on canvas, 63 x 48.3 cm

The painting was first published in 1953 by Giuliano Briganti, who expressed the opinion that the painting was a study from the life, a view shared by Mahon.[1] The gesture of the hand and the particular view of the head are not repeated in any larger composition, so it cannot be stated with certainty that it is a preparatory work. The painting is not a fragment, as three of the original four tacking edges survive. It is likely that Guercino did make oil studies of this type from the model to use for guidance when working on commissioned pictures. The head bears a general resemblance to that of the prophet in *Elijah fed by Ravens* (cat.43) and to the figure of the saint in the *Martyrdom of Saint Peter* (Modena, Galleria Estense).[2] Guercino must also have been aware that he could easily sell a work such as this later on as an apostle or patriarch. The man has no distinguishing attribute but his fervent heavenward gaze and the hazy light around his head, achieved by leaving the warm, almost orange, ground showing, is strongly suggestive of sanctity.

Guercino handles the paint with a remarkable fluency and boldness of touch. Curving impastoed strokes define the curls of the hair and beard and a long snaking brushstroke marks the white border of his cloak. Small dabs of white pigment on the old man's forehead and around his right eye both mark the highlights and emphasise his furrows and wrinkles. In the flesh areas the artist has used the granular consistency of the ground to make the skin seem rough and weathered. The looseness and spontaneity of the execution are characteristic of Guercino's works before his return to Cento from Rome in 1623 and are particularly close to datable works of about 1619–20, like the *Erminia and the Shepherd* (Birmingham City Museums and Art Gallery)[3] and the *Jacob blessing the Sons of Joseph* (cat.44).

A painting in the Hermitage, which appears to be no more than an old copy of this picture (though formerly catalogued there as by the Spanish painter Jusepe de Ribera), was published by Roberto Longhi as an autograph work by Guercino.[4] It shows the original extent of the present painting, which was a few centimetres wider on the left side.

TECHNICAL NOTE

The support is a plain-weave medium-weight canvas. The painting is lined and the stretcher (not original) is of Italian manufacture. The original tacking edges are preserved at the top and bottom and on the right side. The present tacking edge on the left side has the original painted composition continuing on it which means that the painting was once a little wider. The ground is a warm light brown in colour and has a rough consistency; it is visible around the hair of the old man on the left side. There are no obvious pentimenti. The painting is in excellent condition. On the reverse are three red wax seals: one is the seal of the Papal Accademia di Belle Arti in Bologna; another is an unidentified customs seal (Italian); the third (on the stretcher) is that of the excise office of the Grand Duchy of Tuscany and bears the arms of the house of Hapsburg-Lorraine.

PROVENANCE

Lt.-Col. R.W. Barclay, Bury Hill House, Dorking; his sale, Sotheby's, London, 1 February 1950, lot 7, where acquired by the present owner.

EXHIBITIONS

London 1960, no.370; Bologna 1968, no.38; London (National Gallery) 1991, no.7; Bologna 1991, no.41; Frankfurt 1991–2, no.25.

1 Briganti 1953, pp.9, 13 and 17; Mahon (Dipinti) 1968, p.87, under no.38. On this picture see also Salerno 1988, no.62, p.142, and Mahon (Dipinti) 1991, no.41, pp.118–19.
2 Salerno 1988, no.52, p.129.
3 Salerno 1988, no.61, pp.140–1.
4 Longhi 1968, fig.53, p.66.

Guercino (Giovanni Francesco Barbieri) 1591–1666

42 The Mystic Marriage of Saint Catherine

Oil on canvas, 88 x 70 cm
Staatliche Museen zu Berlin Preussischer Kulturbesitz, Gemäldegalerie (Inv.1/70)

The subject of the mystic marriage of Saint Catherine of Alexandria made its appearance in painting in the early fifteenth century and it subsequently became very popular. It has its origin in the story of Catherine's refusal to marry the Emperor Maximian because she claimed she was wed to Christ.

According to Guercino's first biographer, Carlo Cesare Malvasia (1678), the artist made a 'Madonna, and Saint Catherine' for Cavaliere Piombino of Cento in 1620,[1] and Mahon identified it as this work in 1960.[2] The painting is typical of the kind of relatively small commissions that Guercino received from local patrons before his departure for Rome in 1621. Like most of the devotional works of this early period (for example cat.39), it is marked by a modesty and naturalness which belie the sophistication of the design. Guercino conveys a sense of profound human intimacy by means of the physical proximity of the figures to one another and to the viewer. The forms are pressed together within the picture space and they are enlivened by the juxtaposition of areas of light with warm reflective shadows and vibrant midtones. The surface of the painting is animated by individual brushstrokes of great bravura, like the yellow highlight on the sleeve immediately above Saint Catherine's left hand, or the red stroke on her lower lip.

A beautiful preparatory drawing is in the Ashmolean Museum, Oxford (fig.33). It is unusual in so fully anticipating the painting, although there are some significant differences.[3] Generally Guercino's compositions underwent a complex process of change and development in the preparatory stages and the finished painting rarely corresponds very closely with any of the drawings. In the Ashmolean drawing the figures are more spread out and the forms of the two women are broader. The compositional solution adopted in the painting is more daring: the geometry of the design is tighter, the figures are enlarged to fill the picture space and they are brought much closer together; Saint Catherine is placed lower down so that her whole profile is boldly thrown into shadow.

The painting appears to have been given as a gift to Pope Innocent X Pamphilj (reigned 1644–55) in 1652. He had great admiration for Guercino, but, according to Malvasia, found the nudity of the child offensive and asked Pietro da Cortona to add some drapery. Cortona did this reluctantly and wrote a letter of apology to Guercino, which Malvasia must have seen in Casa Gennari after Guercino's death.[4] When Mahon bought the painting there was indeed a drapery covering the offending area but as it was manifestly not part of the original paint surface it was removed. At present there are later additions to three sides of the canvas (2.5 cm to the left, 3 cm to the right and 12 cm at the top, now folded over) but they are not visible, with the exception of part of the strip on the right. The painting is in very good condition. Three copies are recorded by Schleier, all of which were made after Cortona added the drapery to the original.[5]

Later in his career (1650) Guercino painted another version of this subject. It is horizontal in format and completely different in treatment and style.[6]

Fig.33 Guercino, *The Mystic Marriage of Saint Catherine*, 1620. Pen and brown ink over black chalk, 256 x 203 mm. Oxford, Ashmolean Museum.

PROVENANCE[7]
Painted in 1620 for Cavaliere Piombino (or Piombini) of Cento; probably acquired from him or from a family member by Cardinal Niccolò Albergati Ludovisi when he was Archbishop of Bologna, 1645–51; probably the picture given by him to Pope Innocent X in 1652;[8] in the collection of Cardinal Flavio Chigi, nephew of Pope Alexander VII, before 1692;[9] bequeathed by him to 'Card:e de Medici', presumably Cardinal Francesco Maria de' Medici (Cardinal between 1686 and 1709); recorded in the Methuen collection at Corsham Court in 1780, having probably been acquired by Sir Paul Methuen (1672–1757); shortly after 1838 it passed into the collection of Henry Gilbert of Devizes; his sale, Christie's, London, 7 February 1846, lot 38 (bought in); bought by Denis Mahon from Appleby's, London, 1958; acquired from him by the Gemäldegalerie, Berlin-Dahlem, in 1970.

EXHIBITIONS
London 1960, no.369; Detroit 1965, no.98; Bologna 1968, no.40; Bologna 1991, no.42; Frankfurt 1991–2, no.26; Washington 1992, no.21.

1 Malvasia 1678, II, p.364; Baruffaldi (1844–6, II, p.443) gives the subject more accurately as 'lo Sposalizio de s.Caterina martire'.
2 London 1960, no.369, p.139.
3 See the comments in Mahon (Dipinti) 1991, no.42, pp.120 and 122, and Turner and Plazzotta 1991, no.29, pp.58–60.
4 Malvasia 1678, II, p.379; Calvi had also probably seen Cortona's letter, see Calvi 1808, pp.34–5.
5 Berlin Katalog 1975, pp.191–2.
6 Salerno 1988, no.271, p.341.
7 For the provenance of the picture, see Mahon (Dipinti) 1968, no.40, p.90; Salerno 1988, p.371; Mahon (Dipinti) 1991, no.42, p.120, and note 9 below.
8 See Salerno 1988, pp.147 and 371.
9 Sir Denis Mahon has passed on to me a documentary reference to this picture, kindly given him by D.ssa Almamaria Tantillo, Rome, in the inventory of Cardinal Flavio Chigi. The document (Biblioteca Apostolica Vaticana, Archivio Chigi, Inventario 700) is entitled: *Inventario del Cardinale Flavio Chigi, firmato il 1 maggio 1692 da Francesco Corallo Guardarobba*, and item no.166 on f.68 is: *Un Quadro di p.mi 4, e 3 ... con una madonna che tiene il dito à S.Caterina, et il Putto in piedi, con Camiscia [?], et un'Anello in mano in atto di sposarla, mano del Quercino*. On the sheet to the left an annotation (evidently added just after the Cardinal's death in 1693) reads: *Dato per Leg.o al S: Card:e de Medici*.

Guercino (Giovanni Francesco Barbieri) 1591–1666

43 Elijah fed by Ravens

Oil on canvas, 195 x 156.5 cm
Inscribed on the stone slab: *REG.III. / CAP.XVII*
On permanent loan to the National Gallery since 1987

In his account in the *Felsina Pittrice* of Guercino's activities in the year 1620, Malvasia states: 'He was recalled to Ferrara, where he made other paintings for the same legate, and for his nephew, who delighted in drawings; and they were a picture of the prophet Elijah in the desert; Jacob blessing his son, all full length figures.'[1] The Legate was Cardinal Jacopo Serra (1570–1623), Papal Legate of Ferrara (effectively governor of the former Duchy of Ferrara) and an early and enthusiastic patron of the young Guercino; Serra's nephew was Giovan Paolo Serra;[2] the 'Jacob blessing his son' is the *Jacob blessing the Sons of Joseph* in the Denis Mahon collection (cat.44) and the 'Elijah' is the present work.[3]

The inscription refers to a passage in the First Book of Kings (in the *Vulgate* the two Books of Kings and the two Books of Samuel which precede them are called 'The Four Books of Kings', hence the reference in this picture to III Book of Kings) which describes how after prophesying a drought, Elijah was instructed by God to hide himself by the brook of Cherith from which he could drink and where ravens would feed him 'bread and flesh in the morning and bread and flesh in the evening' (I Kings 17:6). In the painting two ravens can be seen delivering bread which in form is similar to the typical bread of Ferrara, still produced today. This episode in the life of the prophet Elijah is the one which is most frequently represented. It is noteworthy that in spite of the inscription the picture appears to have been considered in several seventeenth- and eighteenth-century Barberini inventories to show Saint Paul the Hermit, a fourth-century anchorite, who was also miraculously fed by a raven.[4]

A close examination of the painting, in preparation for this exhibition, revealed that underneath the present inscription there lies another. The following words are readable in an infra-red photograph: *[V]A[DE] CONTRA/ ORIENTEM ET/ ABSCONDERE IN/ TOR[RENTEM]* (Get thee hence, and turn thee eastward, and hide thyself by the brook [Cherith], I Kings 17:3). It was presumably painted out by the artist, perhaps to make that area of the picture less cluttered.

Malvasia records that in the previous year, 1619, Guercino painted three other pictures for Serra. They are *Saint Sebastian Succoured* (fig.32), the *Return of the Prodigal Son* (Vienna, Kunsthistorisches Museum) and the *Samson seized by the Philistines* (New York, Metropolitan Museum).[5] Together with the works painted for Serra in 1620, they form a varied group: there is no consistency of scale or format and no obvious connection in subject matter. Serra appears to have given Guercino a relatively free hand.[6] Recently, however, the subject of the *Elijah fed by Ravens* has been supposed, quite plausibly, to have had some special relevance to Serra's activity as governor of Ferrara. In 1619 Serra had established the Congregazione dell'Abbondanza, an institution devoted to ensuring that Ferrara was supplied with good bread, and this may have had a certain significance for the scene depicted by Guercino.[7]

In his compositions of around 1619–20 Guercino gives the forms massiveness by making them occupy a high proportion of the picture space. This has the effect of bringing them close to the spectator and intensifying their visual impact. Here the figure of Elijah is over life-size and powerfully dominates the picture space; his right foot seems to push through the picture plane into the viewer's space. That the artist sought to dissolve the barrier between the painted world and the real world is evidenced by the shadow cast on the stone slab by an imagined object conceived to be in front of the picture space. Guercino attenuates the massiveness of the figure through the use of light which cuts across the form, breaking it up into patches of light and dark. A variety of juxtapositions and internal overlappings help to create a subtle equilibrium between solidity and dissolution of form. The painting is undoubtedly one of the masterpieces of Guercino's early maturity.

TECHNICAL NOTE
The support is a fairly coarse plain-weave canvas. The painting has an Italian type glue-paste lining dating from before its acquisition by the present owner in 1936. The tacking edges have been removed but the painting does not appear to have been reduced. The picture is on a strainer with a horizontal crossbar which is likely to be original, with the exception of the upper and lower members which are modern, probably substituted when the painting was lined. The stretcher-bar marks on the surface, about 5 cm wide, and especially apparent on the left and right sides, correspond with the present strainer. The ground is warm orange-brown and is visible around the small toe of the figure's right foot and to the right of the mauve cloak above the scroll. There is a retouching the size of a matchbox about 15 cm below the figure's right hand but the painting is in excellent condition.

PROVENANCE[8]
Painted in 1620 for Cardinal Jacopo Serra, Papal Legate of Ferrara; Don Maffeo Barberini, Prince of Palestrina, 1655; listed in Barberini inventories of *c*.1680 and of 1686 (in all three inventories the subject is described as 'Saint Paul the Hermit');[9] upon the division in 1812 of the Barberini entailed estate it passed to the Principi di Palestrina branch of the family ('Il Profeta Elia del Guercino', with a high valuation of 1200 scudi); by descent to Principessa Donna Maria Barberini, from whom acquired by the present owner in 1936. The painting retains its Barberini frame.

EXHIBITIONS
London 1938, no.288; London 1960, no.382; the painting was briefly on loan to the Kunsthistorisches Museum, Vienna, 1955; Birmingham 1955, no.61; Bologna 1968, no.41; Bologna/Washington/New York 1986–7, no.164; London (National Gallery) 1991, no.9; Bologna 1991, no.43; Frankfurt 1991–2, no.27.

1 Malvasia 1678, II, p.364.
2 According to Southorn 1988, p.115; less convincingly, Piero Boccardo has suggested that it could have been Pier Maria Gentile, see Genoa 1992, pp.20–22.
3 The work was identified by Voss in 1922, p.217, and fully published in Mahon 1947, pp.12–31, 67–8, 71, 72.
4 See the painting by Rosa in the present exhibition which shows Saint Paul the Hermit, cat.68.
5 Salerno 1988, nos.54, 57, 58.
6 For Serra as a patron of Guercino, see Mahon 1981 and Southorn 1988, pp.113–15.
7 Southorn 1988, p.114 and note 26 on p.175; Stone 1991, p.86.
8 The provenance is set out in great detail in Mahon (Dipinti) 1968, no.41, pp.91–3. See also Salerno 1988, no.68, p.147, and Mahon (Dipinti) 1991, no.43, pp.122–4.
9 Aronberg Lavin 1975, p.227, no.269; p.376, no.319; p.397, no.76. See also p.715 and the index on p.491 under *Saint Paul, First Hermit*.

Guercino (Giovanni Francesco Barbieri) 1591–1666

45 The Presentation of Jesus in the Temple

Oil on copper, 73.1 x 65 cm
On long-term loan to the National Gallery from the Mahon Trust since 1977

This painting was one of the artist's most celebrated works during his lifetime. Painted in 1623 for Bartolomeo Fabri of Cento, an important early patron of Guercino who also commissioned the *Incredulity of Saint Thomas* (London, National Gallery) and its pendant, the *Taking of Christ* (Cambridge, Fitzwilliam Museum), it was returned to the artist in part settlement of a debt. Malvasia states that the painting hung by Guercino's bed for his personal devotions and adds that it was coveted, 'Penelope-like', by several important collectors, including Cardinal Antonio Barberini, the Duke of Modena Francesco I d'Este, and the Cardinal Prince Leopoldo de' Medici. For many years Guercino refused to part with it but he eventually sold it in 1660 to the learned Frenchman Raphael Dufresne for 100 *doppie* and a flatteringly inscribed copy of Dufresne's edition of Leonardo's *Trattato della Pittura*.[1] Malvasia's account of the sale of 'questo famosissimo rame' is confirmed by an entry in the *Libro dei Conti*, the artist's account book, which refers to it as the 'painting on copper which was near his [Guercino's] bed and was bought by a Frenchman at the cost of 100 Doble'.[2]

The episode of the presentation of the infant Christ in the Temple is recounted in the Gospel of Luke (2:22–39). Mary and Joseph brought Jesus to the Temple in Jerusalem forty days after his birth in order to consecrate him to the Lord, in accordance with the law. The ceremony required a redemptive offering and they presented a pair of turtledoves for the sacrifice, which Guercino shows at the foot of the altar. The priest is Simeon, to whom it had been revealed that he would not die before he had seen the Messiah. In the painting he is about to receive the child in his arms and to utter the words: 'Lord, now lettest thou thy servant depart in peace, according to thy word: For mine eyes have seen thy salvation, Which thou hast prepared before the face of all people' (2:29–31).

Guercino, never an archaeologically minded artist, made no effort to achieve historical accuracy. The architectural details of the scene are wholly Italian and the dancing maenad on the side of the altar is elegant but historically inappropriate. Simeon wears an oriental mitre but his embroidered cope is remarkably similar in pattern and colour to that worn by the Pope in the *Saint Gregory the Great with Saints Ignatius Loyola and Francis Xavier* (cat.47). The decorative carved relief on the dais in that picture is very like the reliefs in this work, confirming that they are quite close in date.

Despite Malvasia's ambiguous reference to the painting, which could be interpreted to mean that it had been begun before Guercino departed for Rome in 1621, Mahon's thorough analysis of the stylistic features of the work when he first published it in 1947 makes it clear that it must date from just after his return to Cento in 1623.[3] The composition, lit by a warm and diffuse light, shows a concern for clearly defined planes and a lucid planimetric arrangement which represent a new departure for the artist and reveal a debt to Domenichino's Roman works, in particular to the fresco of the *Death of Saint Cecilia* in the Polet Chapel in San Luigi dei Francesi.[4] The disposition of the figures and their relationship to the architecture are more nearly related to those in Domenichino's composition than to anything in Guercino's own earlier works. Indeed, the woman kneeling on the right holding a basket with two ducks may be considered an amalgamation of the two women on the right of Domenichino's fresco. With its broad forms and rich colouring the *Presentation* represents a successful fusion of Guercino's North Italian upbringing with its Venetian undertones and the classic point of view in painting which he had encountered in Rome.

Certain technical features are worthy of note. The copper support is the largest Guercino used and suggests that from the start it must have been a costly work and regarded as precious. However, unlike for example Domenichino, Albani and Guido Reni, whose works on copper are executed with great precision and exploit the smooth surface of the support, Guercino did not really adapt his technique when working on copper. Although the tin and lead plating on the painted side gives a brilliant silvery surface, Guercino allows it to play no aesthetic function, completely covering it with the opaque orange ground which he customarily employed throughout his career and which is actually quite similar in hue to the unplated copper. This would seem to indicate that the plating was carried out for purely technical purposes, presumably to prevent corrosion on the painted side.

There are several drawings which are associated in some way or other with this painting.[5]

1 Malvasia 1678, II, p.366, where the dedication is transcribed. Malvasia's mistaken reference to Domenico Fabri is corrected on pp.367–8 where he mentions the *Presentation* again, as having been made for Bartolomeo, see Mahon 1947, p.93 note 149, and Mahon (Dipinti) 1968, p.135.
2 The entry is quoted in Mahon (Dipinti) 1968, p.136.
3 Mahon 1947, pp.93–7.
4 Spear 1982, II, pl.152. Guercino's compatriot, the engraver G.B. Pasqualini, who devoted himself almost exclusively to reproducing Guercino's work, exceptionally made an engraving in 1622 after Domenichino's fresco, see Bagni 1988, p.43, fig.56.
5 See Mahon and Turner 1989, nos.599 and 603 (both offsets); three drawings ascribed to Guercino (Mahon and Turner 1989, nos.350 and 351) and a drawing in the Teylers Museum, Haarlem, (Inv.H.23) seem, however, to be later in date stylistically.
6 The provenance is set out in detail in Mahon (Dipinti) 1968, no.53, pp.135–6; see also Salerno 1988, no.94, p.178, and Mahon (Dipinti) 1991, no.57, pp.170–2.

Guercino (Giovanni Francesco Barbieri) 1591–1666

47 Saint Gregory the Great with Saints Ignatius Loyola and Francis Xavier

Oil on canvas, 296 x 211 cm
The book held by Saint Ignatius is inscribed *IHS* on the binding.
On long-term loan to the National Gallery since 1992

Saint Gregory the Great, monk, theologian and pope (reigned 590–604), sits enthroned on a stone dais receiving the inspiration of the Holy Spirit and the homage of the first Jesuit saints, Ignatius Loyola (1491–1556) and Francis Xavier (1506–1552). He wears a magnificent brocaded and jewelled cope and leafs through the yellowed pages of a book which signifies his holy learning. In the right foreground a wingless putto plays with the papal tiara; the violin-playing angel is perhaps a reference to Gregory's own renowned musical skills. To the left kneels Saint Ignatius, the Spanish founder of the Society of Jesus (the Jesuits). Francis Xavier, on the right was the first great Jesuit missionary. Both saints are dressed in the simple black habit of the order and kneel at the Pope's feet, reflecting one of the Jesuit order's distinguishing characteristics, its allegiance to the papacy. The putti at upper right playfully mimic the scene of veneration below.

Saint Gregory was the namesake and patron of the Bolognese Pope Gregory XV Ludovisi (reigned 1621–3) and it was during his papacy that Ignatius and Francis Xavier were canonised. The ceremonies took place on 12 March 1622, the feast day of Saint Gregory.[1] The Ludovisi were closely tied to the Jesuit order and patronised the construction in Rome of a great church dedicated to the founder. The foundation stone of Sant'Ignazio was laid on 2 August 1626 by Cardinal Ludovico Ludovisi, the Pope's nephew. The subject matter of the painting is so closely linked with these events that it seems extremely probable that Guercino was commissioned to paint it by a member of the Ludovisi family in memory of Gregory XV's connections with the Jesuits. It was perhaps destined to adorn the new church or the adjoining buildings belonging to the order.[2] The Ludovisi had been early patrons of Guercino in Bologna and within a few months of the city's archbishop, Alessandro Ludovisi, being elected to the papacy on 9 February 1621, the artist was called to Rome. During his two-year stay, he produced several ceiling paintings (especially in the Ludovisi villa on the Pincio), the great Santa Petronilla Altarpiece for St Peter's (fig.4), the *Saint Chrysogonus in Glory*, a large canvas commissioned by Cardinal Scipione Borghese for the Roman church of San Crisogono (now in Lancaster House, London), as well as the portrait of the Pope (Malibu, J.Paul Getty Museum). Despite his success in Rome, Guercino decided to return to his native Cento after the Pope's death and remained there until his move to Bologna in 1642.

Before the painting could be permanently installed in its intended location, it was given as a present, presumably by Cardinal Ludovico's brother, Prince Niccolò Ludovisi, who had assumed the headship of the family, to Don Juan Alfonso Enríquez de Cabrera, the 9th Almirante de Castilla, who came to Rome in 1646 as a special envoy of Philip IV of Spain to the recently elected and pro-Spanish Pope Innocent X Pamphilj. The Almirante was a fanatical lover of painting and the subject of *Saint Gregory the Great with Saints Ignatius Loyola and Francis Xavier* could hardly have been more appropriate for him. At about the same time as he received this picture he was also given Guercino's *Jacob blessing the Sons of Joseph* (cat.44) by Cardinal Giulio Sacchetti.

The date of the canonisation in 1622 provides a *terminus post quem* for the execution of the painting but the stylistic features of the work indicate that it should be dated after Guercino's period in Rome to about 1625–6. The monumentality of the composition contrasts sharply with earlier works. The large bulky forms are densely packed into a shallow space, creating an impression of great solidity, a characteristic of the documented *Assumption with Saints Peter and Jerome* (Reggio Emilia, Cathedral) of 1625–6.[3] Differentiation between the forms is achieved in a rather simple but immensely effective manner by contrasting large patches of colour: the black form of Saint Ignatius overlaps the brilliant gold and scarlet of Saint Gregory, which in turn overlaps the silhouette of Saint Francis Xavier. The all black Jesuit habit has always presented painters with a challenge and Guercino's solution in this work is to employ it to give the composition a bold, measured rhythm. The refinement in the types of the angel and putti is consistent with the trend which is apparent in Guercino's works of the mid-1620s.

Three preparatory drawings for the painting are known, one of which, an early compositional drawing, is exhibited here (cat.90).[4]

TECHNICAL NOTE

The support is a single piece of plain-weave fairly coarse canvas. There are remains of the tacking edge on the right side but on the other sides they have been cut off leaving quite ragged edges. The canvas is lined and the stretcher is not original. A band of about 6 cm along the top and bottom edges is repainted. There are several holes in the canvas which have been repaired and retouched, the largest of which is beneath Saint Ignatius's right wrist. There are also several repaired tears. The modern retouching in the sky has discoloured noticeably. The ground is light brown in colour. There are few obvious pentimenti: Saint Gregory's book was extended and the profile of his *camauro* (cap) adjusted.

PROVENANCE[5]

Presumably commissioned by the papal Ludovisi family, probably in 1625–6. Given by Prince Niccolò Ludovisi, nephew of Pope Gregory XV, to Don Juan Alfonso Enríquez de Cabrera (1597–1647), 9th Almirante de Castilla and viceroy of Naples, in 1646;[6] donated to the church of San Pascual Bailon, Madrid, by his son, the 10th Almirante, at his death in 1691 and recorded there by Antonio Ponz in 1776.[7] The painting was removed from the church by 1815, probably by Baron Mathieu de Faviers, Intendant-général of Napoleon's Armée du midi, in whose posthumous sale in Paris it appeared on 11 April 1837, lot 18.[8] Acquired by the 2nd Duke of Sutherland and hung at Stafford (now Lancaster) House, London; sold Christie's, London, 8 February 1908 (Duke of Sutherland sale), lot 82, bought by Sir George Faudel Phillips, Bt, and placed at Balls Park, Hertford. Seen there by the present owner in the mid-1930s and bought by him in 1941 after the death of Sir Lionel Faudel-Phillips (son of Sir George).

EXHIBITIONS

London 1837, no.1; London 1960, no.358; Bologna 1968, no.60; London (National Gallery) 1991, no.17; Bologna 1991, no.66; Frankfurt 1991–2, no.39; Washington 1992, no.31.

1 On the same day Saints Theresa of Avila and Philip Neri were also canonised.
2 Although the painting was given away before the church was consecrated in 1650, it is worthy of note that the first chapel on the left is dedicated to Saint Gregory the Great and now has an altarpiece by Fratel de Lattre showing the saint. An old full-size copy of the Guercino is in the Pinacoteca Vaticana and probably came to the Vatican at the time of the suppression of the Jesuits in 1773 from the Collegio Romano (founded by Gregory XIII) attached to Sant'Ignazio, see Mahon (Dipinti) 1968, pp.150–1.
3 Salerno 1988, no.113, p.194.
4 For the other drawings see Mahon/Turner 1989, no.35, and Mahon (Disegni) 1992, no.45. A fourth drawing in the British Museum may be a rejected study for the figure of Saint Gregory, Turner/Plazzotta 1991, appendix no.13 (not illustrated).
5 For fuller documentation of the picture's history, see the entries in Mahon (Dipinti) 1968, no.60, pp.148–50, and Mahon (Dipinti) 1991, no.66, pp.188 and 190; see also Salerno 1988, no.112, pp.192–3.
6 Listed in his post-mortem inventory of 1647: '637 ytten Vio un lienço gr^de de Sanct Greg^o y sant ignacio y sant fran^co = inventariado a n° 637 = tasolo a quatro mill Reales 4000', revised transcription made by Maria L. Gilbert of the Getty Provenance Index of the entry published by Fernández Duro 1902, p.204 (no.417).
7 Ponz 1772–94 (1988), II, p.43.
8 At De Faviers' death in 1833 the painting was deposited, presumably on account of its size, in the studio of Baron Gérard, see Gotteri 1995, p.141.

Guercino (Giovanni Francesco Barbieri) 1591–1666

48 The Cumaean Sibyl with a Putto

Oil on canvas, 220.2 x 168.8 cm
The stone slab is inscribed: *O LIGNVM/ BEATVM IN / QVO DEVS / EXTENSVS / EST / SYBILLA / CVMANA.*
(O blessed wood upon which God was stretched out. Cumaean Sybil)
On long-term loan to the National Gallery since 1991

The Cumaean Sibyl was one of the twelve pagan sibyls that were adopted by the Christian Church as counterparts to the Old Testament prophets since they were reputed to have foretold the coming of Christ.[1] The Cumaean Sibyl, who takes her name from Cumae near Naples, is alluded to several times in classical literature. In Virgil's *Aeneid* and Ovid's *Metamorphoses* she prophesied Aeneas's future and guided him to the underworld.[2] She was held in honour by the Church because of her prediction that Christ would be born of a virgin in a stable at Bethlehem. The inscription in the painting refers to the cross on which Christ was crucified but the precise source for it has not yet been identified. The Cumaean Sibyl seems to have been the most frequently represented sibyl in Italian painting. Guercino painted another *Cumaean Sibyl* in 1650 known only from copies.[3]

The painting was commissioned in early 1651 by Gioseffo Locatelli of Cesena as a companion to the *King David* now in the Spencer collection at Althorp (fig.34). However, as Malvasia records, before Locatelli had taken delivery of the paintings the *Cumaean Sibyl* was seen in the artist's studio in Bologna by Prince Mattias de' Medici, who coveted it.[4] A generous payment of 197 *ducatoni* was made to Guercino by the Prince's agent, Marchese Bali Cospi, on 26 May 1651.[5] Guercino was then obliged to paint another sibyl for Locatelli as a companion to the *King David*, the *Samian Sibyl*, which is also at Althorp. Naturally it is close in style, figure scale and dimensions to the *Cumaean Sibyl*. Guercino seems to have sought to hide the substitution from Locatelli and it is probable that the patron remained none the wiser. His descendants retained the two paintings until 1768 when they were bought by Gavin Hamilton for the 1st Earl Spencer.[6]

The pairing of David with a sibyl is rare but has its justification in that both played a prophetic role with regard to the coming of Christ. The *Dies Irae*, the famous thirteenth-century funerary hymn, yokes them together: 'The Day of Wrath, the dreadful day, Shall sweep this age in flames away: So David and the Sibyl say.'[7] It would appear to have made little difference to Locatelli whether the *King David* was paired with a Cumaean or a Samian Sibyl. In the inscription that Guercino applied to the substitute *Samian Sibyl*, which refers to 'chaste Sion', he sought to create a clear textual link with the inscription already on the tablet in the *David*, which refers to the 'City of God', a quotation

from Psalm 86. It is, of course, only the inscriptions that provide the identity of the sibyls and so it is also possible that Locatelli may have wanted a Samian Sibyl from the beginning and that when Prince Mattias de' Medici acquired the present picture Guercino made her into the Sibyl of Cumae. Be that as it may, Helston and Henry pay tribute to Guercino's originality and honesty in not merely producing two identical versions of the same composition.[8]

This is one of Guercino's finest late works, noble in composition, rich in colour and dignified in pose and gesture. Mahon has aptly compared the delicate handling to the late work of Murillo and highlighted the quality of execution of the still-life details of the books and the bas-relief.[9] The careful articulation of the folds of the Sibyl's orange cloak and the greenish stole that is draped around her shoulder and tucked into her bodice shows how diligent Guercino was in designing and executing the clothed figure.

TECHNICAL NOTE
The support is a plain-weave, medium-coarse canvas. The painting is lined and has a non-original stretcher with a horizontal cross bar and diagonal corner bars. The stretcher-bar marks which are apparent on the surface of the picture correspond with the present stretcher. There is some abrasion in the area of the floor and along the left edge, but the painting is in very good condition. The ground is a warm orange-brown and is visible at the lower-right corner of the stone tablet. Branch-like forms in green paint are visible underneath the wall behind the Sibyl. The artist seems to have lowered the contour of the orange cloak to the left of the Sybil's foot.

PROVENANCE[10]
Commissioned in 1651 by Gioseffo Locatelli of Cesena but sold by the artist in May of that year to Prince Mattias de' Medici (1613–67), brother of Ferdinando II. The picture is not listed, however, in any known Medici inventories. It was acquired from an unknown source, between 1830 and 1840, by Sir John Forbes, 7th Bt, for the newly completed Fintray House, Aberdeenshire. The picture was sold by his great-grandson, the 19th Lord Sempill, when the house was demolished; it was acquired very soon after, in 1954, by the present owner.

EXHIBITIONS
Rome 1956, no.125; Manchester 1957, no.135; London 1960, no.386; London (Agnew) 1973, no.37; Bologna/Washington/New York 1986–7, no.167; London (National Gallery) 1991, no.27; Bologna 1991, no.134; Frankfurt 1991–2, no.71.

Fig.34 Guercino, *King David*, 1651. Oil on canvas, 223.5 x 167.5 cm. The Collection at Althorp, Northampton.

1 See Marsh 1882.
2 *Aeneid*, VI:10; *Metamorphoses*, XIV:110–56.
3 Salerno 1988, no.281bis, p.351.
4 Malvasia 1678, II, p.378.
5 All the entries from the *Libro dei Conti* are quoted in Mahon (Dipinti) 1968, p.196, and Mahon (Dipinti) 1991, p.348.
6 For these paintings, see Salerno 1988, nos.282–3, pp.352–3; London (National Gallery) 1991, nos.28–9, pp.60–1.
7 Marsh 1882, p.406.
8 London (National Gallery) 1991, p.58.
9 Mahon (Dipinti) 1968, p.197. Such reliefs, where they appear in Guercino's paintings (for example cat.45), seem invented and are rarely of iconographic importance.
10 The provenance is set out in detail in Mahon (Dipinti) 1968, no.90, pp.195–6, and Mahon (Dipinti) 1991, no.134, pp.348–50; see also Salerno 1988, no.281, p.351.

O LIGNVM
BEATVM IN
QVO DEVS
EXTENSVS
EST

SYBILLA
CVMANA

Attributed to Pieter van Laer 1599–after 1642
50 A Franciscan Saint distributing Food to Peasants

Oil on panel, 32.7 x 27 cm

This painting shows a scene from everyday life in Rome. It belongs to a type of painting known as *Bambocciate*.[1] Such subjects, of which there was an established tradition in the Netherlands, were brought to Italy by a group of artists led by Pieter van Laer, known as 'Il Bamboccio' (literally, little doll) because of his hunchback. *Bambocciate* became immensely popular with Roman collectors and the demand for them was met not just by Van Laer and his Netherlandish contemporaries in Rome – among them Jan Miel, Jan Lingelbach and Michiel Sweerts – but also by Italian followers such as Michelangelo Cerquozzi (see cats.12 and 13).

Despite the contemporary fame of Pieter van Laer, relatively little is known about the details of his life and the exact nature of his oeuvre is disputed. Pieter Boddingh van Laer was born in Haarlem in 1599.[2] Nothing is known of his training but his early work seems to reveal the influence of Esaias van de Velde. He travelled to Italy with his elder brother Roelant, who was also a painter, arriving in Rome in 1625 or 1626. Shortly after his arrival, Pieter joined the *Schildersbent*, the association of Netherlandish artists in the city, where he was given the name 'Bamboots' or 'Il Bamboccio'. Van Laer and his friend Giovanni del Campo shared a house, first on the Via Margutta and then on the Via del Babuino in the parish of Santa Maria del Popolo. Van Laer was well known in Roman artistic circles: among many others, he met Claude Lorrain, Nicolas Poussin, Andries Both and Joachim van Sandrart. In the *Teutsche Akademie* Sandrart records that he, Van Laer, Claude and Poussin rode together to Tivoli to draw landscapes from nature. Van Laer enjoyed great success in Rome: his principal patrons included Cardinal Francesco Maria Brancaccio and Ferdi-

nando Afan de Rivera, the Viceroy of Naples, to whom the artist dedicated a series of landscape etchings in 1636.

Van Laer is last recorded in Rome in 1638. He returned to the Netherlands via Vienna where he tried, unsuccessfully, to sell a painting to the Emperor Ferdinand III. He was back in Haarlem in 1639, living with his brother Nicolaes, a schoolmaster. In the same year Van Laer visited Sandrart in Amsterdam and the two artists went to Leiden to see Gerard Dou. Van Laer is mentioned for the last time in his sister's will, drawn up when he left Haarlem in 1642. Theodor Schrevelius, in his history of Haarlem published in 1647, says that he set out for Rome and subsequently disappeared: he compared Van Laer's sudden disappearance to that of the philosopher Empedocles, who fell into the crater of Mount Etna.[3]

Van Laer brings the techniques of Caravaggio and his followers to street scenes painted on dark grounds and small, multi-figured genre compositions. Giambattista Passeri describes them as a 'window onto life'.[4] Van Laer is also mentioned in early biographies and inventories as an animal and landscape painter: his pioneering importance for these subjects has been recognised only relatively recently.

In this small panel a monk with a halo is shown giving soup to the poor. The painting could have been part of a series of the Seven Acts of Mercy similar to that painted by Michiel Sweerts,[5] and should be compared with the latter's *Feeding the Hungry* (fig.35). *A Franciscan Saint distributing Food to Peasants* was catalogued by Borenius as by Van Laer,[6] and there are striking similarities in the restricted dark palette, simple architectural forms and freely drawn treatment of the figures to Van Laer's

Riders at an Inn in the Louvre, also painted on panel (fig.36).[7] However, the painting in the Mahon Collection is thinly painted and the background figures of the monk and the people to whom he is giving the soup are difficult to make out against the dark ground. For this reason, it is catalogued here as 'Attributed to Pieter van Laer'.

C B

TECHNICAL NOTE
The panel is made of a single piece of wood, probably poplar. It is 2 cm thick. The ground is brownish in colour and is in evidence in several areas. There is pronounced craquelure in the paint surface. The reverse of the panel has been painted with a brown pigment.

PROVENANCE
Said to have been purchased by the 2nd Marquess of Clanricarde at Christie's in about 1910; bequeathed by the 2nd Marquess of Clanricarde to the Earl of Harewood;[8] acquired by the present owner at Christie's, London, 29 June 1951, lot 65.

EXHIBITIONS
Not previously exhibited.

1 For the two most recent treatments of the phenomenon of *bambocciate*, see Cologne/Utrecht 1991–2 and Briganti, Trezzani and Laureati 1983. These list previous literature and monographic studies of individual artists who painted *bambocciate*.
2 This biography is based on that by the present author in Philadelphia/Berlin/London 1984, p.231, where all bibliographical references are given in full. The standard catalogue of Van Laer's work is Janeck 1968. See also Briganti, Trezzani and Laureati 1983, pp.39–77, and Cologne/Utrecht 1991–2, pp.188–208.
3 T.Schrevelius, *Harlemum, sive urbis Harlementis Incunabula, incrementa, fortuna varia, in pace, in bello*, Haarlem 1647, p.270.
4 '...li suoi quadri parevano una finestra aperta, per la quale si fussero veduti quelli suoi successi senza alcun divario, et alteratione', Passeri 1934, p.74. The passage is quoted in full in this catalogue, p.46, note 2.
5 Four of this series, *Feeding the Hungry, Refreshing the Thirsty, Clothing the Naked* and *Visiting the Sick* are in the Rijksmuseum (Inv. nos. A 2845, 2846, 2847 and 2848). *Burying the Dead* is in the Wadsworth Atheneum, Hartford, and the two remaining scenes, *Comforting Captives* and *Sheltering Pilgrims*, are in private collections.
6 Borenius 1936, no.170. Briganti also attributed the picture to Van Laer and compared it to paintings by him in the Corsini Gallery, Rome (Briganti 1953, p.12 and no.34, p. 18.)
7 Louvre Inv. no.1417.
8 Borenius 1936, no.170.

Fig.35 Michiel Sweerts, *Feeding the Hungry*, c.1645–50. Oil on canvas, 75 x 97.5 cm. Amsterdam, Rijksmuseum.

Fig.36 Pieter van Laer, *Riders at an Inn*, c.1630-2. Oil on panel, 32 x 43 cm. Paris, Musée du Louvre.

Attributed to Jan Lingelbach 1622–1674
51 Roman Street Scene with Card Players

Oil on canvas, 43 x 34.5 cm

The present painting belongs to a group of *bambocciate* – scenes from everyday life in Rome – many of which show people at work. They are characterised by dramatic contrasts in the fall of light, which have the effect of monumentalising the figures in a manner close to that of Michiel Sweerts, who was in Rome from 1646 until about 1654. They all display a notable simplicity in the architectural and landscape forms in the background. At the core of this group are three paintings in the Galleria Nazionale in Rome which show a Brandy Seller, a Tobacco Seller and a Cake Seller (fig.37).[1] These paintings have traditionally been attributed to Pieter van Laer on grounds of stylistic similarity with signed works and the statement in Sandrart's account of the artist that 'Il Bamboccio, among the various subjects, also painted the trades'.[2] However, in 1968 Janeck removed these paintings from Van Laer's oeuvre[3] – although subsequently Salerno has reattributed them to him[4] – and there is an evident difference in style between this group and the street scenes by Van Laer. Not only are the dramatic lighting and simple backgrounds unlike Van Laer but, as can be seen for example in Van Laer's *Riders at an Inn* (see fig.36), he is far more inventive in his posing of the figures, often showing them twisting in motion, whereas the figures of this group are distinctly stolid. Burger Wegener attributed a number of the paintings to the young Jan Lingelbach[5] and this attribution was supported and the group enlarged by Kren.[6] Kren went so far as to describe the *Cake Seller* as 'the greatest achievement of Lingelbach's Roman period'. More recently this group has been further expanded by Laureati, and its artist given the soubriquet the 'Master of the Small Trades'.[7] However, the present writer finds the attribution to the young Lingelbach convincing.[8] It is based not only on dissimilarities with Van Laer's secure work but on persuasive comparison with Lingelbach's signed and dated works – all of which were painted after his return to Amsterdam – such as the *Dentist on Horseback* of 1651 in the Rijksmuseum.[9] The work of the 'Master of the Small Trades' would, therefore, be part of the early work of Lingelbach painted during his stay in Rome in the 1640s when he closely imitated Van Laer's style.

Jan Lingelbach was born in Frankfurt in 1622 but by 1634 his family had settled in Amsterdam, where his father, David, ran the Nieuwe Doelhof, a successful pleasure garden.[10] The identity of Lingelbach's teacher is unknown. Houbraken says that the artist left Amsterdam in 1642 to travel to France and that two years later he went on to Rome, where he worked until May 1650.[11] This account is supported by the few surviving documents: Lingelbach is recorded in 1647 and 1648 living in Rome on the Strada Paolina delli Greci and in the following year on the nearby Horto di Napoli. In Rome Lingelbach came under the powerful influence of the style of Pieter van Laer; although Van Laer had left Rome by 1639, a number of artists – among them Jan Miel and Michelangelo Cerquozzi (see cats.12 and 13) – continued to work in his style.

Lingelbach is first recorded back in Amsterdam in 1653, when he was married and granted citizenship. He remained there for the rest of his life. After his return Lingelbach became increasingly influenced by the successful and prolific Philips Wouwermans. He also painted Italianate landscapes and seaports in the manner of Jan Baptist Weenix and his son Jan Weenix. Lingelbach also supplied the figures in landscapes by, among others, Jan Hackaert, Philips Koninck, Frederick de Moucheron and Jan Wijnants.

The present painting was probably painted by Lingelbach in the second half of the 1640s, which was a period of remarkable vitality for the Bambocciari, among whom Lingelbach can now be seen as a major figure.[12] It was around this time that Jan Miel painted his *Carnival in the Piazza Colonna* (Hartford, Wadsworth Atheneum)[13] and Michiel Sweerts his series of the *Seven Acts of Mercy*[14] which, along with Lingelbach's Roman street scenes, rank among the greatest achievements of the Bambocciari. There is a copy of the painting, with a pendant, in the Museo di Capodimonte in Naples.[15]

Fig.37 Attributed to Jan Lingelbach, *The Cake Seller*, between 1646 and 1654. Oil on canvas, 33 x 42 cm. Rome, Galleria Nazionale d'Arte Antica di Palazzo Barberini.

TECHNICAL NOTE
The support is a coarse plain-weave canvas. The painting was lined in the nineteenth century by Leedham (inscription on stretcher). The stretcher-bar marks apparent on the surface of the painting indicate that the original stretcher/strainer members were about 3.5 cm wide. The paint is applied thinly and the surface is slightly abraded. The ground is orange-brown and is quite visible. There is some retouching in the area of the blue sky and grey cloud. The lower basin of the fountain appears to have been painted over the completed figures of the donkey and his master, and the upper part of the fountain may have been an afterthought, apparently painted over the finished sky and landscape.
CB

PROVENANCE
Joseph Gillot before 1872; his sale, Christie's, 3 May 1872, lot 324, bought by Colnaghi; Mrs G. C. H. Kwantes before 1958; her sale, Sotheby's, 2 April 1958, lot 1, bought by Colnaghi, from whom acquired by the present owner in 1959.

EXHIBITIONS
Not previously exhibited.

1 Briganti, Trezzani and Laureati 1983, pp.250–7. *The Brandy Seller* is illustrated as fig.9.1.
2 Sandrart 1675 (1925), pp.183–8.
3 Janeck 1968, pp.143–7. These three paintings are nos.C11, 12 and 13 in Janeck's catalogue.
4 Salerno 1977–80, I, pp.307–9.
5 Burger Wegener 1976, p.219.
6 Kren 1982, especially p.45.
7 Briganti, Trezzani and Laureati 1983, pp.250–7.
8 I have argued this attribution in greater detail in the catalogue of the exhibition, *Masters of Seventeenth-Century Dutch Genre Painting*, see Philadelphia/Berlin/London 1984, no.62. Sir Denis Mahon does not concur in this identification of the Master of the Small Trades with the young Lingelbach.
9 Oil on canvas, 68.5 x 86 cm, signed and dated: *J. Lingelbach Ao 1651*, Rijksmuseum Inv. no.A226.
10 For Lingelbach's biography see Burger Wegener 1976, and Philadelphia/Berlin/London 1984.
11 Houbraken 1718–21, II, pp.145–7.
12 For references to this painting, see Nicolson 1963, pp.120 and 124 (as Van Laer); Burger Wegener 1976, p.219, note 3 (as Lingelbach); Briganti, Trezzani and Laureati 1983, p.250, note 5, and plate 9.8.; Kren 1982, pp.50–3.
13 Oil on canvas, 89 x 176 cm, Wadsworth Atheneum Inv. no.1938.603, see Kren 1979, cat.A15, and Philadelphia/Berlin/London1984, no.73.
14 Kultzen 1996, cats.47–53.
15 Both oil on canvas, 42 x 33 cm, Inv.nos. 537 and 538 (as Pieter van Laer). No. 537 appears to be a seventeenth-century copy of *Roman Street Scenes with Card Players*. Its pendant shows two riders, one of whom has dismounted, in the shadow of an arch.

Johann Liss *c.*1597–1631
52 *The Fall of Phaeton*

Oil on canvas, 129.2 x 110.3 cm (original canvas 126.5 x 108.5 cm)

In 1948 this picture appeared at auction in London as 'The Fall of Icarus' by Francesco Albani. Mahon and another distinguished collector, Vitale Bloch, had identified it as the lost *Fall of Phaeton* by the German painter Johann Liss and at the sale it was 'hotly contested'.[1] Mahon succeeded in acquiring the work for himself but allowed Bloch to publish the discovery, which he duly did in *The Burlington Magazine* in 1950.

Painted with a typically brazen flamboyancy, the *Fall of Phaeton* is one of Liss's most striking works. Sandrart, who met Liss in Venice in 1628–9, noted: 'In equally brilliant manner he painted the *Fall of Phaeton*, with his chariot, and beneath on earth the water nymphs looking up so terror-stricken, with which beautiful nude nymphs, as well as with the graceful landscape and flaming clouds Liss proved that he was a master of colour and of charming hues.'[2]

The subject of the painting is taken from Ovid's *Metamorphoses* (Book 2). Phoebus, god of the sun, was persuaded by his son, Phaeton, to let him drive his chariot, but Phaeton quickly lost control of the horses who took a wild course across the sky. They are just visible in the painting in the fiery clouds at upper right. The chariot came too near the earth, setting it aflame, destroying cities and forests and drying up rivers, springs and even the sea. In the left foreground are scattered seashells and coral stranded on dry land. To prevent the destruction of heaven and earth Jupiter hurled a thunderbolt at the chariot which smashed it to pieces and sent Phaeton hurtling to his death.[3] His body was received by the river Eridanus that meanders and glistens through the landscape and breaks into a small waterfall beside the recumbent figure of Eridanus.[4] The nymphs on the left, their poses and gestures eloquent of fear, are among the most brilliant passages of the painting. The sensuous subject matter is matched by the luscious, creamy handling, with the softness of the flesh and the glowing skin tones conveyed with assured blended strokes of green, pink and violet.[5] On the large boulder on the right the winged Heliades, the grieving daughters of Phoebus, mourn the death of their brother.

Liss was born in Holstein, just north of Lübeck, in about 1597. He was in the Netherlands between about 1615 and 1619 and although Sandrart says only that he visited Amsterdam, where he adopted a 'Heinrich Golzii manier', his work shows the influence of Rubens, who was in Antwerp, and of the so-called Haarlem Mannerists. He visited Paris and by 1621 was in Venice where he came under the influence of Domenico Fetti, who was there from 1622 to 1623. Liss subsequently went to Rome where he became a member of the Netherlandish painters' club, the Bent, and was given the sobriquet *Pan*, which reflected his reputation for riotous living. He was again in Venice by 1628 and died in Verona in 1631, probably of the plague.[6] His career was brief and his oeuvre is small but he is one of the most attractive, poetic and technically accomplished painters of the seventeenth century.

As there is only one dated painting by Liss,[7] a chronology must be deduced principally from stylistic analysis and an assessment of the various influences on him. Bloch noted that the composition of the *Fall of Phaeton* lacks unity – a perfectly valid criticism – and that certain aspects of the work were indebted to Cornelis van Haarlem. This suggested a date in the artist's 'middle period', which Bloch did not care to define too closely.[8] Klessmann's dating of the picture to around 1624 seems reasonable, although it is still not clear if Liss was in Venice or Rome at this time.[9]

Feyken Rijp, author of a chronicle of the Dutch town of Hoorn (in which he claims Liss was born) published in 1706, noted the existence of two paintings of Phaeton by Liss, one in the collection of Mr Procurator Hooft (in Amsterdam?), which measured six feet, and another in the Pamphilj Palace (in Rome) which was even larger.[10] We may be sceptical about the latter, as there is no corroborating evidence of any kind and other pronouncements of Rijp's to do with Liss are manifestly untrue, but there is a good probability that the painting belonging to Hooft is identical with the present work.[11]

A preparatory drawing for the nymph with her back turned, made from the life, was in a private collection in Paris in 1975.[12] Two compositional drawings of the *Fall of Phaeton* on the *recto* and *verso* of a sheet in a private collection formerly thought to be by Liss are now attributed to Paolo Pagani (1661–1716).[13]

TECHNICAL NOTE
The support is a plain-weave, medium-weight canvas. There is a horizontal seam running across the picture about 25 cm from the top and a vertical seam at the right end of this section of canvas, about 10 cm from the right edge. The original tacking edges have been removed. Some abrasion of the paint surface is apparent. The ground is a dark reddish brown. The sea-green cloak of the standing nymph has darkened so as to seem now almost black. Originally the cloak had a fold which billowed out to the right but this was covered over by the waterfall. The contour of the figure of the river-god was adjusted by the artist.

PROVENANCE
Colonel M.A. Swinfen-Broun, Swinfen Hall, Lichfield; Christie's, London, 10 December 1948, lot 76 (as Albani), where acquired by the present owner.

EXHIBITIONS
London (Hazlitt) 1952 , no.5; Zurich 1956, no.156; Venice 1959, no.58; Manchester 1961, no.186; briefly on loan to Berlin, Gemäldegalerie, to hang with the permanent collection there (August-November 1962); London (Agnew) 1965, no.8; Berlin 1966, no.44; Augsburg/Cleveland 1975–6, no.A.26; London (National Gallery) 1979, no.16.

1 Bloch 1950.
2 Sandrart 1675 (1925), p.187.
3 Ovid refers to the 'axle torn from the pole' which may explain the form behind Phaeton's left foot.
4 Klessmann (Augsburg/Cleveland 1975–6, English edn., p.94) identified the figure as Neptune (who plays a part in the Phaeton story) but the figure rests on a vase which is typical of river deities. The object resembling a trident is probably an oar.
5 A similar group appears in the contemporary Pommersfelden *Toilet of Venus*, Augsburg/Cleveland 1975–6, no.A.28.
6 Antoniazzi 1975.
7 *The Agony in the Garden*, signed and dated 1628, formerly in a Swiss private collection and now in a British private collection, see Klessmann 1996, p.191, note 31, and Mantua 1996, no.69.
8 Bloch 1950, p.282.
9 Augsburg/Cleveland 1975–6 (English edn. only), p.95, and Klessmann 1996, p.190. Klessmann dates the Roman period about 1622–6 (1996, p.187). Mahon has observed to the present writer that the figures in this painting suggest that Liss was familiar with the sculptures Bernini made for Cardinal Scipione Borghese in the early 1620s, particularly the *Pluto and Persephone* and the *Apollo and Daphne*.
10 'By de Heer Fiscaal Hooft is een Phaëton, ses Voet groot dat ook in't Paleys der Pamphiliën door hem nog grooter geschildert is', F. Rijp, *Chronijk van Hoorn*, Hoorn, 1706, pp.318–19, quoted in Steinbart 1940, p.159.
11 See Steinbart 1958–9, p.192. What is almost certainly the Hooft painting was described by J.C. Weyerman in 1729, see Augsburg/Cleveland 1975–6 (German edn. only), p.192, no.22.
12 Black chalk heightened with white on grey paper, 253 x 183 mm, see Augsburg/Cleveland 1975–6 (English edn. only), no.B56a, fig.61a. A compositional drawing in the Herzog Anton Ulrich-Museum, Braunschweig, showing a different subject, *The Death of Phaeton* (197 x 296 cm), has a similar disjointed composition to the Mahon painting and may record an earlier idea of Liss for the painting.
13 Pen and brown ink over grey wash and faded colour washes, 335 x 528 mm, see Augsburg/Cleveland 1975–6, no.B56, figs.59–60; for the attribution to Pagini see Bean 1976.

Andrea Locatelli 1695–1741

53 Rocky Landscape with a Natural Arch and Distant Tower

Oil on canvas, 18.5 x 108.2 cm

54 Landscape with a Waterfall and Distant Lake

Oil on canvas, 18.4 x 108 cm

Andrea Locatelli was one of the foremost painters of classical landscape in eighteenth-century Rome.[1] According to the biographical notes written by Nicola Pio in about 1723, Locatelli was trained first by his father and then by 'Monsù Alto', a northern painter who specialised in marine subjects.[2] In about 1712 he passed to the studio of Bernardino Fergioni, another marine specialist, and before 1723 he was an independent master. He was a prolific artist and worked for distinguished patrons, including Cardinals Albani and Ottoboni; he painted frescoes in Palazzo Ruspoli, and decorated an entire room in Palazzo Colonna with landscapes pictures. Two of Locatelli's most prestigious commissions were due to the architect Filippo Juvarra; in 1723–4 he painted two large perspective views of the façades of the projected Castello di Rivoli, based on Juvarra's designs, for Vittorio Amedeo II of Savoy[3] (two others were painted by Pannini), and in 1735 he was commissioned to paint two overdoors for the Chinese Room designed by Juvarra in the Palace of Sant'Ildefonso in Segovia, Spain.[4] The figures in his landscapes were sometimes painted by other artists, among them Batoni and Subleyras. Pio states that he was much employed by 'Roman and English gentlemen and other foreigners'. An inscription on a portrait drawing of Locatelli by Pier Leone Ghezzi states that he fancied himself as a poet, although to date none of his verse has been identified.[5] Despite his earlier success, he apparently died in poverty at the age of 46.

The proportions of this pair of landscapes indicate that they were made as overdoors but their original location remains unknown. The serene Arcadian vision they offer, in which the figures, engaged in rustic activities or resting, are at one with their natural surroundings, has its origin in the landscapes of Claude and Poussin and is characteristic of much of Locatelli's oeuvre. His immediate precursor in propounding this poetic view of the Roman Campagna was the Antwerp painter Jan Frans van Bloemen, known as l'Orizzonte (1662–1749), who settled in Rome in 1688 and had a lengthy and productive career as a painter of placid and charming classical landscapes. Locatelli, however, also adopted something of the more energetic handling of Gaspar Dughet and Salvator Rosa in

his works. Here he provides an anthology of motifs from the classical landscape tradition – the natural arch, the rocky outcrop, the waterfall and lake, and the diagonal tree – and successfully integrates them into convincing compositions by means of the lighting, in one case the bright clear light of day and in the other the warmer light of evening. While the paintings are thus to some extent artificial and contrived they nonetheless give a sense of the timeless quality of the Roman countryside.

The sweeping wide-angle view adopted by the artist in which the specatator has the impression of turning 180 degrees in a landscape has few precedents. Gaspar van Wittel painted two

panoramic views of the Abbey of Grottaferrata in about 1710 in which a similar wide-angle view is adopted,[6] but Locatelli's pictures are extraordinary for their narrow proportions: the length is nearly six times the height. Two similar works formerly with Agnews have even narrower proportions (19 x 124 cm),[7] and these too must have been conceived as decorative panels for a large room.

The chronology of Locatelli's works remains a matter of speculation since there is only a handful of dated works and his style remained fairly homogenous throughout his career,[8] but, given the boldness of the design, one may speculate that these works date from the later part of his career, perhaps from the 1730s.[9]

TECHNICAL NOTE

Both paintings are on plain-weave, medium-coarse canvas. Both are lined and have the same non-original stretchers. However, the *Rocky Landscape with a Natural Arch and Distant Tower* retains its original tacking edges, while *Landscape with a Waterfall and Distant Lake* does not. The lining canvases are different and the former is nailed into the stretcher with hand-made tacks, the latter is not. This indicates that *Landscape with a Waterfall and Distant Lake* has been lined one more time than its companion. From the stretcher-bar marks on the canvases it is possible to tell that the original stretcher/strainer was about 3 cm wide. The ground is a warm brown colour. Both paintings are in good condition. *Landscape with a Waterfall and Distant Lake* has a repaired small hole just above the waterfall with a corresponding patch on the reverse, and a repaired vertical tear about 6 cm long in the trees at the left. It has noticeable retouching along the bottom edge.

PROVENANCE

Sir George Warrender, 6th Bt (1825–1901), Bruntisfield House, Edinburgh;[10] Sotheby's, London, 21 June 1950, lot 50, where acquired by the present owner in 1950.

EXHIBITIONS

London 1960, nos.422 and 425.

1 For Locatelli's life and work, see Busiri Vici 1976.
2 See Pio 1977, pp.185–6, 252, 309–11. For Monsù Alto, see Chiarini 1970, who identified several of his works.
3 Busiri Vici 1976, figs.10 and 11.
4 See Urrea Fernández 1977, pp.275–6, 477–8. They are reproduced in Battisti 1958, figs.13 and 14.
5 The drawing is reproduced in Busiri Vici 1976, fig.9; see also Busiri Vici 1967.
6 Briganti 1966, nos.136–7, p.221.
7 Busiri Vici 1976, nos.140 and 141.
8 There are dated landscapes in the years 1721, 1725, 1731 and 1736, see Busiri Vici 1976, nos.40, 17, 279 and 289, respectively.
9 In London 1960, p.174, they are tentatively dated 'relatively early in the career of Locatelli, and before his dated work in the 'twenties'.
10 A paper label on the reverse of *Rocky Landscape with a Natural Arch and Distant Tower* is inscribed in pen: 'From Bruntisfield Ho. Edin./ Library no.9', then in pencil: 'no.7'.

Pier Francesco Mola 1612–1666

56 Landscape with Saint Bruno in Ecstasy

Oil on canvas, 73.2 x 97.3 cm
Inscribed lower-right-hand corner: *K.K.K.K.*

Mola painted several Carthusian subjects – two of which are in the Mahon collection – although there is no evidence that he had any special relationship with the order. This painting probably dates from the period before 1647, the year in which Mola made his definitive return from the north of Italy to Rome.[1] His most frequently copied easel painting is the *Vision of Saint Bruno* (Malibu, J. Paul Getty Museum), which shows the founder of the order reclining in a landscape witnessing a heavenly apparition with cherubs. It was probably made for Cardinal Flavio Chigi (1631–93), the nephew of Pope Alexander VII, in the early 1660s.[2] A painting of *Saint Bruno in a Landscape* was recorded in a Roman collection in 1935 and would appear to be autograph.[3]

Saint Bruno (*c*.1035–1101) was born in Cologne and studied at Reims and Tours. He founded the charterhouses of Grenoble and La Torre in Calabria and gave his followers, some of whom lived as hermits in the wilderness, an austere pattern of life based on prayer, manual work and silence. He was beatified by Leo X in 1514.[4] His canonisation by Gregory XV Ludovisi in 1623 gave rise to several cycles of paintings of his life, including those by Giovanni Lanfranco, Eustache Le Sueur and Vicente Carducho.[5] Mola's Carthusian subjects are related to the taste for anchorite themes which developed in

Rome in the 1630s, and is exemplified in the works of Poussin, Claude, and then Salvator Rosa (see cats.68–9).

Mola shows Saint Bruno levitating on a cloud, his arms raised in prayer. The pose may derive from Krüger's engraving of the *Apotheosis of Saint Bruno* after Lanfranco,[6] but it is a fairly standard ecstatic pose. A drawing by Mola in Darmstadt (Hessisches Landesmuseum) shows Saint Bruno in a similar pose but seems to date from some years later and is perhaps a first idea for the Getty painting.[7] Mahon has emphasised the naturalism of the landscape, drawing attention to the detail of the reflection in the water of the cloud which supports the saint, which is indebted to the early paintings of Guercino, as is also the rather dark and intense colour.[8] The significance of the inscription has not been established.

TECHNICAL NOTE
The support is a moderately coarse, open plain-weave canvas. The painting is lined. There are stretcher-bar marks apparent on all four sides, about 5.5 cm from the edges, which correspond with an earlier stretcher or strainer. There is some retouching in the corners but the painting is in generally good condition. The ground is a warm reddish brown and is particularly apparent in the lower left-hand corner of the painting.

PROVENANCE
Listed in the manuscript catalogue of the paintings of Thomas Worsley (1718–78), Hovingham Hall, Yorkshire;[9] by descent until 1957; acquired by the present owner from Agnew in 1957.

EXHIBITIONS
London 1960, no.407; Lugano/Rome 1989–90, no.I.2.

1 See Sutherland Harris 1974, p.290, and Laureati in Lugano/Rome 1989–90, no.I.2, p.148; Cocke, however, dates the picture to the later Roman period (1972, cat.15, p.48).
2 See Carr 1991, which lists the known copies.
3 Buscaroli 1935, p.294, pl.LIV; Cocke accepts it as autograph (1972, cat.70, p.63.).
4 Mrs Jameson noted with irony that the 'most humble and self-denying of ascetics was beatified by the most luxurious and profligate of churchmen' (1880, p.127).
5 See Baticle 1958.
6 See Baticle 1958, p.27, fig.20. Cocke refers to an engraving by A.E. Rousslet after a lost Mola of the same subject in which the pose is very similar (1972, pp.47–8).
7 The drawing (red chalk and red wash on laid paper, 22.3 x 17.8 mm) is reproduced in Carr 1991, fig.13. A painting based on this drawing is in a Swiss private collection, but is probably a workshop picture, see Genty 1979, p.137.
8 London 1960, no.407, pp.166–7.
9 'Fran Mola, S.Bruno in a Landscape', see London 1960, p.166.

57 Landscape with Two Carthusian Monks

Oil on canvas, 51.3 x 68.2 cm

Two Carthusians, in their distinctive white habits, are engaged in meditation in a wild landscape. In the middle distance there is a third monk with a companion. The pose of the recumbent monk on the left is similar to that of the saint in the Getty Museum's *Vision of Saint Bruno*, which is datable to the early 1660s. The crossed trees in this picture also appear in that work and in the preparatory drawings for it. Although this is a favourite motif of the artist, the fact that one of the trees is a palm tree suggests that here it is intended to have iconographic significance: Saint Bruno, the founder of the Carthusians, has as one of his attributes a cross shaped from a palm tree, in reference to his having brought the cross of Christ into the wooded wilderness.[1]

The date of the work is a matter of dispute as with so much of Mola's oeuvre. However, the similarities with the Getty painting and the loose

and confident handling indicate a late date, close to 1660.[2] Mola was in personal contact with Poussin in Rome and certain aspects of this work, the careful planning of the zig-zag recession into depth in the landscape, the varied lighting effects, and the treatment of the foliage on the rocks to the left, suggest that he paid careful attention to Poussin's landscapes.[3]

TECHNICAL NOTE
The support is a quite a coarse, open plain-weave canvas. There is a raised vertical thread about 6 cm from right which looks like a seam but is in fact a fault. The painting is lined and the tacking edges have been cut off. The edges and corners are retouched and there is some abrasion in the darks and in the lower left part of the painting due to heat lining. The ground is a warm reddish brown.

PROVENANCE
Probably acquired by Charles Ingram, 9th Viscount

Irwin (1727–78); recorded in the 1808 inventory of the Ingram collection, Temple Newsam House, Leeds;[4] by descent to the Earl of Halifax; sold Christie's, London, 12 December 1947, lot 113; acquired by the present owner in 1947.

EXHIBITIONS
Lugano/Rome 1989–90, no.1.14.

1 Bibliotheca Sanctorum, III, col.569; see the Wierix print of *Saint Bruno* reproduced in Mauquoy-Henrickx 1978–83, part 2, no.1084, which bears the inscription 'sicut oliva fructifera' (Psalm 5:10).
2 A late dating is proposed by Arslan 1967, p.199, note 25, and supported by Laureati (Lugano/Rome 1989–90, no.I.14, p.165). Cocke, however, dates the work to the 1640s on the basis of the handling (1972, pp.12 and 48).
3 See Cocke 1969.
4 The inventory is published in the *Leeds Art Calendar*, nos.99 and 100, 1987, p.9, '26. A Landscape Mola 20 [guineas]'. The picture is recorded at Temple Newsam by Neale, V, no pagination; Waagen 1854/7, III, p.322, and in Temple Newsam 1879, p.344.

TECHNICAL NOTE

Both paintings are on plain-weave, medium-coarse canvas. Both are lined and have the same non-original stretchers. However, the *Rocky Landscape with a Natural Arch and Distant Tower* retains its original tacking edges, while *Landscape with a Waterfall and Distant Lake* does not. The lining canvases are different and the former is nailed into the stretcher with hand-made tacks, the latter is not. This indicates that *Landscape with a Waterfall and Distant Lake* has been lined one more time than its companion. From the stretcher-bar marks on the canvases it is possible to tell that the original stretcher/strainer was about 3 cm wide. The ground is a warm brown colour. Both paintings are in good condition. *Landscape with a Waterfall and Distant Lake* has a repaired small hole just above the waterfall with a corresponding patch on the reverse, and a repaired vertical tear about 6 cm long in the trees at the left. It has noticeable retouching along the bottom edge.

PROVENANCE

Sir George Warrender, 6th Bt (1825–1901), Bruntisfield House, Edinburgh;[10] Sotheby's, London, 21 June 1950, lot 50, where acquired by the present owner in 1950.

EXHIBITIONS

London 1960, nos.422 and 425.

1. For Locatelli's life and work, see Busiri Vici 1976.
2. See Pio 1977, pp.185–6, 252, 309–11. For Monsù Alto, see Chiarini 1970, who identified several of his works.
3. Busiri Vici 1976, figs.10 and 11.
4. See Urrea Fernández 1977, pp.275–6, 477–8. They are reproduced in Battisti 1958, figs.13 and 14.
5. The drawing is reproduced in Busiri Vici 1976, fig.9; see also Busiri Vici 1967.
6. Briganti 1966, nos.136–7, p.221.
7. Busiri Vici 1976, nos.140 and 141.
8. There are dated landscapes in the years 1721, 1725, 1731 and 1736, see Busiri Vici 1976, nos.40, 17, 279 and 289, respectively.
9. In London 1960, p.174, they are tentatively dated 'relatively early in the career of Locatelli, and before his dated work in the 'twenties'.
10. A paper label on the reverse of *Rocky Landscape with a Natural Arch and Distant Tower* is inscribed in pen: 'From Bruntisfield Ho. Edin./ Library no.9', then in pencil: 'no.7'.

Pier Francesco Mola 1612–1666

55 Mercury and Argus

Oil on canvas, 31.2 x 40.8 cm

Jove was in love with the nymph Io whom he transformed into a heifer to prevent his wife Juno from becoming suspicious. Juno asked for the heifer as a gift and set Argus, the many-eyed herdsman, to guard it. After some time Jove sent Mercury, who took the form of a shepherd, to kill Argus. Mercury lulled the herdsman to sleep with music and stories and then cut off his head. Juno, who in Mola's painting appears looking down from the clouds, took his eyes and set them on the tail of the peacock, the form of which is suggested just behind the goddess. Eventually Io was transformed into a nymph again and bore Jove a son, Epaphus. The story is recounted by Ovid in his *Metamorphoses* (Book I).

This is probably the earliest of Mola's four treatments of the myth. Two other paintings (one in Berlin and the other at Oberlin), and an etching, show a different moment in the narrative – Mercury playing his pipe to entertain Argus.[1] Ovid makes reference to Mercury's winged sandals, his 'sleep-producing wand' (*virgam potenti somniferam*) and his cap and sword, all of which appear in the Mahon painting. Mola, however, made no effort to represent the hundred eyes around Argus's head.

Mola was born in Coldrerio in the Canton of Ticino, Switzerland, the son of the architect Giovanni Battista.[2] By 1616 the family was living in Rome and Pier Francesco was apprenticed to the successful, if by then rather elderly, Cavaliere d'Arpino in the second half of the 1620s. From 1634 until 1646 he seems to have been living mostly in northern Italy. He worked in the studio of Albani in Bologna for about two years, probably during 1634–5;[3] in 1637 he was in Lucca with Pietro Testa and in 1644 he was in Venice. During these years he became familiar with the work of Guercino, whose influence is strongly apparent both in his paintings and in his drawings. He painted frescoes in the parish church of his home town in 1641–2 and in 1647 he was back in Rome. The dating of his early works is not straightforward. In Rome he received public commissions for altarpieces and frescoes and this period is better documented. The style of his later Roman works is indebted to Pietro da Cortona, Andrea Sacchi and Poussin. Mola's most original works, however, are the small-scale landscapes with figure subjects for which he is best known. In 1655 he became a member of the Accademia di San Luca. He received commissions from Pope Alexander VII (indirectly), Cardinal Luigi Omodei, the Costaguti family and from Prince Camillo Pamphilj, nephew of Pope Innocent X. The commission from Pamphilj to decorate the family palace in Valmontone led to a lengthy court case (1659–64) which ended with the judgement going against the artist.

The *Mercury and Argus* appears to be part of a group of early works by the artist, perhaps dating to the mid-1630s. These works tend to be small in scale and betray the influence of both Albani and Guercino; they include the Ashmolean Museum's *Echo and Narcissus*, the Berlin *Mercury and Argus* and the National Gallery's *Rest on the Flight into Egypt*.[4]

TECHNICAL NOTE
The support is a plain-weave, medium-coarse canvas. The painting is lined and the tacking edges have been cut off. Linear crack losses along the edges are consistent with the painting having been put on a smaller stretcher between the original stretcher/strainer and the present stretcher. There is a repaired tear to the left of Mercury's sword; a patch has been applied to the reverse in this area. The surface is a little worn and the cloud upon which Juno sits is considerably retouched but the painting is generally in good condition. The ground is a warm reddish brown.

PROVENANCE
A label on the reverse is inscribed 'Stacy Marks', presumably the painter H. Stacy Marks, RA (1829–98), and another similar label has the following inscription in the same hand: 'Landscape/ Argus & Mercury by/ Poussin';[5] K.R. Mackenzie of Gillotts, Henley-on-Thames; his sale, Christie's, London, 4 June 1917, lot 136 (bought Cohen); acquired by the present owner at Sotheby's, London, 29 November 1950, lot 80 (as 'POUSSIN').

EXHIBITIONS
Not previously exhibited.

1 Cocke 1972, plates 31 and 21, respectively; the etching is plate 22. In Mola's post-mortem inventory there is a reference to 'Un abbozzo d'una favola d'Argo in tela d'imperatore cop.a', although no painter's name is given, see Lugano/Rome 1989, p.53.
2 For Mola's life, see the biographies by Passeri (1942, pp.367–72) and Pascoli (1730/6, I, pp.122–9); see also: Sutherland Harris 1964; Cocke 1972, pp.1–10; Lugano/Rome 1989–90.
3 The date of Mola's association with Albani is disputed: Cocke, following the sequence of events given by Passeri in his Life of the artist, situates it in 1645–7, Cocke 1972, pp.3–4. For the earlier dating see Schleier in Lugano/Rome 1989–90, pp.60–1 with references.
4 Cocke 1972, plates 17, 31 and 24, respectively.
5 There is a white chalk inscription on the stretcher: *CAREY*.

Pier Francesco Mola 1612–1666

56 Landscape with Saint Bruno in Ecstasy

Oil on canvas, 73.2 x 97.3 cm
Inscribed lower-right-hand corner: *K.K.K.K.*

Mola painted several Carthusian subjects – two of which are in the Mahon collection – although there is no evidence that he had any special relationship with the order. This painting probably dates from the period before 1647, the year in which Mola made his definitive return from the north of Italy to Rome.[1] His most frequently copied easel painting is the *Vision of Saint Bruno* (Malibu, J. Paul Getty Museum), which shows the founder of the order reclining in a landscape witnessing a heavenly apparition with cherubs. It was probably made for Cardinal Flavio Chigi (1631–93), the nephew of Pope Alexander VII, in the early 1660s.[2] A painting of *Saint Bruno in a Landscape* was recorded in a Roman collection in 1935 and would appear to be autograph.[3]

Saint Bruno (*c*.1035–1101) was born in Cologne and studied at Reims and Tours. He founded the charterhouses of Grenoble and La Torre in Calabria and gave his followers, some of whom lived as hermits in the wilderness, an austere pattern of life based on prayer, manual work and silence. He was beatified by Leo X in 1514.[4] His canonisation by Gregory XV Ludovisi in 1623 gave rise to several cycles of paintings of his life, including those by Giovanni Lanfranco, Eustache Le Sueur and Vicente Carducho.[5] Mola's Carthusian subjects are related to the taste for anchorite themes which developed in

Rome in the 1630s, and is exemplified in the works of Poussin, Claude, and then Salvator Rosa (see cats.68–9).

Mola shows Saint Bruno levitating on a cloud, his arms raised in prayer. The pose may derive from Krüger's engraving of the *Apotheosis of Saint Bruno* after Lanfranco,[6] but it is a fairly standard ecstatic pose. A drawing by Mola in Darmstadt (Hessisches Landesmuseum) shows Saint Bruno in a similar pose but seems to date from some years later and is perhaps a first idea for the Getty painting.[7] Mahon has emphasised the naturalism of the landscape, drawing attention to the detail of the reflection in the water of the cloud which supports the saint, which is indebted to the early paintings of Guercino, as is also the rather dark and intense colour.[8] The significance of the inscription has not been established.

TECHNICAL NOTE

The support is a moderately coarse, open plain-weave canvas. The painting is lined. There are stretcher-bar marks apparent on all four sides, about 5.5 cm from the edges, which correspond with an earlier stretcher or strainer. There is some retouching in the corners but the painting is in generally good condition. The ground is a warm reddish brown and is particularly apparent in the lower left-hand corner of the painting.

PROVENANCE

Listed in the manuscript catalogue of the paintings of Thomas Worsley (1718–78), Hovingham Hall, Yorkshire;[9] by descent until 1957; acquired by the present owner from Agnew in 1957.

EXHIBITIONS

London 1960, no.407; Lugano/Rome 1989–90, no.I.2.

1 See Sutherland Harris 1974, p.290, and Laureati in Lugano/Rome 1989–90, no.I.2, p.148; Cocke, however, dates the picture to the later Roman period (1972, cat.15, p.48).
2 See Carr 1991, which lists the known copies.
3 Buscaroli 1935, p.294, pl.LIV; Cocke accepts it as autograph (1972, cat.70, p.63.).
4 Mrs Jameson noted with irony that the 'most humble and self-denying of ascetics was beatified by the most luxurious and profligate of churchmen' (1880, p.127).
5 See Baticle 1958.
6 See Baticle 1958, p.27, fig.20. Cocke refers to an engraving by A.E. Rousslet after a lost Mola of the same subject in which the pose is very similar (1972, pp.47–8).
7 The drawing (red chalk and red wash on laid paper, 22.3 x 17.8 mm) is reproduced in Carr 1991, fig.13. A painting based on this drawing is in a Swiss private collection, but is probably a workshop picture, see Genty 1979, p.137.
8 London 1960, no.407, pp.166–7.
9 'Fran Mola, S.Bruno in a Landscape', see London 1960, p.166.

57 Landscape with Two Carthusian Monks

Oil on canvas, 51.3 x 68.2 cm

Two Carthusians, in their distinctive white habits, are engaged in meditation in a wild landscape. In the middle distance there is a third monk with a companion. The pose of the recumbent monk on the left is similar to that of the saint in the Getty Museum's *Vision of Saint Bruno*, which is datable to the early 1660s. The crossed trees in this picture also appear in that work and in the preparatory drawings for it. Although this is a favourite motif of the artist, the fact that one of the trees is a palm tree suggests that here it is intended to have iconographic significance: Saint Bruno, the founder of the Carthusians, has as one of his attributes a cross shaped from a palm tree, in reference to his having brought the cross of Christ into the wooded wilderness.[1]

The date of the work is a matter of dispute as with so much of Mola's oeuvre. However, the similarities with the Getty painting and the loose

and confident handling indicate a late date, close to 1660.[2] Mola was in personal contact with Poussin in Rome and certain aspects of this work, the careful planning of the zig-zag recession into depth in the landscape, the varied lighting effects, and the treatment of the foliage on the rocks to the left, suggest that he paid careful attention to Poussin's landscapes.[3]

TECHNICAL NOTE

The support is a quite a coarse, open plain-weave canvas. There is a raised vertical thread about 6 cm from right which looks like a seam but is in fact a fault. The painting is lined and the tacking edges have been cut off. The edges and corners are retouched and there is some abrasion in the darks and in the lower left part of the painting due to heat lining. The ground is a warm reddish brown.

PROVENANCE

Probably acquired by Charles Ingram, 9th Viscount

Irwin (1727–78); recorded in the 1808 inventory of the Ingram collection, Temple Newsam House, Leeds;[4] by descent to the Earl of Halifax; sold Christie's, London, 12 December 1947, lot 113; acquired by the present owner in 1947.

EXHIBITIONS

Lugano/Rome 1989–90, no.I.14.

1 Bibliotheca Sanctorum, III, col.569; see the Wierix print of *Saint Bruno* reproduced in Mauquoy-Henrickx 1978–83, part 2, no.1084, which bears the inscription 'sicut oliva fructifera' (Psalm 5:10).
2 A late dating is proposed by Arslan 1967, p.199, note 25, and supported by Laureati (Lugano/Rome 1989–90, no.I.14, p.165). Cocke, however, dates the work to the 1640s on the basis of the handling (1972, pp.12 and 48).
3 See Cocke 1969.
4 The inventory is published in the *Leeds Art Calendar*, nos.99 and 100, 1987, p.9, '26. A Landscape Mola 20 [guineas]'. The picture is recorded at Temple Newsam by Neale, V, no pagination; Waagen 1854/7, III, p.322, in Temple Newsam 1879, p.344.

Pierre Patel the Elder *c.*1605–1676

58 *Landscape in the Roman Campagna*

Oil on canvas, 40.7 x 60.6 cm

The subject of this painting is based on no identifiable literary source, but is typical of the kind of painting of figures in the Roman Campagna which became especially popular in Rome from the 1630s. Stylistically the landscape at the left recalls Paul Bril (see cat.6) who worked mainly in Rome, and the composition is like that of his *Landscape with Saint Eustace and the Stag* (London, Apsley House).[1] The prominent tree left of centre, the ruined temple on a cliff top, and especially the delicate gradations of light at the right, show the influence of another painter working in Rome, Claude Lorrain. Furthermore, the painting as a whole has some compositional resemblance to works of Swaneveldt, for example his *Classical Landscape* in the Hunterian Collection, University of Glasgow. However, the attribution to Swaneveldt, who also worked in Rome, made in the first half of the last century (see Provenance and Exhibitions) cannot be retained: his trees are more feathery than those in this painting and his architectural elements more sharply defined. The original attribution to Patel, the French seventeenth-century landscapist who was most influenced by Claude, is surely correct,[2] particularly given the compositional resemblances between the present painting and Patel's *Rest on the Flight into Egypt* in Tours (fig.38). But how are the Roman stylistic elements in the painting to be reconciled with the fact that no documentary evidence has yet been found that Patel ever visited Rome?

The absence from the painting of elaborate architecture, seen for example in Patel's *Rest on the Flight into Egypt* in the National Gallery, in any case suggests that this is an early work made before Claude's paintings with architecture of this type started to arrive in France from around 1639.[3] If Patel did go to Rome and painted the work there, he may have done so as early as 1634. However, if he painted it in Paris, as seems more likely, it may have been in response to one of Claude's earlier paintings to reach that city. A candidate which has some affinity with the present painting is Claude's *Pastoral Landscape* in Raleigh (North Carolina Museum of Art), although Patel's hill-top temple is more prominent than Claude's. The latter's picture was painted probably in 1637–8, and certainly for a Paris patron. This would be consistent with a date of about 1638–9 for Patel's picture, which could therefore have been painted in Paris notwithstanding its Roman elements.[4] The figures, however, are painted with a solidity and assurance which at this period are more Roman than Parisian and which are not typical of Patel.

This might suggest, if not a Roman origin for the painting, the collaboration of an artist who had trained in Rome but who was in Paris in the late 1630s.[5] However, as Natalie Coural has pointed out, the figures are well integrated into the landscape, making the work of a second hand less likely.[6] In the present state of knowledge, therefore, it is better to conclude that at this stage of his career Patel was borrowing from a variety of sources, both Northern and Italian.

The picture is first recorded in this country in the collection of Lord Burlington who built his celebrated villa at Chiswick in the 1730s. The Red Closet at Chiswick House in which the painting once hung probably housed his favourite paintings.[7]

HW

TECHNICAL NOTE
Painted on fine canvas, lined with a paste lining probably during the early nineteenth century. There is a damage at top left, and some wear. There is some blanching in the greens.

PROVENANCE
Collection of Richard Boyle, 3rd Earl of Burlington (1694–1753), in the Red Closet at Chiswick House (as by Patel);[8] by inheritance with Chiswick House to the Dukes of Devonshire;[9] probably in the Green Velvet Room (as by Swaneveldt) by 1845;[10] in the Red Velvet Room *c.*1885;[11] removed from Chiswick House to Chatsworth by 1892;[12] sold Christie's, London, 27 June 1958, lot 21 (as by Swaneveldt), bought Agnew; acquired by the present owner in the same year.

EXHIBITIONS
London (Agnew), 1958, no.7 (as Swaneveldt); Cardiff 1960, no.65 (as Swaneveldt).

Fig.38 Pierre Patel the Elder, *Landscape with the Rest on the Flight into Egypt*, signed and dated 1658? Oil on canvas, 40 x 57 cm. Tours, Musée des Beaux-Arts.

1 Bril's painting has been dated after *c*.1615: Kauffman 1982, p.34.
2 As Natalie Coural has kindly written to confirm.
3 For example, the *Seaport*, dated 1639 (Paris, Louvre, inv. 4715).
4 Natalie Coural has dated the Mahon painting 'avant 1640 (dans une fourchette qui va de 1630 à 1640, autour de 1635).' She notes similarities in the foreground and tree masses between the Mahon painting and early works by Patel in public collections in Cherbourg, Amiens and Basle. The painting in Tours is, however, signed and apparently dated 1658 (Coural 1990, p.309, n.22). I have been unable to confirm whether this reading of the date is correct.
5 Although Jean Lemaire, who was in Rome for some dozen years from 1624 but had returned to Paris by 1638, would fit such a description, the figures are not by him (letter to the author from Maurizio Fagiolo).
6 Letter to the author.
7 Rosoman 1985, p.670.
8 Manuscript list, probably in Lady Burlington's hand, preserved at Chatsworth, and written soon after her husband's death in 1753: '13 – a Landskip – Patel'. The painting is recorded as by Patel in the Red Closet in Dodesley, II, p.120; in Martyn I, p.35, and in Anonymous 1774, p.32, as by Patel. The Red Closet is a small room on the west side of Chiswick House (Rosoman 1985). There is another manuscript list of paintings preserved in Chatsworth believed to date from about 1745 and perhaps in Lord Burlington's hand. It contains no reference to any painting by either Patel or Swaneveldt, but the list is not necessarily complete.
9 The sole heir of Burlington was his youngest daughter, Charlotte (1731–54), who married Lord Hartington, son and heir to the 3rd Duke of Devonshire, in 1748 (see Nottingham 1973, p.25).
10 Thomas Faulkner, 1845, pp.387ff. Faulkner records (p.403) in the East Saloon, apparently the same room as the Green Velvet Room, 'A Landscape – Swaneveldt. Trees in the foreground, a piece of water, the ruins of a temple in the distance.' Then in a different East Saloon he records (p.414) 'Landscape – Swaneveldt. A Sketch.' As Mahon has noted (unpublished note), no Patel is recorded by Faulkner in this apparently complete catalogue, but earlier sources (see note 8 above) record both a Patel and a Swaneveldt, and it seems reasonable to conclude that the so-called Swaneveldt noted by Faulkner at p.403 is the Patel now in the Mahon collection.
11 See photograph reproduced as fig.6 and p.667, n.14 of Rosoman 1985.
12 Rosoman 1985, p.664.

Giovanni Antonio Pellegrini 1675–1741
59 *Jephthah returning from Battle is greeted by his Daughter*

Oil on canvas, 121.8 x 99.3 cm

The story is taken from the Book of Judges (11:30-40). Jephthah the Gileadite was judge over Israel and led the Israelites against the Ammonites. Before joining battle he swore an oath that if he were victorious he would offer up as a sacrifice to God the first creature that came out of his house to meet him. After delivering a crushing defeat on the Ammonites, he made his return to Mizpeh and as he approached his house his only daughter came out to meet him 'with timbrels and with dances' (verse 34). Pellegrini shows the moment of the tragic encounter when Jephthah recoils from the sight of his beloved child whom he has inadvertently condemned to death. She selflessly submitted to her father's rash vow.

Pellegrini painted several half-length pictures with biblical heroines as protagonists, for example the *Rebecca at the Well* in the National Gallery[1] and the *Judith with the Head of Holofernes* at the Barber Institute in Birmingham,[2] and several versions of *Bathsheba at her Toilet*.[3] These form part of a larger group of works of feminine subjects taken from the Old Testament, classical antiquity and mythology, as well as from Ariosto, which are about the same size, and are similar in figure scale, colour and handling. The earliest datable works of this kind are the two pendant overdoors showing *Susannah and the Elders* and *Angelica and Medoro* which were made for the Saloon at Burlington House in Piccadilly in about 1709–10, but were soon afterwards moved to Narford Hall, Norfolk, where they remain.[4] As a result, all the works in the group are normally dated to the artist's first stay in England (1708–13).[5] This date is acceptable for the Mahon painting, too.[6] It is possible that some of these paintings were conceived as pairs or even as parts of larger series, although most were probably painted as single works.

The bold brushwork and luminosity of the palette reflect Pellegrini's Venetian inheritance, but also the technique of late seventeenth-century painters such as Giovanni Battista Gaulli and Luca Giordano (see cats.25 and 28–38). Like certain works by the latter, Pellegrini's pictures often have the character of oil sketches painted large. Pellegrini has made use of a light sandy yellow ground which has the effect of increasing the brilliance of his colours. The paint is applied rapidly and with great confidence, creating a shimmering, vibrant effect. Typically, Pellegrini has placed a figure, seen from behind, at the lower right corner to increase the immediacy and drama of the scene. The heavy impasto on his helmet conveys superbly the shiny reflective surface of the metal. The heightened emotion of the participants, especially the young woman's tender appeal to her father, has a lyrical character which finds a parallel in several contemporary operas.

Pellegrini was born in Venice and trained with the Milanese painter Paolo Pagani. He had a very successful career working mostly in north and central Europe, where his luminous and elegant Rococo style was much admired by aristocratic patrons. Pellegrini came to England in 1708 with Marco Ricci in the retinue of the 4th Earl of Manchester, ambassador to Venice, and executed frescoes and decorative canvases at Kimbolton Castle, Castle Howard and Burlington House. He painted stage sets for operas at the Queen's Theatre, Haymarket, and competed unsuccessfully for the commission to paint the dome of St Paul's Cathedral.[7] He left England for Düsseldorf in 1713 and worked for the Elector Palatine Johann Wilhem in Bensberg Castle. He was in the Low Countries in 1716–18, where he painted decorative canvases in the Mauritshuis in The Hague. After returning briefly to England in 1719 he went to Paris. In the 1720s he was travelling in central Europe (Dresden, Vienna, Würzburg, Prague) and in the mid-1730s he was again in Germany. With Sebastiano Ricci and Jacopo Amigoni, who also enjoyed great international success, he was one of the most important Venetian history painters of the early eighteenth century.

TECHNICAL NOTE
The support is a plain-weave medium-weight canvas (original canvas dimensions: 120.2 x 98 cm). The painting is lined on a non-original stretcher. Stretcher-bar marks on the surface of the painting show that the original stretcher/strainer was about 4 cm wide. The ground is a sandy yellow colour. When the sky was painted the artist left some areas in reserve for the figures, which suggests that he had a fairly clear idea of the composition when he started the painting. There are no signifcant pentimenti. In a few places the impasto has been slightly crushed as a result of lining but in general the painting is in good condition.

PROVENANCE
Acquired by the present owner from the Koetser Gallery, London, in 1959.

EXHIBITIONS
London (Koetser) 1959, no.34 (as 'Mars and Venus'); London 1960, no.461; Kingston-upon-Hull 1967, no.43; Venice 1969, no.28; Venice 1995, no.9.

1 Levey 1971, p.177. Another version of the subject was formerly in the Kress Collection, Washington, see Levey 1959, p.27, where it is reproduced.
2 London/Washington 1994–5, no.40.
3 For the version in Dublin, see Young 1969, pp.197–8, fig.3; two other versions were exhibited in Venice 1969, nos.25–6.
4 Knox 1988, and Knox 1995, pp.52–3, 62–3, figs.50–1.
5 See Knox 1995, p.62, note 31.
6 See the entry in London 1960, no.461; Nicolson (1960, p.79) suggested that it was no later that 1710. All subsequent scholars have agreed with a dating in the English period.
7 For Pellegrini's English career, see Croft-Murray 1970, II, pp.13–15 and 253–6; Knox 1995, pp.47–88.

Nicolas Poussin 1594–1665

60 Rebekah quenching the Thirst of Eliezer at the Well

Oil on canvas, 93.3 x 117.5 cm
Inscribed on the back of the original canvas: RACHEL.SITIENTEM.SOLANS.POVSSINI: OPVS
(Rachel quenching the thirst of a parched man, the work of Poussin)[1]
Private collection

In spite of the inscription on the back of the canvas and early references to the picture as showing the story of Rachel,[2] the subject is undoubtedly the meeting of Rebekah and Abraham's servant, Eliezer, as related in the Book of Genesis (chapter 24). Abraham sent Eliezer to find a wife for Isaac from among Abraham's kindred in Mesopotamia. One evening at a well outside the city of Nahor, Eliezer prayed to the Lord that whoever was intended as Isaac's future wife might reveal herself by offering water both to Eliezer and to the ten camels in his train. The moment shown is that in verse 18: 'And [Rebekah] said, Drink, my lord; and she hasted, and let down her pitcher upon her hand, and gave him drink.' The subject, together with its pendant, *Christ and the Woman of Samaria* (fig.39), which also showed a meeting at a well, was particularly appropriate for Poussin's Roman patron, Cassiano dal Pozzo (since *pozzo* means 'well' in Italian). The careful and prominent depiction of the camels would also have appealed to Cassiano who had a strong interest in natural history.[3]

Poussin subsequently painted the subject twice more, for other patrons, once in 1648, showing a later moment in the story when Eliezer presented Rebekah with jewels (Paris, Musée du Louvre), and once in about 1661 showing Eliezer drinking (Cambridge, Fitzwilliam Museum).[4] In 1965, at a time when Poussin's oeuvre in his earliest years had been less fully investigated, the present version was dated by Mahon to 1629,[5] and the fact that there is an 'exceptionally close similarity of canvas weave' between this painting and *The Virgin and Child appearing to Saint James* (Paris, Musée du Louvre),[6] itself datable to 1629–30, supported such a dating. However, the hot colours found, for example, in *Acis and Galatea* (Dublin, National Gallery of Ireland), are also apparent in this painting; both (and this has for some time been the view of Mahon) must precede the more accomplished *Death of Germanicus* (Minneapolis Institute of Arts), itself finished by the end of 1627. It is, therefore, reasonable to suppose that the *Rebekah* was painted after the return of Cassiano to Rome from Madrid in September 1626, and, for reasons of style, before the winter of 1627–8.[7]

Typically, Poussin has treated a biblical text with care. Although, not unreasonably, he shows three camels rather than ten, the action takes place outside a city as related in the Bible, albeit one reminiscent of ancient Rome. The maiden in the centre with her back turned to Eliezer may be taken to represent the other women who also came to the well but who were not chosen. Furthermore, the principal action in which Rebekah 'let down her pitcher upon her hand, and gave him drink' is faithfully shown, although probably derived from a print of the same subject after Primaticcio.[8] When Mahon published the painting in 1965 he noted that Eliezer was a young man (contrasting this with Poussin's other two treatments of the encounter) and (as he acknowledged) he fantasised that Eliezer 'may in some sense be symbolical' of Poussin and of his relationship to his patron Cassiano dal Pozzo. 'What we see is a youngish man, fatigued by his travels and exertions in the heat of the Mediterranean summer's day, at length attaining his goal and receiving solace and refreshment from the well (*pozzo*) at the hands of a dignified and statuesque figure worthy of typifying the eternal city – in a setting which indeed evokes the environs of Rome.'[9] In fact, it was pointed out by Ralph Holland,[10] there were reasons for supposing the setting to be more specifically related to the very centre of Rome. Poussin may well have seen his painting as acknowledging his indebtedness to Rome and to his patron, even though the same cannot be said of its pendant, *Christ and the Woman of Samaria*. Indeed, the transformation of Primaticcio's voluptuous Rebekah into an antique Roman type makes Mahon's fantasy more credible, as does the hypothesis of Ralph Holland mentioned above.

A early copy with slight but infelicitous variations (59 x 72 cm) is in the Musée de Tessé, Le Mans.[11]

HW

TECHNICAL NOTE
A report on the materials and technique of the painting was published by Joyce Plesters in *Apollo* (vol. LXXXI, 1965, pp. 203–4). The picture was cleaned and relined in 1964–5 by Arthur Lucas (Chief Restorer at the National Gallery).

PROVENANCE
Painted for Cassiano dal Pozzo and thence by inheritance to Giuseppe Boccapaduli, by whom sold in 1779, together with its pendant, *Christ and the Woman of Samaria*, to the painter and art dealer Gavin Hamilton (1723–98);[12] probably sale of the former French First Minister Charles Alexandre de Calonne (1734–1802), London, Skinner and Dyke, 28 March 1795, where sold together with a companion picture for £145 to an unknown buyer;[13] next known to have been at Middlewood Hall, Darfield, Yorkshire, in the collection of R.H.H. Taylor, by whom sold without an attribution in a local auction in 1960; sold at Sotheby's, London, 24 June 1964, lot 68 (as by Pietro Testa), where bought by Oscar & Peter Johnson Limited on behalf of Sir Denis Mahon; bought from him by Messrs Wildenstein in 1977.

EXHIBITIONS
Rome, Cloister of S. Salvatore in Lauro, 1715 (exhibition of the Dal Pozzo Collection in honour of the Holy House of Loreto);[14] Tokyo (Wildenstein) 1983, *Ten Masterpieces of European Painting*, no number; Fort Worth 1988, no. 42; London (Royal Academy) 1995, no.5.

Fig.39 Nicolas Poussin, *Christ and the Woman of Samaria*, c.1627. Oil on canvas, presumably 93.3 x 117.5 cm. Present whereabouts unknown.

1 See the reproduction in Mahon 1965b, fig.5 on p.204. For a discussion of such inscriptions on the backs of paintings in the Dal Pozzo collection, see Mahon 1985, Standring 1988, passim, and Fagiolo dell'Arco 1995, pp.58–60.
2 The painting was called 'Rachele' as early as 1689 in the post-mortem inventory of Cassiano dal Pozzo's brother, Carlo Antonio, where it and its pendant are described as 'Due quadri compagni, uno rappresentante la Samaritana e l'altro Rachele tele d'Imperatore per traverso cornici dorate si credono di Posino': Sparti 1992, p.187. For references to the painting as of Rachel by Giuseppe Ghezzi in 1715 and Jonathan Richardson in 1722, and as of Rebekah by De Cotte c.1689 and De Brosses in 1739–40, see Mahon 1965, pp.198–9. Significantly the protagonist was corrected to Rebekah in the French edition of Richardson's work (1728). The over-cautious notary who drew up the Dal Pozzo inventory applied the expresssion 'si credono di Posino' to all of the pictures by Poussin in the collection (including the *Seven Sacraments*!).
3 The point was made by Mahon (1965b), but see also, for example, two essays by David Freedberg (Freedberg 1989 and Freedberg 1993).

4 The Cambridge picture was once thought to be that painted for Dal Pozzo, see Blunt 1966, no.9, but the documentation brought forward later by Standring 1988 conclusively excludes this.

5 Mahon 1965b, p.202.

6 According to Joyce Plesters, see Mahon 1965b, p.203.

7 The painting has been dated to 1627 by, for example, Oberhuber (1988, p.271), and by Richard Verdi in London (Royal Academy) 1995, p.156, who gave convincing reasons for his conclusions.

8 As pointed out in Mahon 1965b, p.203, where reproduced as fig. 4.

9 Mahon 1965, pp.202–3.

10 *Apollo*, LXXXI, 1965, p.409.

11 See reproduction in *Apollo*, LXXXI, 1965, fig.3, on p.203.

12 Standring 1988, pp.623–4. The identification of the painting with that once in the Dal Pozzo Collection was first proposed by Denis Mahon (1965b) but is irrefutably established by Standring. The attribution of the painting to Poussin has been accepted by all (including Rosenberg in Paris1994, p.383) save Jacques Thuillier who tentatively suggested it might be by Charles Errard (Thuillier 1978, pp.160 and 171, nn. 59, 60) without, as Denis

Mahon informs me, having at that time examined the painting. Moreover, there are, as Mahon points out, a number of discrepancies in Thuillier's argument, including the surprising suggestion that the figure of Eliezer could have been derived from the figure of a drinker in the Sutherland *Moses striking the Rock* (*c*.1637) rather than vice versa, as previously argued by Mahon; in addition, Thuillier attempts to discount the attributions to Poussin in the Pozzo inventories of this picture and also of the *Hannibal crossing the Alps* (which there are now excellent reasons for believing to have been painted by Poussin as early as the end of 1625) and suggested that they could both be works by Charles Errard (who, although a well-known painter in Rome towards the end of his life, does not appear in any of the Pozzo inventories, several of which were published after 1978). Further, it is worth stressing that authenticated paintings by Charles Errard are particularly rare and there is no evidence, or indeed probability, that he could ever have produced, or indeed wished to produce, works so close in colour and handling to Poussin's very earliest work in Rome. Notwithstanding all this, however, Thuillier cites anew in his monograph of 1994 (no.B13) his suggestion

of Errard advanced tentatively in his article of 1978.

13 Described in the sale catalogue as 'N. Poussin 15 Rebecca at the Well. This and the companion picture are the test of the great genius and superior abilities of Poussin.' Since Thiéry (1787, I, p.172) records only one (unidentified) Poussin in Calonne's collection in Paris (vol.1, p.172), it is possible that Calonne acquired the two Poussins referred to above after he came to England in 1787. The companion picture must have been the *Christ and the Woman of Samaria* bought by Hamilton from Boccapaduli. Its present whereabouts is unknown, but the composition is likely to have been that shown in a reproduction of a painting in an advertisement of the Sackville Gallery in *The Burlington Magazine*, XLVIII, 1926, p.xxiii of no.274 (reproduced by Verdi, London (Royal Academy) 1995, fig.35 on p.156). The composition is entirely compatible with a dating of *c*.1627, though one cannot be certain from the reproduction whether the painting was an original or a copy.

14 Haskell and Rinehart 1960, pp.324–6, and De Marchi ed., 1987, p.304.

Guido Reni 1575–1642

61 Saint Francis consoled by the Musician Angel

Oil on copper, 44.4 x 34 cm

The subject of the angelic consolation of Saint Francis became popular in the second half of the sixteenth century as a result of the post-Tridentine Church's fresh appreciation of the mystical experiences of the saint, almost to the exclusion of the more picturesque episodes of his life that characterised the traditional iconography.[1] According to the *Little Flowers of Saint Francis*, a fourteenth-century compilation of stories in Italian about the saint, Francis was keeping a rigorous fast on Mount Alverna when 'suddenly there appeared to him an angel in great splendour, who had a viol in his left hand and in his right hand a bow; and whilst St Francis stood stupefied at the vision the angel drew the bow once across the viol, and immediately there was heard such a sweet melody that his soul was inebriated with sweetness, and he lost all bodily sense.'[2] Saint Francis's ecstatic experiences were understood as both the sign and the reward of his perfect conformity to Christ. The parallel between this episode and the angelic consolation afforded to Christ in the Garden of Gethsemane is evident.

In Reni's painting the saint is positioned at the mouth of a cave which the musician angel has just entered. A cool evening light throws the figures into relief and picks out the skull, books and crucifix, the objects of Saint Francis's meditation. In the lower left-hand corner is a basket with some radishes. This detail has its source in the print of 1595 by Agostino Carracci (fig.40) after the Sienese painter Francesco Vanni which served as Reni's iconographical and, to some extent, compositional prototype.[3]

Several of Reni's early works are on copper, a support which had come into vogue among painters in Italy in the second half of the sixteenth century. The smooth surface and relatively small size of the copper panels meant that they were suited to small-scale figure compositions with a large amount of delicate detail.[4] Malvasia states that Reni painted on copper in emulation of his first teacher, Denys Calvaert, a Flemish painter who had settled in Bologna, but Ludovico Carracci was also employing copper panels in the 1580s.[5]

Reni's earliest painting on copper is the so-called Sampieri *Assumption of the Virgin* (present whereabouts unknown) which is usually dated 1596–7. During the years when he was mainly based in Rome (1601–14) Reni painted several works on copper of exquisite quality and refinement. These include the *Holy Family with Saint John the Baptist* (London, Pat Coombes), the *Virgin and Child with Saint John* (Paris, Louvre), the *Agony in the Garden* (also Louvre) and the

Fig.40 Agostino Carracci (after Francesco Vanni), *Saint Francis consoled by the Musician Angel*, signed and dated 1595. Engraving, 308 x 342 mm. London, British Museum.

two versions of the *Martyrdom of Saint Apollonia* (formerly New York, M.Roy Fisher Fine Arts, and New York, Richard Feigen). Reni's *Coronation of the Virgin* in the National Gallery of about 1607 is painted on a copper panel, the recto of which is coated with a lead-tin alloy. The reason for this is not entirely clear (but see cat.46). Reni's interest in painting on a small scale on copper seems to have declined after about 1614.

The *Saint Francis consoled by the Musician Angel* was first published by Giuliano Briganti as a work by Annibale Carracci dating from before Annibale's move to Rome in 1595 and it was subsequently exhibited as such on two occasions.[6] Briganti remarked upon its similarity to works by the young Reni, but it was Roberto Longhi who identified it definitively as a work by Reni dating from 1605–10 and exactly contemporary with the National Gallery *Coronation of the Virgin*.[7] Similarities in style and in the typology of the figures have subsequently been noted between the present work and the *Martyrdom of Saint Catherine*, the large altarpiece Reni made for the church of Sant'Alessandro, Conscente (Liguria), which is dated on quite firm grounds to 1606–7, and so the generally accepted view is that the *Saint Francis consoled by the Musician Angel* is a work of about 1606–7.[8]

A seventeenth-century copy of the painting in tondo format and on poplar (45cm diameter) is in the collection of Campion Hall, Oxford.[9]

TECHNICAL NOTE
The support is a copper panel. There are two holes 5 mm from the top edge about 2 cm either side of the centre. They have been pushed through from behind and may have served for a fixing to hang the picture; they have been subsequently filled in and retouched. There are diagonal deformations in the copper at the upper-right, lower-right and lower-left corners. There appears to be a reddish underlayer beneath most of the painted surface. Few pentimenti are apparent, the most significant being in the angel's robe, which originally billowed out about 6 cm further to the right before being covered with sky. The darker areas have suffered from pinpoint flaking but in general the painting is in good condition. On the reverse are several daubs of yellowish oil paint which do not seem to be significant.

PROVENANCE
Acquired by the present owner at Christie's, London, 21 January 1951, lot 101 ('Guercino, Vision of St Anthony').

EXHIBITIONS
Manchester 1957, no.88 (as Annibale Carracci); London 1960, no.399 (as Annibale Carracci); London (Agnew) 1973, no.42 (as Reni); London (Harari and Johns) 1987, no.9; Bologna 1988, no.10; Los Angeles/Fort Worth 1988–9, no.6; Rome 1996, no. 100.

1 Réau 1958, III (1), pp.529–30, and especially Askew 1969, pp.280–2.
2 Little Flowers, pp.183–4.
3 De Grazia Bohlin 1979, no.204, pp.329–30. The print is, in its turn, based in great part on an etching by Vanni (ibid., fig.204a). Agostino knew Vanni from the time they were in Passerotti's workshop in 1577. Reni met Vanni in Rome in 1602/3, see Bellori 1976, p.495, but see also D.S. Pepper's comments in Rome 1996, pp.554 and 556, note 8.
4 Andrews 1977, pp.169–70; Horovitz 1986; Bowron 1995.
5 Malvasia 1678, II, p.5. For example, Ludovico Carracci's Marriage of the Virgin (London, Private collection) is on copper, Bologna/Fort Worth 1993–4, no.29 .
6 Briganti 1953, p.5; Manchester 1957, no.88; London 1960, no.399, pp.159–60.
7 Longhi 1960, p.61.
8 Matthiesen and Pepper 1970, p.462, note 45; Pepper 1984, no.28, pp.222–3; Pepper 1988, no.28, p.227; Andrea Emiliani in Los Angeles/Fort Worth 1988–9, p.164.
9 This painting was probably acquired in Rome by the Hon. John Barry of Marbury Hall, Northwich, Cheshire, in the late eighteenth century. The Catalogue of Paintings, Statues, Busts, &c. at Marbury Hall, Warrington, 1819, p.3, lists it as '52. St.Francis, Domenichino'. It left Marbury Hall to be sold at Sotheby's on 21 June 1933, lot 63. For this picture, see Oxford 1996, no.5, pp.16–17, and Brett 1993 (unpublished).

Guido Reni 1575–1642
62 A Sibyl

Oil on canvas, 74.2 x 58.3 cm (original canvas 70.7 x 55.3 cm)

The sibyls were pagan seers who were believed to have foretold the coming of Christ (see cat.48). In medieval Christian imagery they are frequently paired with Old Testament prophets but in seventeenth-century Italian painting they were treated as subjects for the representation of idealised female beauty. The sibyls of Reni and Domenichino are often recognisable as such only by their vaguely oriental or antique dress and their upraised eyes; their specific identity was not usually considered important.

Reni's unnamed Sibyl wears a turban made from a long strip of cloth that comes down her right shoulder and over her breast and left arm, inscribing a delicate and elegant arabesque which defines the limits of the composition. The outline of the turban is dented on the right by a stroke of the warm grey-green paint used for the background, introducing variety to the soft rounded forms of the picture and drawing attention to the Sibyl's upturned eyes. She is receiving heavenly inspiration and enumerates on her fingers the parts of the prophecy she must communicate. The type of Guido's Sibyl conforms to his Magdalens and Cleopatras (cat.64) and reflects a conception of beauty based on the adaptation of classical forms and the art of Raphael.

The handling is spontaneous and confident and the painting clearly belongs to the late phase in Reni's career when he customarily employed a light palette, applying the paint thinly and intentionally leaving areas of transparency. Reni is unlikely to have made preparatory studies on paper for a painting such as this (certainly none is known), indeed his 'drawing' is apparent in the light brown contours of the hands and in the dark lines in the white chemise. The visibility of the pentimenti should not lead one to the conclusion that the picture is unfinished.

When the painting was first published it was dated to the artist's very last years, about 1639–42,[1] but the discovery of a reference to it in the 1637 inventory of the paintings of Cardinal Prince Giovan Carlo de' Medici (see under cat.66) at his villa of Mezzomonte near Florence indicates an earlier date. Pepper has dated it 1635–6 and proposed that it is identical with the 'Head of a Sibyl in the act of looking towards Heaven' which the Florentine writer Filippo Baldinucci saw in the collection of the Florentine Monsignore Jacopo Altoviti, titular Patriarch of Antioch, and which, he says, Altoviti had commissioned directly from the artist.[2] If Pepper is correct then Altoviti must have commissioned the work on behalf of Giovan Carlo and then acquired it for himself after the Prince's death in 1663, when his collection was sold.

Two copies of the painting are cited by Pepper.[3]

TECHNICAL NOTE

The support is a fine-weave canvas and is lined. The tacking edges have been cut off. The original canvas has been extended at a later date by about 2.5 cm on the left side and 1.5 cm at the top. The ground is warm orange-brown. There are small pentimenti: the cloth forming the turban which comes over the figure's left shoulder originally came a little higher and covered more of her breast; the index finger of her left hand was originally shorter and the tip turned up. The painting is in excellent condition.

PROVENANCE

Cardinal Prince Giovan Carlo de' Medici (1611–63), Villa di Mezzomonte near Florence, 1637; listed in his post-mortem inventory of 1663;[4] possibly identical with a picture described by Baldinucci in the collection of Jacopo Altoviti (1604–93), titular Patriarch of Antioch; George Nassau, 3rd Earl Cowper (1738–1789), Florence, by 1779;[5] later at Panshanger, Hertfordshire;[6] by descent to Lady Desborough; her sale, Christie's, London, 16 October 1953, lot 117; bought by Agnew, whence acquired by the present owner in January 1954.

EXHIBITIONS

Bologna 1954, no.50; Birmingham 1955, no.62; London 1960, no.378; Detroit 1965, no.83; Bologna/Washington/New York 1986–7, no.186; Bologna 1988, no.61; Los Angeles/Fort Worth 1988–9, no.49.

1 Cavalli in Bologna 1954, no.50, p.109, and Mahon in London 1960, no.378, p.146.
2 Baldinucci 1845–7, IV, p.28; Pepper 1984, no.159, p.274; Pepper 1988, no.157, pp.286–7. In a footnote to Baldinucci's statement about the Altoviti picture in the 1845–7 edition of the *Notizie*, F. Ranalli notes that the painting was visible in the Tribuna in the Real Galleria di Firenze (IV, p.28, note 2). However, the Sibyl that Ranalli must have been referring to is a mediocre school picture in the Uffizi collection (Inv.762, oil on copper, 59 x 43 cm), see Borea 1975, no.117, and Uffizi Catalogo 1979, no.P1317.
3 Pepper 1984, p.274.
4 Mascalchi 1984, pp.271–2. The painting is listed in the following inventories: Villa di Mezzomonte, 2 August 1637; Casino di Via della Scala, 1 January 1647; post-mortem inventory of the Casino di Via della Scala, 1663, where it appears as: 'Un quadro in tela, entrovi la Testa, con il Busto nudo, di una Sibilla scollacciata, con sciugatoio avvolto in Testa, con adornamento liscio e dorato, di mano di Guido Reni'; in an associated inventory of 1663, which lists pictures that should be put up for sale, the height (presumably including the frame) is given as 1 1/2 braccia, equivalent to 87.54 cm, Mascalchi 1983–4 (unpublished), I, p.272, and II, pp.409, 495 and 611–12.
5 Inventory of Pictures belonging to William 3rd Lord Cowper c.1779 in Villa Palmieri and Villa Cipresso, Florence: 'No.17. Una Sibilla di Guido, Larghezzo [sic] 1 Piedi 9 Pollici (Mesura del Piede, Parigine) Altezza 2 Piedi 3 Pollici', Sutton 1956, p.83.
6 Where seen by Waagen (1854, III, p.15).

Guido Reni 1575–1642

63 The Rape of Europa

Oil on canvas, 177 x 129.5 cm

In his biography of Reni, Malvasia records that the artist made three paintings of Europa: one was for King Charles I of England, another was commissioned by the Duke of Guastalla for an eminent Spanish collector (the Marqués de Leganés, Viceroy of Milan), and the third was for the King of Poland, Wladislaw IV.[1] It is highly doubtful if the first of these ever existed; the second is the painting recently acquired by the National Gallery of Canada (fig.41), which bears a Leganés inventory number, and dates from 1636–7;[2] and the third must be the present picture.[3] Although there is a gap in the provenance of this painting of just over fifty years (between 1687 and 1741), the circumstantial evidence for its identification with the painting Reni sent to Poland, and which subsequently passed to France, is strong.

In early 1640 King Wladislaw wrote to the artist from Warsaw expressing his satisfaction with the picture he had received: 'To the very illustrious and excellent Sig. Guido Reni. Ladislaus IV, by the grace of God King of Poland and Sweden. Illustrious and Excellent Signore: It is not possible for us to express by any means other than our letters how pleased we are with the Europa, which you sent to us through our secretary Puccitelli ... and how great is the esteem we have of your renowned ability. Give

us then the opportunity to be able to demonstrate this to you with deeds for in this you will always find us ready, and may Our Lord keep you. Warsaw 3 March 1640. Ladislaus Rex.'[4]

After the king's death in 1648 the picture passed to his brother and successor, John II Casimir, who abdicated in 1668 and retired to Nevers in France.[5] It was acquired from John Casimir's estate by Charles III Duc de Créquy, one of the great French collectors of the seventeenth century.[6] The painting has a superb Régence frame which must have been made for it in France early in the eighteenth century before it came into the possession of the London dealer Samuel Paris, who acquired large numbers of pictures in France.[7]

Europa was the daughter of Agenor, King of Tyre. Zeus was in love with her and took the form of a docile bull which made its way to the shore where she was playing, in order to abduct her. She climbed on its back and they swam away to Crete where she eventually bore Zeus three sons, Minos, Rhadamanthys and Sarpedon. Reni shows Europa's wailing companions on the shore. The myth, with its dark erotic undertones, was one of the most frequently represented themes in the seventeenth-century repertoire of classical subjects. Reni's treatment is unusual because of the inclusion of the cupid at upper right. Europa is shown at the moment when her disquiet at being carried out into the water begins to give way to love.

The distinctive features of Reni's late style – the luminous tonality, the sapient juxtaposition of pale colours, the studied elegance of the pose and draperies and the subtle balance between movement and stasis – are here crystallised in an image of extraordinary refinement. The scene is bathed in a clear Mediterranean light almost to the complete exclusion of shadow. Europa's golden tresses, cloak and sleeve billow out in the wind but she effortlessly retains her composure and her balance.

TECHNICAL NOTE

The support is a coarse-weave twill canvas. The ground is a warm red. The canvas was lined in the nineteenth century and the original tacking edges survive. Prior to conservation treatment and relining at the National Gallery in 1996 the painting showed pronounced horizontal craquelure consistent with the canvas having been rolled up at some point, perhaps for transport. A repaired vertical tear about 30 cm long runs through the lower part of the bull's neck and into the water. Diagonal stretcher-bar marks are apparent on the surface, particularly at upper left. The surface is quite worn in the area of the sea to the right of the figure and to the left of the

bull's neck, and in the sky. Following the removal of the old lining canvas the painting received moisture treatment which has succeeded in significantly reducing the craquelure. The more obvious areas of wear have been retouched. There are several pentimenti: the position of the cupid's bow was altered and Europa's right hand and wrist appear originally to have been a little further up the bull's neck.

PROVENANCE

Painted for Wladislaw IV, King of Poland; King John II Casimir, his brother and successor, who retired to France (d.1672); acquired by Charles III Duc de Créquy in 1673 and recorded in his post-mortem inventory of 1687; acquired from Samuel Paris, importer of pictures from the Continent, by Sir Jacob de Bouverie (afterwards 1st Viscount Folkestone, and father of the 1st Earl of Radnor) on 20 November 1741 for £152 14s. 11d.;[8] Radnor collection at Longford Castle until 1945; acquired by the present owner at Christie's, London, 27 July 1945, lot 37.

EXHIBITIONS

Bologna 1954, no.53; Manchester 1957, no.127; London 1960, no.397; London (Agnew) 1973, no.47; Bologna 1988, no.69; Los Angeles/Fort Worth 1988–9, no.57.

1 Malvasia 1678, pp.30, 41 ,61.
2 See Zeri 1976; Pepper 1984, no.164, pp.275–6; Pepper 1988, no.155, pp.285–6; Sybille Ebert-Schifferer in Frankfurt 1988–9, no.A30, pp.207–8.
3 The painting was first published by Mahon in 1947 as a late work, quoting the opinion of Otto Kurz, p.51; see also Pepper 1984, no.184, p.285; Pepper 1988, no.176, p.296; Cristina Casali Pedrielli in Bologna 1988 and Los Angeles/Fort Worth 1988–9, no.57 (English edn.), p.304.
4 The letter is quoted by Malvasia (1678, p.61) and Bellori (1976, pp.527–8). Mahon has wondered whether the Italian draft of the letter might have been made by Giacinto Campana, who was at that time painter at the court of Wladislaw IV.
5 Recorded in his post-mortem inventory of 1672 as no.37, Tomkiewicz 1959, p.143.
6 Jean-Claude Boyer has drawn the attention of Sir Denis Mahon to a document in the Archives Nationales, Paris, recording the sale of John II Casimir's possessions: 'Procès verbal de vente des meubles du Roy Casimir. 15 février 1673 [...] Item un tableau représentant l'enlevement d'Europpe peint sur toille garny de sa bordure prisé par le vingt troisieme article dudit inventaire la somme de quatre cent livres, crié audit prix, vendu, adjugé et dellivré apres plusieurs & diverses encheres & proclamations à monsieur le duc de Créquy pour la somme de deux cent vingt cinq livres commes plus offrant et dernier enchérisseur, cy IIc xxv' (KK534.1, fol.44r and v). The painting is listed in the Duc de Créquy's post-mortem inventory of 1687: 'Guide: un autre [tableau] representant l'Europe estimé trois cens livres', Magne 1939, p.190. For Créquy as a collector, see Schnapper 1994, pp.81 and 384–5.
7 For Samuel Paris's activities, see Pears 1988, pp.87–92.
8 Radnor 1909, I, no.103, p.76. This was almost certainly a private transaction rather than an auction purchase.

Fig.41 Guido Reni, The Rape of Europa, 1636–7. Oil on canvas, 157.5 x 115.3 cm. Ottawa, National Gallery of Canada.

Guido Reni 1575–1642

64 Cleopatra

Oil on canvas, 77 x 65.1 cm
Inscribed in the lower left corner: 81 and 209

Cleopatra was the Queen of Egypt, renowned in the ancient world for her beauty and eloquence. She was loved first by Julius Caesar and then by Mark Antony. After the latter was defeated by Augustus at the Battle of Actium in 31 BC Cleopatra's downfall quickly followed. When Augustus resolved to bring her as a captive to Rome she put an end to her own life with the poison of an asp. Cleopatra was one of the heroines of classical history, together with Portia, Lucretia and others, who were much admired in the Renaissance.

Reni made several pictures of Cleopatra, the earliest of which seems to be the half-length painting in Potsdam dating from the mid-1620s.[1] The style of this picture and the particularly languid pose indicate that it is a much later work and Pepper has dated it 1639–40.[2] The very thin paint, loosely applied, the transparent veils of soft colours and the unfinished appearance are hallmarks of Reni's distinctive 'seconda maniera'. Whereas there may be some doubt as to whether certain late works such as the Edinburgh *Moses with Pharaoh's Crown*, or the astoundingly beautiful *Holy Family with Saints Elizabeth and John the Baptist*,[3] are actually finished, there can be no doubt that the present work is as finished as the artist intended it to be. All the elements of the

composition are resolved: the arrangement of the draperies, the positions of the hands, the expression of anguish and despair, even the dramatic detail of the drops of blood staining the expanse of pallid flesh.

Guido Reni's late manner has not always found favour. Malvasia, Reni's Bolognese biographer, claimed that he was expressing a widely held view when he declared that Reni's later works are far less good than his early ones, lacking vigour and boldness.[4] This prejudiced view persisted into the twentieth century but with the advent of modern studies of the artist (Voss, Kurz, Gnudi and Cavalli, and more recently Emiliani and especially Pepper) there has developed a more profound and sympathetic appreciation of Reni's artistic intentions at the end of his career.[5] The presentation of newly cleaned works from the artist's last years at the great monographic exhibition in Bologna in 1954, of which Denis Mahon was a member of the 'Commissione Consultativa', proved to be something of a revelation and since then the late period has come to be seen as the culmination of the artist's career.

A poor copy with many paint losses, on canvas (86 x 61 cm, with a curved top), is in the possession of a member of the Patrizi family in Rome.

TECHNICAL NOTE
The support is a fine-weave canvas and is lined. The tacking edges have been cut off. The ground is a pale orange-brown and the paint is very thinly and loosely applied. There are some retouched losses but the painting is in very good condition.

PROVENANCE
The early provenance of the picture is not known;[6] a label on the reverse which probably dates from the early nineteenth century indicates that it was then in a British collection;[7] acquired by the present owner at Christie's, London, 8 November 1957, lot 60.

EXHIBITIONS
Bologna 1988, no.76; Frankfurt 1988–9, no.A.36.

1 Pepper 1984, no.106, p.254, pl.131; for other Cleopatras, see ibid., nos.111, 136, 181, 189, 210.
2 Pepper 1984, no.189, p.287; Pepper 1988, no.181, p.298.
3 Pepper 1984, nos.213 and 214, figs.241 and 246 (for the latter see also colour plate XVI).
4 Malvasia 1678, II, p.49.
5 Specifically on the late works, see Cuppini 1952 and Pepper 1979.
6 The numbers 81 and 209 in the corner of the picture have not yet been connected with any inventory.
7 The label is printed: 'No.13 GUIDO – Cleopatra applying the Asp to her Bosom. Her exquisitely lovely face is in contortions from the deadly bite of the Asp. This picture is of very high quality: it looks like a large Pearl. 23 – 29 [inches] On canvas Price 500 Guineas.' The label appears to be cut out of a private sale catalogue. A picture described with similar wording was offered for sale at auction in London by John 2nd Baron Crewe (1771–1835) in 1809 and 1810: European Museum, May 1809, lot 89, 'Guido, Cleopatra applying the asp to her bosom', remained unsold?; European Museum, 26 February 1810, lot 89, remained unsold?; Farebrothers, 14 July 1810, lot 68, 'Guido, Cleopatra applying the Asp to her Bosom', sold £4.10. It may be the same picture, but the low price it fetched is a little surprising.

Giovanni Francesco Romanelli *c.1610–1662*

65 *Angelica encountering the Wounded Medoro*

Oil on canvas, 61.6 x 76.3 cm

The subject is from Ariosto's epic poem, *Orlando Furioso*, and shows Angelica, daughter of the king of Cathay, finding the handsome Moorish knight Medoro. He had been wounded in a skirmish with a group of Scottish knights which left his companions Cloridano and Dardinello dead. Angelica had disdained love up to this moment and Cupid here saw his opportunity:

> Such reckless pride the god of love resents.
> Resolved that he will suffer it no more,
> He waits beside Medoro and with craft
> He fixes to his bow a piercing shaft.[1]

The painting shows Cupid firing his bow at Angelica as she gazes at the wounded warrior. Her cold heart was melted with compassion and she tended him, eventually confessing her love.

The work was almost certainly made for Cardinal Mazarin, First Minister to the Queen Regent of France, Anne of Austria, during Romanelli's first visit to France (1646–8).[2] Romanelli had been a pupil of Domenichino and then of Pietro da Cortona, whom he assisted in the decoration of the ceiling of the Salone in Palazzo Barberini. He enjoyed an exalted position in Rome during the years of Cortona's absence in Florence from 1637, but with the death of Urban VIII Barberini in 1644 he fell out of official favour and two years later he followed Cardinal Francesco Barberini, the Pope's nephew and a close ally of Mazarin, to Paris. There he painted the ceiling of the Galerie Mazarine in the Cardinal's palace with scenes from ancient history and mythology in a stately classic Baroque style which exerted a great influence on painters like Eustache Le Sueur and Charles Le Brun.[3] After a period in Rome he was again in Paris from 1655 to 1657 to decorate a suite of rooms in the Queen Regent's summer apartments in the Louvre. While lacking the vigour of Cortona's art, Romanelli's dignified monumental compositions helped to define the character of public painting in both Italy and France in the second half of the seventeenth century.

The identification of the subject matter of the present work proved a challenge from very early on. In the 1653 inventory of the collection of Cardinal Mazarin (and in that of 1661) it is said to represent the wounded Tancredi with Armida and the dead Argante, and thus a subject from Tasso's *Gerusalemme Liberata*.[4] An engraving after the painting by Jean Charles Le Vasseur (1734–1816), presumably made when it was still in France, identifies it as 'Tancred and Erminia'. When it was in the collection of the Earls of Ellesmere at Bridgewater House it was entitled 'Cephalus and Procris' and attributed to 'Filippo Monzani'. Mrs Jameson noted in her description of the Bridgewater House collection published in 1844 that she had no familiarity with this artist.[5] When Mahon acquired the picture in 1952 it had been overpainted to transform it into a 'Venus and Adonis': the bodies of Cloridano and Dardinello had been painted out and Medoro held a hunting spear in his hand. On cleaning, the original composition was revealed and the subject was correctly identified.[6]

TECHNICAL NOTE

The support is a fairly coarse plain-weave canvas (painted canvas dimensions: 60.6 x 75.2 cm). The painting was lined, probably in the nineteenth century, and the original tacking edges have been cut off. Wooden strips about 1 cm wide have been attached to the top and bottom edges of the stretcher. There is some abrasion, probably due to cleaning, below Medoro's left leg and left elbow, but the painting is in good condition. The ground is light brown. A pentimento is apparent in the centre of the picture: the arrow flying towards Angelica was originally positioned further to the right.

PROVENANCE

Cardinal Jules Mazarin (1602–61) by 1653; possibly identifiable with a picture in the collection of the Marquis of Stafford, Cleveland House, London;[7] Earls of Ellesmere, Bridgewater House, by 1833;[8] Christie's, London, 18 October 1946 (Ellesmere sale), lot 120 ('Filippo Monzani, Cephalus and Procris', bought by Lawrence); acquired by the present owner at Sotheby's, London, 22 October 1952, lot 103 (as 'Rinaldo and Armida' by Albani).

EXHIBITIONS

London (Wildenstein) 1955, no.66; London 1960, no.409; Bologna 1962, no.141.

1 'Tant'arroganzia avendo Amor sentita,/ più lungamente comportar non volse:/ dove giacea Medor, si pose al varco,/ e l'aspettò, posto lo strale all'arco', Canto XIX, 19. The passage is quoted from Barbara Reynolds's translation, Penguin Books, Harmondsworth, 1975.

2 As recognised by Kerber (1973, p.163, note 11, and 1979, p.12, note 29). The painting is listed in the two inventories of Mazarin's collection, 1653 and 1661. In both instances the subject is misidentified. 1653: '210. Un petit paysage, long de travers, avec Tancrède blessé, Argante morte et Erminie avec deux enfants en l'air, long en travers, sans bordure … Romanelli.' (Duc d'Aumale 1861, p.318, no.210). Laurain-Portemer (who had not made the link between the inventory entry and the Mahon picture) expressed the view that the pictures by Romanelli and by his assistant Paolo Gismondo Perugino listed in the 1653 inventory were probably painted by them in France (1973, p.154). 1661: '1044. Un autre faict par Romanelli, sur toille représentant un Petit Paysage où est Tancrède blessé, Argant mort et Armide, avecq deux enfans en l'air, hault d'un pied dix pouces et large de deux piedz quatre poulces, garny de sa bordure de bois doré, prisé la somme de deux cens livre, cy … 200 L.T.' (Comte de Cosnac 1885, p.311, no.1044).

3 For Romanelli in France, see Laurain-Portemer 1973; Paris 1988–9, pp.334–7. For paintings by Romanelli sold in France in the eighteenth century (including an 'Angelique et Medore'), see Wildenstein 1982, p.44.

4 See note 2.

5 Jameson 1844, p.109, no.62. Giuliano Briganti suggested that 'Monzani' was Filippo Menzani, an obscure follower of Albani (none of whose works is known) mentioned by Malvasia. He added that in late eighteenth-century England it was thought that any Italian Seicento painting with small figures in a landscape must have some connection with Albani and this attribution was interesting for its enterprising character, see Briganti 1953, p.15.

6 Briganti 1953, p.15.

7 Westmacott 1824, p.206: '287. Story of Cephalus and Procris'.

8 See the *Catalogue of the Bridgewater Collection of Pictures*, 5th edn, London, 1851, p.19, no.107. The painting is not marked with an asterisk which means that it was in the collection before 1833.

Salvator Rosa 1615–1673

66 *Landscape with Travellers asking the Way*

Oil on canvas, 108.3 x 174.2 cm
Signed on the rock to right of centre with monogram, *SR* interlaced

Rosa was invited to Florence in 1640 by Prince Giovan Carlo de' Medici (1611–63), brother of Ferdinand II, Grand Duke of Tuscany. Giovan Carlo had been appointed Generalissimo of the Spanish fleet by King Philip IV in 1638 but quickly proved himself a seaman of no ability. He was created a cardinal in 1644 and is sometimes referred to as Giovan Carlo the Younger to distinguish him from his uncle Cardinal Carlo de' Medici (1596–1666). He was a patron and collector of great discernment, and owned works by Raphael, Piero di Cosimo, Parmigianino and Rubens. Three pictures formerly in his collection are in the National Gallery: Filippino Lippi's *Adoration of the Kings*, Correggio's *Madonna of the Basket* and Poussin's *Adoration of the Shepherds*. He was a patron of Pietro da Cortona, the Bolognese Agostino Mitelli and Angelo Michele Colonna, and of Rosa himself.[1] He was also the owner of two works now in the Mahon collection, this one and Reni's *Sibyl* (cat.62). Between 1641 and 1645 Rosa received a small monthly salary from Giovan Carlo and individual payments for each work he made for him. Altogether Rosa produced some fifteen paintings for the Prince. The *Landscape with Travellers asking the Way*, probably painted in 1641, was one of the first.[2] Among the others are the *Diogenes and Alexander* and the *Cincinnatus recalled from the Plough* (both Althorp, Earl Spencer collection), and the *Temptation of Saint Anthony* (Florence, Palazzo Pitti).[3] He also executed frescoes in Giovan Carlo's apartment in Palazzo Pitti.

The painting has no specific subject. Two riders seek directions from a trio of peasants by the side of the road. The setting is a bend in the path adjacent to a rocky outcrop and two of the figures point towards a vast sunlit valley beyond. In the middle distance are the silhouettes of two peasants making their way home after a day in the fields. Rosa had painted a similar subject at least once before when he was in Rome (fig.42), although the figures in that work are larger in scale and it is more a *bambocciata* than a landscape painting. Rosa's debt to the Bamboccianti – the artists, mostly foreigners, who lived in Rome and specialised in low-life genre subjects (see cats.50–1) – is obvious, particularly in the figures. In Rome Rosa was certainly familiar with Herman van Swanevelt and Jacques Courtois as all three had been engaged to paint landscapes for the Duke of Modena in 1640, and Rosa probably also knew Claude and Jan Asselijn. This work has perhaps most in common with the sunlit evening landscapes of

Jan Both, who was in Rome from about 1635 to 1641, although the execution is broader and the general effect more dramatic. Rosa was later to react violently to the subject matter of the Bamboccianti in his satire *Painting* written in 1650.[4]

Rosa makes a great show of the picturesque motifs for which his landscapes came to be admired: the sinewy twisting trunks with split and broken branches, the trailing ivy growing on the trees, the curious rock formations with cavernous recesses, and the heavy-leafed plants languishing in the foreground. In particular Rosa exploits the effects of evening light to create interesting juxtapositions of light and dark areas. The foreground gloom is enlivened with a shaft of warm yellow light that cuts through the trees and rocks at the left and picks out the figure group in the centre. The dramatic foreground contrasts are balanced by the placid evenly-lit distant view. The technical evidence suggests that the composition was carefully planned: the area occupied by the dark trunk on the right, for example, was left in reserve when the sky was being painted. The figures were painted after the landscape was completed.

TECHNICAL NOTE
The support is a moderately coarse twill canvas; a horizontal seam about 12 cm from the top edge runs along the whole width of the painting. The painting has been lined in the present century and the tacking edges have been cut off. The ground is brown but it has been thoroughly covered by the upper layers of paint. There is a repaired horizontal tear extending about 8 cm in from the left edge of the picture about two thirds of the way up. There is some retouching around the edges, at the corners and along the seam. A loss about the size of a new penny to the left of centre at the top edge has also been retouched. The browns in the painting have darkened a little and there has probably been some discoloration in the red lake on the saddle and breeches of the horseman on the right.[5] However, the painting is in very good condition.

PROVENANCE
Cardinal Prince Giovan Carlo de' Medici;[6] sold with most of his collection after his death in 1663; George Nassau, 3rd Earl Cowper (1738–89), Florence, by 1779;[7] later at Panshanger, Hertfordshire; Christie's, London, 16 October 1953 (Lady Desborough sale), lot 119, where acquired by the present owner.

EXHIBITIONS
Birmingham 1955, no.91; London 1960, no.364; London (Hayward Gallery) 1973, no.4; Cologne/Utrecht 1991–2, no.31.1.

Fig.42 Salvator Rosa, *Travellers asking the Way*, signed, late 1630s. Oil on canvas, 143.5 x 170.2 cm. Formerly with Matthiesen Fine Art Ltd, London.

1 See Mascalchi 1984; see also Mascalchi 1983–4 (unpublished).

2 Salerno (1963, p.370) correctly dated the work to the beginning of the 1640s before the connection with Giovan Carlo de' Medici was known. Helen Langdon pointed out the similarities with the Modena *Landscape with Erminia* painted in Rome in 1640, London (Hayward Gallery) 1973, p.20, under no.4.

3 Salerno 1975, nos.68, 69 and 73, respectively.

4 Scott 1995, pp.86–7.

5 Waagen described the painting when it was at Panshanger as follows: 'Another large landscape with horsemen, is carefully executed; but it wants keeping, as the foreground and middle distance have become dark', Waagen 1854/7, III, p.15.

6 Mascalchi 1984, pp.268 and 272. The painting is listed in the inventory of 1 January 1647, Casino di Via della Scala; also in the post-mortem inventory of 1663, Villa di Castello: 'Dua Quadri Bislunghi in Tela lunghi b.a 3–1/2 alti b.a 2–1/3 in c.a entrovi Paesi che uno vi è Albero e

Masso con Dua Viandanti e tre Villani che gl'inseguono la Strada con dua figurine più lontane et uno dei Viagganti sop.a un Cavallo Bianco e nel'Altro [...]. Adornamenti intagliati e dorati del Rosa', Mascalchi 1983–4 (unpublished), II, pp.557 and 708–9.

7 Inventory of Pictures belonging to William 3rd Lord Cowper c.1779 in Villa Palmieri and Villa Cipresso, Florence: 'No.20. Un Paese del Medesimo [Salvatore], Larghezzo [sic] 5 Piedi 5 Pollici (Mesura del Piede, Parigine) Altezza 3 Piedi 4 Pollici', Sutton 1956, p.83.

Salvator Rosa 1615–1673

67 Head of a Man with a Turban

Oil on canvas, 59.5 x 49.5 cm

This painting is of a type known in the seventeenth century as a 'testa di fantasia' or 'testaccia'. In a letter addressed to Giovanni Battista Ricciardi in Florence, written in Rome in January 1650, Rosa referred to two 'testace' he was sending.[1] Following his departure from Florence in 1649, Rosa seems to have nourished the friendships he had formed in Tuscany with gifts of paintings such as this one. On 16 February 1651 he wrote again to Ricciardi saying that he had sent him three 'heads, one for signor Lanfreducci and two for Signor Pandolfini'.[2] Rosa perhaps deemed them suitable presents on account of their strong characterisations, their antique or philosophical flavour and also, perhaps, the limited amount of effort required to produce them. Other works of this kind include the so-called *Diogenes*, formerly in the Bedford collection, the *Portrait of a Man* (New York, E.V.Thaw), and the octagonal so-called *Self Portrait* in a Roman private collection.[3] These pictures are all very similar in size.

Only the Mahon painting, however, has a recorded Florentine provenance. According to a mid-nineteenth-century manuscript catalogue of the Sebright pictures at Beechwood Park, the painting came from Palazzo Ridolfi in Florence.[4] In Baldinucci's Life of Salvator Rosa, which is rich in information concerning Rosa's contacts with Florence, two members of the Ridolfi family are named: the Marchese Ferdinando Ridolfi who, according to Baldinucci, commissioned a battle painting from Rosa when the artist was in Florence, and Luigi Ridolfi, who took part in the theatrical performances organised by the Accademia dei Percossi, the literary society established in Florence under

Rosa's auspices.[5] Since the 'testacce' seem to have been destined for his friends then the most likely recipient of the picture is Luigi Ridolfi. The picture is difficult to date but the confident technique and the brooding character of the image suggest a date in the 1650s.

In his subject paintings taken from classical history Rosa used this kind of turban-like headdress for sages or philosophers. The stern expression and the piercing gaze invest the figure with a deep seriousness that Rosa may have wanted viewers to associate with his pretensions to be recognised as a modern Stoic. The painting has been called 'an informal self portrait',[6] and although the resemblance with the certain self portraits (including the recently published *Self Portrait as Pascariello*)[7] is not especially compelling, the dark almond-shaped eyes, the long eyebrows and the elegant nose are certainly comparable. Baldinucci states that Rosa made use of a mirror in his room to study his own gestures and expressions in order to make pictures from them and perhaps this is the kind of painting that would have resulted.[8] It is not a self portrait, strictly speaking, therefore, but rather a 'testa di fantasia' based on his own features.

There are several drawings of 'teste di fantasia' which show men wearing turbans.[9] Some of these are executed in coloured chalks and must have been intended as finished works in their own right. Mahoney has proposed that a drawing in the collection of M. Alfred Norman, Paris, *A Bearded Man in a Cap*, may show the same sitter who posed for the Mahon painting, but the similarity is more likely due to the generic familial resemblance of Rosa's types.[10]

TECHNICAL NOTE
The support is a medium-weight plain-weave canvas. The tacking edges have been cut off but the painted area of the canvas has not been reduced. The painting was lined probably in the late nineteenth century. The ground is a brownish red but very little of it shows through. The surface is a little abraded and the lake pigment used for the thinly painted jacket has faded. By contrast the face and headgear are quite densely painted and survive in good condition.

PROVENANCE
(?) Ridolfi collection, Florence; Sebright Collection, Beechwood Park, by the mid-nineteenth century; Christie's, London, 2 July 1937 (Sir Giles Sebright, Bt, sale), lot 127 (bought in); Christie's, London, 18 January 1946 (Sir Egbert Saunders Sebright, Bt, sale), lot 77 (the lot included another Rosa of 'Four men conversing in a woody landscape'); Christie's, London, 26 April 1950, lot 97, where acquired by the present owner.

EXHIBITIONS
Barnard Castle 1962, no.43; London (Hayward Gallery) 1973, no.32.

1 De Rinaldis 1939, letter 1, p.5.
2 De Rinaldis 1939, letter 6, p.16; see also Limentani 1950, letters IV and V, pp.67 and 71–2. In April 1651 Pietro Pandolfini, who was from Siena and was then in Rome, commissioned a 'Testuccia' from Rosa to give to the Maestro di Camera of the papal Secretary of State, Cardinal Panziroli, see Limentani 1950, letter VII, pp.74–5.
3 Respectively: Christie's, 19 January 1951, lot 53, 64.8 x 48.3 cm, reproduced in Mahoney 1977, II, 31.12A; Salerno 1975, no.163, p.98, 63 x 47 cm; Salerno 1975, no.100, p.92 (no dimensions given).
4 'Beechwood Pictures: Oriel Room: Head by Salvator Rosa, From Ridolphi Palace Florence', presumably the Palazzo Stiozzi Ridolfi is meant. The manuscript catalogue (of which there is a typewritten copy in the National Gallery Library) can be dated to the mid-nineteenth century (because there is a reference to a picture by Champaigne as coming from the Louis Philippe Gallery which was sold in London in 1853). The picture was noted at Beechwood Park by Waagen (1854/7, supplement, p.329).
5 Baldinucci 1845–7, V, pp.449 and 452.
6 Briganti 1953, p.12.
7 Scott 1995, p.59 and fig.74. The portrait was exhibited at the National Gallery in 1993.
8 'Teneva egli però per entro la sua ben chiusa stanza un chiarissimo specchio di grandezza di più che mezz'uomo, davanti a cui si metteva a formare attitudini colla propria persona, e talora a comporre o scomporre la propria faccia, per quivi interamente cavare, o positure, o azioni, o affetti, secondo ciò, che richiedeva suo bisogno', Baldinucci 1845–7, V, p.487. Mahoney (1977, I, p.360) states that 'Rosa intensely studied his own face in a mirror, and thus probably absorbed his own features into his general repertoire of facial types'.
9 See Mahoney 1977, II, nos.31.3–7, 31.9, 31.11.
10 Mahoney 1977, II, no.31.2.

Salvator Rosa 1615–1673

68 *Landscape with Saint Anthony Abbot and Saint Paul the Hermit*

Oil on canvas, 67 x 49.2 cm

69 *Desolate Landscape with Two Figures*

Oil on canvas, 67.3 x 49.9 cm
Signed lower left with monogram: *SR* interlaced

In this pair of pictures, dating from the first half of the 1660s,[1] Rosa combines a popular religious subject, the meeting of Saints Anthony Abbot and Paul the Hermit, with an apparently subject-less secular scene. In spite of the figural presence the paintings are primarily evocative landscape paintings which have as their subject the awesomeness and grandeur of nature. The dramatic contrasts of scale and tone serve to heighten the sense of mystery and convey a mood of gloom and menace. In an often-quoted letter of 1662 written to his friend Giovanni Battista Ricciardi after he had returned from a trip to Loreto, Rosa expressed his appreciation of the 'wild beauty' of the Apennine mountain scenery and his longing for the 'most solitary hermitages' that he had passed along the way.[2] The paintings seem to express one of the paradoxical themes of Rosa's late work: the artist's yearning for withdrawal from the corruption and stresses of urban life and the savage and inhospitable character of nature.

Late in his career Rosa seems to have preferred to paint small landscapes. They continued to be much sought after, a fact which was the cause of increasing irritation to him since he felt that his success as a painter of landscapes eclipsed his achievement as a figure painter. In a wry comment in a letter to Ricciardi in 1666 Rosa referred to the physical deterioration which some of his landscapes had suffered due to poor technique: 'I'm delighted that many of these paintings of mine are going to ruin so that people will forget that I ever painted landscape.'[3] These two modest but impressive paintings are unlikely to have been commissioned works.

The fourth-century founder of monasticism, Saint Anthony Abbot, sought out Saint Paul, the first hermit, in the wilderness he had made his home. Each day at noon a raven delivered bread to Saint Paul for his sustenance and the bird can just be made out above the saints. By the time Rosa painted this picture the landscape with anchorite subject was an established genre. An entire series of anchorite landscapes was commissioned in Rome in the mid-1630s from Claude, Poussin, Gaspard

Dughet, and other painters, to hang in the newly built Buen Retiro Palace in Madrid, which was set in gardens dotted with hermitages.[4] Rosa's interest in hermit subjects was long standing but became especially marked towards the end of his career. In about 1661, near to the time when he executed these pictures, he also painted the large

Saint Paul the Hermit for the church of Santa Maria della Vittoria in Milan, commissioned by Cardinal Luigi Omodei, in which the saint is shown by a brook in a forest of gnarled trees.[5] He also produced in the same period the two etchings of Saint William of Maleval and his disciple Albert, two particularly austere twelfth-

century hermits who had lived in Malevalle, close to Ricciardi's villa, Strozzavolpe, near Siena, where Rosa spent many pleasurable months. Two other paintings by Rosa, similar in style, date and subject to the Mahon pictures, have been thought to belong to the same series.[6]

Briganti has highlighted the importance of these kinds of pictures by Rosa for the landscapes of the Genoese Alessandro Magnasco and the Veneto painter Marco Ricci.[7]

TECHNICAL NOTE

The pictures form a pair. They are painted on plain-weave, moderately coarse canvas. Both paintings are lined, probably in the later nineteenth century and the stretchers date from the same time. Parts of the tacking edges survive. The ground is a warm terracotta but the artist has allowed it to show through only in very few areas. The surface of both pictures is moderately worn and there are retouchings in the ultramarine skies which have discoloured. The general tone of the pictures has darkened a little with the passage of time. There are no obvious pentimenti. Both stretchers are inscribed in ink: *SALVATORE ROSA, BORN 1615, DIED 1673.*

PROVENANCE

Andrew Hay, by whom sold to Edward Harley, 2nd Earl of Oxford (1689–1741), before 1716;[8] his sale, 8–13 March 1742, day three, lots 50 and 51 ('50. A Landskip and Figures, Salvator Rosa; 51. Its companion.'), bought by the Duchess of Bedford; Dukes of Bedford, chiefly at Woburn Abbey;[9] acquired by the present owner at Christie's, London, 19 January 1951 (Duke of Bedford sale), lot 52.

EXHIBITIONS

Zürich 1956, nos.224 and 225; London 1960, nos.405 and 410; Bassano del Grappa 1963, nos.1 and 2; *Landscape with Saint Anthony Abbot and Saint Paul the Hermit* was shown in Detroit 1965, no.157; *Desolate Landscape with Two Figures* was shown in London (Kenwood) 1967, no.17.

1 Salerno (1963, p.127, nos.56–7) dates them to about the same time as the *Crucifixion of Policrates* (Chicago, Art Institute), painted shortly after 1662.
2 The relevant section is quoted in London (Hayward Gallery) 1973, p.15.
3 Quoted in Scott 1995, p.192.
4 Brown and Elliott 1980, pp.125–7.
5 Salerno 1963, no.52, p.126; Salerno 1975, no.157.
6 Salerno 1975, nos.250 and 251. A copy, possibly autograph, of the Mahon *Desolate Landscape with Two Figures* is in Nantes, see Sarrazin 1994, no. 175, p.228.
7 Briganti 1953, p.12.
8 '4. Two fine pieces of Salvador Rosa, (price paid: £60)', in a list of 1716 of pictures bought by Edward Harley from Andrew Hay, see Goulding and Adams 1936, p.XXX.
9 For references to the pictures while at Woburn, see London 1960, p.165, under no.405.

Andrea Sacchi 1599/1600–1661

70 Saint Anthony of Padua reviving a Dead Man

Oil on panel, 110.7 x 76.2 cm

The work is a reduced replica of the altarpiece Sacchi painted in 1633–4 for a chapel in the newly built Capuchin church of Santa Maria della Concezione, Rome. The church, which was dedicated in August 1636, was under the protection of the Barberini who undertook to adorn the chapels. Altarpieces were commissioned from Guido Reni, Mario Balassi, Giovanni Lanfranco, Cortona and two from Sacchi (*Saint Anthony* and *The Vision of Saint Bonaventure*). All, except for Lanfranco's *Immaculate Conception*, which was destroyed by fire in 1813, are still *in situ*. Domenichino donated his *Stigmatisation of Saint Francis*, now on the third altar on the right of the church, in fulfilment of a vow. Although payments for Sacchi's altarpieces are not documented, both Passeri and Bellori state that they were commissioned by Cardinal Antonio Barberini the Elder (1569–1646), brother of Pope Urban VIII.[1] In both the present painting and the related altarpiece (which measures approximately 290 x 200 cm) a Barberini bee appears in the corner of the niche.

The *Saint Anthony* altarpiece was certainly in place for the dedication of the church in 1636 and the stylistic evidence of the surviving preparatory drawings suggests a date between 1632 and 1635.[2] The statue seen in the niche, which is a recognisable portrayal of the *Santa Susanna* by the Flemish sculptor François Duquesnoy (1597–1643), helps to establish a more accurate date for the altarpiece. Duquesnoy's statue was placed on the high altar of the church of Santa Maria di Loreto in Rome in the early spring of 1633,[3] and since it is extremely unlikely that Sacchi would have preempted its unveiling, that date can probably constitute a *terminus post quem*. The altarpiece may be supposed to have been completed shortly afterwards. The presence of the *Santa Susanna* in the painting should be considered a *petit hommage* by Sacchi to his friend,[4] but the story of the biblical Susannah, who was unjustly accused of a crime she did not commit and was eventually proved innocent (Daniel 13), has parallels with the narrative of the altarpiece.

Saint Anthony was miraculously transported from Padua to Lisbon, where his father had been accused of murdering a youth (Sacchi shows the knife wound in the chest). The saint had the corpse exhumed, revived the young man and commanded him to prove his father's innocence. The pallid colour of the revived youth is contrasted with that of the ruddy sextons, one of whom emerges dramatically from the burial vault holding a candle. The composition and the poses of the two protagonists recall Sebastiano del Piombo's *Raising of Lazarus* (London, National Gallery).[5] The two putti bear the saint's traditional attributes of book and lily.

The painting has been considered Sacchi's preparatory *modello* for the altarpiece.[6] Although it is painted with great freedom, the composition, gestures and expressions correspond more closely with the altarpiece than one would expect in a *modello* and the absence of any significant pentimenti confirms the impression that this is a reduced replica rather than a preparatory oil sketch.[7] The picture was presumably made for the patron himself, or for a member of his family, soon after the execution of the altarpiece. There are several instances of Sacchi making copies of his own works for important clients.[8]

There are three references to paintings of *Saint Anthony of Padua reviving a Dead Man* in the published Barberini inventories of the seventeenth century.[9] The post-mortem inventory of Sacchi's possessions also lists a version of the composition, but this has not been identified.[10] Two other painted versions of the composition associated with Sacchi belong to the Galleria Nazionale d'Arte Antica in Rome. One came from the Corsini collection and is still in the Galleria in Palazzo Corsini (oil on canvas, 67 x 51 cm), and the other is in Palazzo Barberini (oil on canvas, 64 x 48.5 cm). Neither is of autograph quality.[11]

TECHNICAL NOTE

The support is made up of two vertical planks. The join has been strengthened on the reverse with oak butterflies. There is a vertical split in each of the two planks forming the panel and the split on the right-hand plank, about 14 cm from the right edge, has a thin wooden insert which is visible from the back. The splits have also been strengthened with oak butterflies. At the lower edge of the painting a strip about 7 mm wide remains unpainted. The painting is in excellent condition. Two minor pentimenti are apparent: the outline of the top of the saint's head has been slightly modified and the little finger of the left hand of the acolyte in the left foreground has been altered.

PROVENANCE

Probably identical with a picture listed in the 1692 inventory of paintings belonging to Cardinal Carlo Barberini (1630–1704), Rome;[12] with Malcolm Waddingham (according to Colnaghi files); noticed by chance by the present owner in a warehouse in Paris around 1960 and acquired in London from Colnaghi in 1961. The frame is an original Barberini frame but comes from the *Saint Bernard offering his Rule to the Virgin* by Pietro da Cortona now in the Toledo Museum, Ohio.

EXHIBITIONS
London (Colnaghi) 1961, no.2; Bologna 1962, no.135.

1 Passeri 1934, p.297, and Bellori 1976, pp.549–50. Saint Anthony was, of course, the patron saint of Cardinal Antonio; for the *Vision of Saint Bonaventure*, painted 1635–6, see Sutherland Harris 1977, pp.78–9.
2 Sutherland Harris (1977, pp.70–1) lists seven preparatory drawings for the *Saint Anthony*.
3 Mahon 1962, pp.66–7.
4 Passeri, who reports Sacchi's great enthusiasm for the sculpture, puzzlingly states that he included it in his picture because he wanted to offend another artist, but he mentions no names (1934, p.108). Hess assumed this was Bernini, but see Sutherland Harris 1977, p.31.
5 It is not clear whether Sacchi could have known it, since it was in Narbonne. It bears a closer resemblance to the Sacchi than Cigoli's altarpiece of *Saint Peter healing the Lame Man* made for St Peter's (now lost) which is usually proposed as the source (and which Sacchi is known to have admired).
6 Nicolson 1961, pl.1; Andrea Emiliani in Bologna 1962, pp.331–2.
7 The preparatory *modello* is almost certainly identifiable with the painting on panel (65.3 x 43 cm) now in the collection of Prince Augusto Barberini, Rome.
8 A full-scale replica (now untraced) of the *Three Mary Magdalenes* was made for Cardinal Antonio Barberini, probably in the 1640s, and Sacchi made for Pope Alexander VII Chigi a reduced version of his celebrated *Vision of Saint Romuald* of 1631, receiving payment for it in 1658, see Sutherland Harris 1977, pp.68 and 61, respectively. Several reduced versions of Sacchi's public commissions are listed in the artist's own inventory.
9 Two are listed in the 1671 post-mortem inventory of Cardinal Antonio Barberini the Younger (1607–71), nephew of Pope Urban VIII. The first (see Aronberg Lavin 1975, p.306, no.299) is identifiable as the painting in the collection of Prince Augusto Barberini, see note 7; the second (ibid., p.313, no.426) is described as on copper and remains untraced (it is probably the picture which was seen by De Cotte in Palazzo Barberini in about 1689 and was then referred to by Rossi and Panciroli in 1719, see Sutherland Harris 1977, p.70). The third is almost certainly the Mahon painting, see under Provenance. I am indebted to Rossella Vodret for help with these identifications.
10 'Un quadro con S[an]to Antonio di Padova, che risuscita un morto con altre figure con cornice negra e dorata', Sutherland Harris 1977, p.121 (no.197).
11 A third version in a private collection in Rome mentioned by Posse (1925, p.60) was declared by Emiliani in Bologna 1962, p.331, to be a copy of the altarpiece by a hand other than Sacchi's.
12 'Un S.Antonio che risuscita un morto con Cornice di ebano fatto a Prospettiva con un S.Michele Arcangelo in cima al:p.mi 5.1:4 [presumably 5 1/4] di Andrea Sacchi', Aronberg Lavin 1975, p.435, no.174. Although the support is not identified in the entry, the height given is equivalent to 117.1 cm, which is close to the Mahon picture's 110.7 cm.

Andrea Sacchi 1599/1600–1661

71 *The Baptism of Christ*

Oil on panel, 29.7 x 40.3cm (oval)
Inscribed on reverse: *Andreę Sacchi Pict.*

The painting is a reduced version of the central part of Sacchi's *Baptism of Christ* (fig.43), one of the series of eight canvas paintings of stories of Saint John the Baptist painted between 1641 and 1649 for the lantern of the Lateran Baptistery (known as San Giovanni in Fonte), Rome. The paintings measure 310 x 250 cm and they now hang in the adjacent Lateran Palace. In 1968 they were replaced in the lantern by copies. The series formed part of a larger decorative scheme which includes fresco scenes of the stories of Constantine, an allegory of Innocent X, *trompe l'oeil* bronze medallions and flying putti. The frescoes were only partly executed by Sacchi. His increasing lack of self-confidence at this time led him to entrust the large fresco scenes to Carlo Maratti, Camassei and others.[1]

Sacchi's *Baptism* is one of his most famous compositions and was much copied in the seventeenth and eighteenth centuries.[2] Four 'Baptisms of Christ' are recorded in the artist's post-mortem inventory of 1661, one of which would appear to be identifiable with the present picture, and the Barberini, who had paid for the reconstruction and redecoration of the Lateran Baptistery, themselves owned three.[3]

Sacchi's composition is indebted to the equally celebrated *Baptism of Christ* by his teacher Francesco Albani, made for the church of San Giorgio in Bologna and now in the Pinacoteca Nazionale (428 x 224 cm). Sacchi visited Bologna during the trip he made to northern Italy between July 1635 and August 1636 and would have seen the painting then. While in Bologna he made a portrait of Albani, which is now in the Prado. Albani's painting has a tall altarpiece format and shows God the Father surrounded by angels at the top of the picture. Sacchi's *Baptism* is less tall and only the head of God the Father is seen (although the surface of the painting is now so worn that it is hardly visible) rather than a whole figure group. It does, however, have the clarity and simplicity of composition of Albani's work and it shares the lyrical sentiment expressed in the poses and gestures of Albani's figures. In both paintings there are two attendant angels who take hold of Christ's garments, one of whom looks at Christ and the other at the descending dove of the Holy Spirit.

As might be considered appropriate for a reduced version, any extraneous detail is excluded in this picture: the angels and the distant figures are not shown and the background is muted. The luminosity of the picture is particularly striking given the much darkened state of the Baptistery picture. The figures are very close to those in the larger picture and they are painted with extraordinary delicacy. The principal difference, of course, is that they are half length. Sutherland Harris thought that the painting had been trimmed from a rectangular or square format and considered that the wooden support was so unusual for Sacchi that the painting might be by Sacchi's pupil Maratti.[4] Although an examination of the panel suggests that it was trimmed after the execution of the painting, there is no way of knowing how soon after it was done; nor is it possible to tell whether the painting was originally square or rectangular and if the figures were ever shown full length. The absence of the angels and the smaller figures indicate that it was never an exact replica on a reduced scale of the Baptistery picture.

The picture should, it seems, be identified with the 'small oval painting showing Saint John and Jesus Christ being baptised', which is listed in the artist's post-mortem inventory of 1661 (see Provenance). No other oval painting of this subject by Sacchi or Maratti is recorded in the seventeenth-century or later sources. The entry does not state that the picture is on panel, but only very rarely is the type of support specified in the inventory. Sacchi is known to have painted on panel on several occasions and stylistically the work is acceptable as by him rather than by Maratti. If an autograph work by Sacchi it must date from no earlier than 1644, when a *Baptism* by Sacchi, presumably based on the Baptistery picture, was listed in the collection of Cardinal Antonio Barberini the Younger (1607–71).[5] The present picture should probably be situated in the second half of the 1640s.

TECHNICAL NOTE

The support is a single piece of poplar approximately 1.1 cm thick. The paint surface continues to the very edge of the panel. The edge is roughly sawn and it would appear to have been cut after the painting was finished. There is a repaired split which runs diagonally across the lower half of the panel. Two battens, applied cross grain, have been nailed and glued to the reverse, presumably after the panel split. The painting is in excellent condition. There are no signs of pentimenti. The ground is a warm reddish brown.

Fig.43 Andrea Sacchi, *Baptism of Christ, c.*1643. Oil on canvas, 310 x 250 cm. Rome, Lateran Palace.

PROVENANCE
Probably identical with a painting in Sacchi's post-mortem inventory of 1661: '40. Un Quadretto ovato con San Gio[vanni] Batt[ist]a e Giesù Christo che si battezza';[6] acquired by the present owner from Colnaghi's in 1972.

EXHIBITIONS
London (Colnaghi) 1972, no.60.

1 Sutherland Harris 1977, pp.84–9.
2 Bellori singled it out as the finest of the series, Bellori 1976, p.563.
3 Sutherland Harris 1977, pp.88–9. Several others are listed there.
4 Sutherland Harris 1977, p.89.
5 '28 Un quadro p sopraporto con Cristo battezato nel Giordano da S. Gio.ta di mano del Sacchi con cornice tutta dorata', inventory of April 1644, Aronberg Lavin 1975, p.159.
6 Sutherland Harris 1977, p.119.

Lo Scarsellino (Ippolito Scarsella) *c.*1550–1620

72 The Holy Family with Saint John the Baptist

Oil on panel, 28 x 20.8 cm
Inscribed on the reverse: *SCHEDONE*

Scarsellino was the leading painter in Ferrara in the late sixteenth and early seventeenth centuries, in the period when the city passed from the courtly but inefficient government of the Este Dukes to the stern control of the Church. Together with the late Mannerist painter Domenico Mona (*c.*1550–1602), he designed and painted the triumphal arches which greeted Pope Clement VIII Aldobrandini when he came to reclaim the city for the papacy in 1598. The event left a profound mark on the city and on Scarsellino, who all but abandoned non-religious painting and adopted a more introverted and meditative manner in the last two decades of his activity.

According to Baruffaldi, writing nearly a century after the artist's death, when Scarsellino was 17 he went to Bologna for nearly two years to study the works of contemporary artists, including the Carracci, and subsequently spent four years in Venice where he was a pupil of Veronese.[1] Although a measure of scepticism with regard to this source may be appropriate – the Carracci were not yet active when Scarsellino was learning to paint – the apprenticeship with Veronese rings true, since Scarsellino's early works reveal an evident debt to the forms and bright saturated colours of Veronese. He was employed by the Este in the early 1590s to paint decorative canvases in the Palazzo dei Diamanti in Ferrara, together with Gaspare Venturini (1570–1617) and Ludovico Carracci. There seems to have been a fruitful artistic exchange with Ludovico. From an early date Scarsellino showed an interest in landscape which seems to anticipate some of Annibale Carracci's concerns. He painted altarpieces and frescoes and after 1598 he was engaged with Carlo Bononi (1569–1632) to make copies of the sixteenth-century altarpieces in Ferrarese churches which were to be removed and taken to Rome; his copy of Girolamo da Carpi's *Virgin appearing to Giulia Muzzarelli* (Washington, National Gallery of Art) is in the church of San Francesco. Scarsellino's painting is rooted in the rich native tradition of Ferrara, but it shows fascinating and continuing links with Venetian and Bolognese painting, with Palma Giovane and with Guido Reni, for example. Scarsellino was admired by Guercino[2] and the rich pastose handling, spontaneous, but often jerky and nervous, had an influence on the work of Giuseppe Maria Crespi (cats.15–17).

The present work is one of a group of small devotional paintings showing the Virgin and Child or the Holy Family, which Scarsellino made mostly in the early part of his career. They are often datable only on stylistic grounds. There are two other versions of the Mahon picture: one, on panel, is in the Uffizi and has usually been thought of as the earliest version,[3] and another, on copper, is in the Molinari Pradelli collection in Bologna.[4] Because of its 'Venetian' colouring, Francesco Arcangeli dated the Molinari Pradelli picture to about 1585, adding that the Mahon picture, which had a more typically Scarsellinesque character, probably dated from a few years later.[5] The composition and colouring of all three pictures show a debt to Venice: the elegant turn of the head of the Virgin, the foreshortened view of Christ and the animated pose of Saint Joseph recall Tintoretto, and the intense colours are reminiscent of early works by Titian.

TECHNICAL NOTE
The support is a single-member wood panel with two battens (almost certainly not original) applied horizontally, cross-grain. Four strips of wood approximately 2–3 mm wide have been applied to all four sides. The reverse of the panel has been covered with a gesso-like material. There is evidence of worm damage on the reverse of the panel at upper left. There is a small area of retouching in the sky and there are signs of abrasion (probably from cleaning) on the flank of the sheep in the lower left-hand corner but in general the painting is in a good state. The ground is a warm ochre. There are no obvious signs of underdrawing or pentimenti.

PROVENANCE
Earls of Pembroke, Wilton House, before 1731, as by Schedoni;[6] by descent until sold at Christie's, 22 June 1951 (Pembroke sale), lot 57 (as 'Bartolommeo Schedoni'), where acquired by the present owner.

1 Baruffaldi 1844–6, II, pp.67–9.
2 See Mahon 1937, and Briganti's comments on this picture (1953, p.8).
3 27 x 20 cm, Uffizi Catalogo 1979, Inv.P.1428, p.474; Novelli 1964, no.140, pp.38–9.
4 26.4 x 22.6 cm, see Bologna 1959, no.126; Novelli 1964, no.11, pp.27–8.
5 Bologna 1959, no.126.
6 The painting is described in Carlo Gambarini's 1731 catalogue of the Wilton House collection: 'Bart. Schedoni; Christ in the Virgin's arms and St John hugging him; Joseph and the lamb looking on; his very best manner so that some have taken it for Correggio' (quoted in Wilkinson 1907, II, p.267, no.81).

Bartolomeo Schedoni 1578–1615

73 *The Coronation of the Virgin*

Oil on panel (possibly oak), 47 x 38 cm

Schedoni was the son of a maskmaker employed at the ducal courts of Modena and Parma. He was precociously gifted as an artist and in 1595 was sent by Duke Ranuccio I Farnese of Parma to Rome to train with Federico Zuccaro; by 1597 he was officially in the Duke's employ as a painter.[1] He was prone to a disorderly life of fighting and gambling, however, and after a short spell in prison in 1600 he left Parma for Modena where he became court painter to Cesare d'Este. He executed numerous works for the Duke and decorative canvases with obscure classical subjects for the Palazzo Comunale (1607).[2] His early works show a clear debt to Correggio, and Schedoni came to be thought of as 'Correggio reborn'.[3] The contrast between his unruly and violent life and his refined and delicate style has often attracted comment. After another brief prison term in 1607 he returned to Parma and signed a contract to work exclusively for Ranuccio Farnese, who held him in great esteem. Almost all the important works he painted between 1608 and his early death (apparently by suicide) in 1615 were made for the Duke and today they are principally in Parma and in the Museum of Capodimonte in Naples. In addition to the altarpieces and small easel paintings of devotional subjects for which he is best known, he painted numerous frescoes but of these lamentably little survives. His activity as a sculptor has just begun to be studied.[4]

Schedoni's distinctive style, so evident in the two paintings in the Mahon collection, is rooted in the art of his native Emilia. Correggio and Parmigianino were his constant points of reference but he was alive to the innovations of the Carracci in Bologna, to their naturalism and their novel use of light. There remains in his painting, however, something courtly, highly refined and precious. This is especially apparent in the small devotional pictures in which these qualities appear in distilled form.

The *Coronation of the Virgin*, the same subject as the Annibale Carracci in this exhibition (cat.8), corresponds with the fifth Glorious Mystery of the Rosary. Cherubs frolic among the clouds, disregarding the solemnity of the divine event. A warm light gently radiates from the dove of the Holy Spirit and illuminates the figures from above, throwing the elegant profile of Christ into shadow and highlighting the Virgin's bright red robe and the right palm of God the Father. The crystal globe, signifying the Father's majesty, also catches the light. The

modelling of the forms and draperies is simplified and the painter uses mid-tones sparingly. The colouring is delicate and the overall effect of the painting is defined by the subtle juxtapositions of green and blue-grey, rose and grey-white. One of Schedoni's favourite motifs, that of a head turned to look out at the viewer over an extended arm, is repeated here several times.

The chronology of Schedoni's oeuvre is uncertain and as regards the small devotional pictures one is forced to rely on stylistic analysis. Generally speaking, Schedoni's paintings become increasingly graceful in style and refined in execution during the course of his brief career. Miller has sought to define a small corpus of Modenese works on the basis of stylistic and typological similarities with the documented works in the Palazzo Comunale.[5] The present work does not conform closely with these and a date in the early years after his return to Parma, perhaps about 1608–10, seems most likely.[6]

Technical note

The panel support is probably oak; two hardwood battens are inserted horizontally into the reverse. There is a brand, repeated once, on the back, probably the mark of the panel maker. An inscription in a dark pigment states '[Sc]hidone', the first two letters hidden by a paper label. The painting is in good condition. Originally Christ's robe would have been redder, but the red lake pigments have faded; the Virgin's robe is almost certainly azurite and has darkened considerably. The contours of the right arms of God the Father and Christ, as well as those of their heads, have been adjusted by the artist. The upper section of God the Father's cloak above his left shoulder may have been added once the painting was in its frame as it stops abruptly a few millimetres from the right edge of the panel.

Provenance

Acquired from a 'célèbre galerie italienne' by Rénault-César-Louis de Choiseul, Duc de Praslin (ambassador at Naples, 1766–71);[7] his sale, Paris, 21 February 1793, lot 8 (bought by the dealer Jean-Baptiste Pierre Lebrun); Colonel John Trumbull (1756–1843), the American painter, who held a diplomatic post in Paris; his sale, Christie's, London, 17 February 1797, lot 37 (with Duc de Praslin provenance given);[8] Dukes of Hamilton; Christie's, London, 24 June 1882 (12th Duke of Hamilton sale), lot 372; 1st Earl of Plymouth (1857–1923), Hewell, Worcs;[9] his daughter, Lady Phyllis Benton; her sale, Sotheby's, London, 26 April 1950, lot 131, where acquired by the present owner.

Exhibitions

London 1960, no.374.

1 For Schedoni, see Moschini 1927; Miller 1973; Lodi 1978; Miller 1986; Negro/Pirondini 1994, pp.235–60 (an extensive bibliography is on pp.239–40).
2 See Vedriani 1662, pp.108–12, and Miller 1979; two scenes from the Palazzo Comunale decoration are reproduced in colour in Negro/Pirondini 1994, figs.320–1.
3 See, for example, Vedriani (1662): 'Se vera fosse la pazza opinione ... che teneva la trasmigrazione delle anime ... dir si potrebbe, che quella d'Antonio da Correggio fosse passata ... ad informare il corpo di Bartolomeo Schidoni', quoted in Negro/Pirondini 1994, p.236.
4 See Negro/Pirondini 1994, p.236 and figs.299–302.
5 Miller 1979. He includes among the Modenese works the *Holy Family* at Burghley House, another in the Audisio collection, Parma, and two full-length groups of the *Holy Family with Saint John the Baptist* in the Palazzo Pitti, Florence, and in the Galleria Corsini in Rome (all illustrated).
6 Briganti thought it should be dated to shortly before 1600 because it is 'more Parmese in feeling' (1953, p.8). However, it should be noted that he thought this when it was still believed that Schedoni was born in about 1570 rather than 1578.
7 A.J. Paillet, *Catalogue des Tableaux ... de feu M.Choiseul-Praslin*, Paris, 1792, p.4, no.8.
8 See Waagen 1854/7, III, p.304, who misidentifies the subject: 'SCHIDONE – The Assumption of the Virgin; a beautiful little picture, of nobler conception than usual'.
9 A paper label on the reverse of the panel states 'The Earl of Plymouth/ –P[?] 9'.

Bartolomeo Schedoni 1578–1615

74 The Holy Family, with the Virgin teaching the Child to read

Oil on panel (possibly fruitwood), 33.8 x 28.2 cm

Schedoni painted numerous small paintings of the Holy Family, sometimes with the addition of Saint John.[1] They mostly seem to date from the years when he was settled in Parma, from 1607 to 1615, in the service of Ranuccio I Farnese, although he certainly also painted them earlier (see under cat.73). According to the terms of his contract, he could work for other patrons only if the Duke permitted it, but it seems clear that Ranuccio had no objection to Schedoni producing these modest works for domestic devotion.[2] There are also numerous workshop copies and versions of these pictures.

This painting, executed with great delicacy and skill, is one of the most beautiful and of the finest quality. The influence of Correggio's small religious paintings is apparent but the dark tone has been thought to reflect Schedoni's interest in the later works of Ludovico Carracci.[3] The close-knit composition, the nearness of the figures to the picture plane, and the golden light that bathes the scene, create a powerful sense of human intimacy and familial warmth. The lack of self-consciousness of the figures and the tender gestures, like the child's hand resting on his mother's thumb, enhance the naturalness of the representation. It is paintings of this kind which seem to have had a formative influence on the young Guercino (see for example cat.39).

An autograph variant of the painting in the Ashmolean Museum, probably earlier in date, includes the figure of the young Saint John the Baptist, who is being helped to read by the Christ Child.[4] A variant of that picture is in the Palazzo Pitti in Florence.[5]

According to an inscription on the reverse, the Mahon painting belonged to Schedoni's wife, Barbara Saliti, whom he married in 1613. She gave it to her mother, Violante Cacciardina, who sold it in 1618. It is thus probable that the painting dates from the last two years of Schedoni's life. Indeed, the painting may have been occasioned by the birth of the couple's son, Ranuccio, in July 1615.

TECHNICAL NOTE

The support is a single panel of hardwood, possibly fruitwood. There are two inset battens on the reverse. Old handmade nails are inserted in all four edges, conceivably to stretch a piece of fabric over the reverse. The painting is in good condition, although there is a small vertical split at the top. The ground layer is dark in colour. The azurite of the Virgin's robe has darkened considerably.

A paper label on the reverse is inscribed: 'Schidone 80/ La vierge ensignats/ a lire a l'enfant J[esus]'; in ink on the panel itself: '7bre 1645/ Da M. l'Arcivescovo d'Es'[6] and then a separate large inscription in ink: *225*; another pen inscription below: 'Opera del Sig.ʳ Bartol:ᵒ Schedone comprata dalla Sig.ʳᵃ Violante/ Cacciardina sua socera [added above the line: l'anno 1618 il di 7ᵒ di Novembre (the last three words uncertain)] et a lei donata dalla Sigʳᵃ Barbara sua figliola/ che era [the word moglie crossed out] pri[ma] moglie del dᵒ Sigʳ Schedone hora Moglie/ del Sʳ flaminio Scotti[?] Parmeg.ᵒ'

PROVENANCE[7]

The painter's wife, Barbara Saliti; given by her to her mother Violante Cacciardina; sold by Violante in 1618;[8] Michel Mazarin (1607–48), Archbishop of Aix, by 1645, and (presumably) donated by him to his brother Cardinal Jules Mazarin (1602–61) in September 1645;[9] listed in the inventories of his collection in 1653 and 1661;[10] Monsieur Coypel (a member of the family of painters, probably Antoine, 1661–1722, or his father Noël, 1628–1707); Ducs d'Orléans;[11] remained in the Palais Royal until the French Revolution, when imported into England and acquired by the Duke of Bridgewater; Lord Francis Egerton (afterwards 1st Earl of Ellesmere), Bridgewater House, London; acquired by the present owner at Christie's, London, 18 October 1946 (Ellesmere sale), lot 150.

EXHIBITIONS

Rome 1956–7, no.278; Bologna 1959, no.106; London 1960, no.408.

1 See Kultsen 1970.
2 The contract is quoted in Lodi 1978, pp.51–2; Miller 1982 discusses the episode in 1611 in which an altarpiece painted by Schedoni for the Magnanini chapel in Fanano Cathedral (the *Holy Family in Glory worshipped by Saints*, now Naples, Museo di Capodimonte) was sequestrated by the agents of the Duke and a declaration issued that no works by the artist should be taken out of the city.
3 London 1960, p.168, under no.408.
4 Inv.A789, oil on panel, 23 x 21 cm.
5 Oil on panel, 25.5 x 20.2 cm, see Borea 1975, no.52; workshop copies of the Pitti picture are in the Galleria Estense, Modena (oil on panel, 31 x 24 cm), the Kerr collection, Melbourne, Derbyshire (oil on panel, 10 x 8 inches, see Courtauld Institute photograph B62/691), and Christie's, London, 19 January 1951 (Duke of Bedford sale), lot 59 (oil on panel, 10 x 8 inches).
6 The 'Arcivescovo d'Es', or Archbishop of Aix, at this date, September 1645, was Michel Mazarin, younger brother of Cardinal Jules Mazarin. Michel was made a cardinal in 1647.
7 The provenance is fully set out in London 1960, no.408.
8 This information is gleaned from the inscription on the reverse.
9 Mahon has suggested very plausibly that it was given to Jules Mazarin as a token of gratitude for his part in Michel's elevation to the archbishopric of Aix, see London 1960, p.168, under no.408.
10 The number 225 on the reverse of the panel corresponds with the number of the picture in the Mazarin inventory of 1653: '225. Nostre Dame et nostre Seigneur qui lisent et St Joseph auprès, en petit, la bordure dorée ... Schidone' (Duc d'Aumale 1861, p.319, no.225). In the 1661 inventory it is given the relatively high valuation of 500 *livres tournois*, but erroneously stated to be on canvas: '1057. Un autre faict par Schidonna, sur toille, représentant une Nostre-Dame avecq Nostre-Seigneur qui lizent et sainct Joseph, hault d'un pied et large de dix poulces, garny de sa bordure de bois doré, prisé la somme de cinq cens livres, cy ... 500 L.T.' (Comte de Cosnac 1885, p.312, no.1057).
11 Dubois de Saint Gelais 1727, p.90 (with provenance from 'M.Coypel'); Galerie du Palais Royal 1786/1808, I, no.1 of Schedoni, engraved in reverse by Romanet, and with an account of the picture including a faulty but recognisable transcription of the handwritten statement on the reverse.

Francesco Solimena 1657–1747

75 Madonna and Child enthroned with Saint Peter Martyr and Two Warrior Saints

Oil on canvas, 75 x 59.5 cm

The painting is a preparatory oil sketch for Solimena's altarpiece of *Santa Maria dei Martiri* (fig.44) in the church of San Pietro Martire in Naples.[1] The altarpiece was made for the Cafatino Chapel, the fourth chapel on the left, which houses the tomb of Giovanni Cafatino (died 1540), a generous benefactor of the church, and his brother Paolo. The chapel was originally dedicated to Saint Dominic but towards the end of the seventeenth century it was rededicated to the Virgin of Martyrs and Saint Lucy.[2] A stone tablet on the left wall records that the chapel was restored in 1705. Solimena received payments for the altarpiece in 1707.[3]

Solimena was the leading painter in Naples after Luca Giordano's departure for Spain in 1692. His style is similarly flamboyant, although he had a lighter touch, and in the later decades of

his lengthy career it became more classicising. He painted large history pictures, altarpieces and frescoes, as well as portraits and small-scale paintings; his work was admired throughout Europe and much in demand among the princes and aristocracy of France, Spain and Austria. He had a large number of pupils, among them the Scottish painter Allan Ramsay.[4]

The sketch shows the Virgin enthroned on a classical altar with a sculpted relief of a bull being led to sacrifice. The Christ Child is about to hand down the palm of martyrdom, while the angel to the left holds the crown of victory. The Dominican saint with a rope around his neck is Saint Peter Martyr, who was murdered by heretics in 1252. The two soldiers are the Roman martyrs Paul and John, the patron saints of the Cafatino brothers, who were members of the imperial household and were put to death by Julian the Apostate in 362 when they refused to abjure their Christian faith.[5] The differences between the oil sketch and the altarpiece are few: the pose of the central putto in the present work is a little more dynamic and he looks up instead of straight ahead; the shape of the shield on which he sits is slightly different, and the sculpted relief on the base of the Virgin's throne is less elaborate than in the altarpiece. The sketch includes an architectural setting of stone arch and pilasters which approximates the arrangement in the chapel itself.

The painting is a striking example of the technique which Solimena developed to enable him to paint elaborate figure compositions with great rapidity. The warm reddish-brown ground is used as a mid-tone and the highlights are deftly touched in so that a convincing illusion of modelling is achieved. This may be clearly seen in the left hand of the standing Roman saint. The darker pigment used around the hand defines the contour of the form and acts as the shadow. This simplified scheme was employed with great virtuosity by Solimena, particularly in his oil sketches. His large finished paintings sometimes lack the finesse of the smaller works.

There is a double-sided sheet of studies for the painting in a private collection in Naples[6] and a compositional drawing in the Albertina, Vienna.[7] Solimena painted another preparatory oil sketch, similar in size to this one but without the arched top, which is now in the Minneapolis Institute of Art.[8] A weak copy of the Mahon painting is apparently in the Schönborn collection at Pommersfelden.[9]

TECHNICAL NOTE
The support is a fairly fine plain-weave canvas. It has a glue-paste lining, probably dating from early this century, and the tacking edges have been cut off. The edges are obscured with repaint. The artist has used a reddish-brown ground which is left fully exposed in several areas, as is customary in Solimena's sketches, although it is now more visible in the half-tones and shadows than was first intended due to wear and abrasion. In general the painting is in good condition. The technique is remarkably fluent and economical and no pentimenti are apparent.

PROVENANCE
Rev. D.T. Reynolds Carlin, Bugthorpe, York, by 1958;[10] acquired by the present owner in 1961.

EXHIBITIONS
Barnard Castle 1962, no.64.

Fig.44 Francesco Solimena, *Santa Maria dei Martiri*, 1707. Oil on canvas, 342 x 185 cm. Naples, San Pietro Martire.

1 For the altarpiece, see Bologna 1958, pp.91, 93, 187 and 264.
2 Chiarini's nineteenth-century guide to Naples states that there is a figure of Saint Lucy in Solimena's altarpiece (Celano-Chiarini 1856–60, IV, p.271) but this seems to be an error. It is repeated by Galante 1872 (1975), p.196; see also Bologna 1958, pp.187 and 319 (index).
3 He received 50 ducats on account in March and the balance of 150 on 19 August, from Fra Casulano Causidio, Procuratore of San Pietro Martire, see Pavone and Fiore 1994, pp.33 and 90, doc.13g. The altarpiece must have been delivered very soon after. In his article on the history of the church and monastery, G. Cosenza states that a payment was made for the altarpiece on 25 July 1705 and cites Archivio di Stato, Naples, *Monasteri Soppressi*, San Pietro Martire, vol.744 (see Cosenza 1900, p.117). I have not been able to check this archival reference.
4 There is no recent monograph on Solimena. Bologna's important work of 1958 is invaluable but see also Spinosa 1988, Nocera Inferiore 1990 and Vienna/Naples 1993–4.
5 Bibliotheca Sanctorum, VI, pp.1046–8.
6 See Vitzthum 1970, fig.29 and accompanying text.
7 Inv.630, 280 x 158 mm, pen and ink and chalk, see Albertina 1926–41, VI, no.360.
8 Inv.70.14, 29 1/2 x 19 1/2 in. (69.5 x 49.5 cm). The painting was reproduced, and accompanied by an informative caption, in *The Burlington Magazine* when it was with Seligman and Co., New York, ('Notable Works of Art now on the Art Market', 104, December 1962, plate XVII); see also Spinosa 1988, cat.23, p.107, fig.27. Two studio copies of this painting are recorded: one is in the Kunsthistorisches Museum in Vienna (Inv.6397), and another was on the art market in London in 1969, London (Heim) 1969, no.16, and recently appeared at Sotheby's, London, 11 December 1991, lot 21.
9 Inv.543, according to Barnard Castle 1962, no.64.
10 According to a label on the reverse: 'Bugthorpe Vicarage, York; Rev. D.T.Reynolds Carlin' followed by a pen inscription: 'September 1958'.

Attributed to Francesco Solimena 1657–1747

76 The Rest on the Flight into Egypt

Oil on copper, 32.3 x 38.9 cm

The painting, of which there are several versions, has a complicated attributional history. It was acquired by the present owner at a sale in which it was catalogued as 'Carracci'; it was later attributed to the Roman painter Giuseppe Chiari (1654–1727), a pupil of Carlo Maratti.[1] In 1967 the eminent specialist of eighteenth-century Italian painting Anthony M. Clark drew attention to an engraving by Bernard Baron (c.1700–66) published in London in 1724 which shows the composition in reverse and bears the inscription 'Fran.s Solimene pinx.' (fig.45). Paradoxically he proposed that the Mahon picture was not by Solimena but that it was an early work by his pupil, Sebastiano Conca (1680–1764).[2] He also noted that there was another version (strictly speaking a variant) of the painting at the Spencer Museum of Art, Lawrence, Kansas. That painting, which is on canvas (30.8 x 37.5 cm) and seems to be of similar quality to the present work, was donated to the museum in 1950 as a work by Sébastien Bourdon.[3] It, too, acquired an attribution to Giuseppe Chiari,[4] but when it was de-accessioned in 1985 it was catalogued as 'Attributed to Giovanni Battista Rossi'.[5] It is now in the collection of Everett Fahy, New York. Recently it was published by Nicola Spinosa as a work by Solimena and dated about 1695.[6]

This rich menu of attributions requires some digestion. The ascriptions to 'Carracci' and to Bourdon are quickly dismissed as fanciful; Chiari's figure types, his Marattesque palette and handling, are quite distinctive and differ considerably from this painting.[7] Giovanni Battista Rossi (documented 1749–82) was a Neapolitan follower of Solimena but may not even have been born when the picture was painted.[8] The painting does show several similarities, compositional and iconographic, with the work of Conca,[9] but they are insufficient to sustain an attribution to him.

After the death of Giordano, Solimena became the leading painter in Naples and in addition to his public commissions for the city he also made many pictures for foreign collectors.[10] Although the present writer finds it difficult to support without any reservations an attribution to Solimena for the Mahon painting, since the stylistic comparisons with the works which Spinosa dates to the same period – like the

Finding of Moses in the Hermitage, St Petersburg, a much more typical work – are not completely compelling, yet he is obliged to recognise that powerful evidence for Solimena's invention of the composition is offered by the inscription on the Baron print. Solimena was in the full flower of his career when the print was made in 1724 and we must assume that the attribution to him was based on some fairly firm foundation. Interestingly, the print was not made after the Mahon picture, which by virtue of its very high quality and the small pentimenti in it (see Technical Note) should be considered the prime version, but after the Fahy picture (or some copy of it),[11] since both that work and the print lack the charming detail of the plate of fruit which the standing putto is about to offer the Christ Child.

TECHNICAL NOTE

The copper panel has a silver-coloured coating on the recto, probably a lead-tin alloy. This reflective surface has optical qualities which have been exploited by the artist: for example, in the areas which are covered only by the reddish-brown ground the support takes on the appearance of gold, enhancing the jewel-like quality of the painting. There is some retouching in the darks at lower left but the painting is generally in very good condition. There are some small pentimenti: the extent of the orange drapery of the left-hand putto has been reduced since it originally passed over his back; there are small changes apparent in Christ's drapery.

Fig.45 Bernard Baron after Francesco Solimena, *The Rest on the Flight into Egypt*, 1724. Engraving. London, The British Museum.

PROVENANCE
Duke of Norfolk, Norfolk House, St James's Square, London;[12] Christie's, London, 11 February 1938 (Norfolk House sale), lot 72 ('CARRACCI, The Repose in Egypt'), where acquired by the present owner.

EXHIBITIONS
Not previously exhibited.

1 Briganti 1953, pp.15 and 16. Briganti's attribution followed an oral one by Federico Zeri.
2 See Clark 1981, p.8, note 5.
3 That attribution was rejected in Rosenberg 1964, p.299, note 15.
4 Fredericksen and Zeri 1972, p.52.
5 Sotheby's, New York, 6 June 1985, lot 97.
6 Spinosa 1988, no.13, p.104, and fig.16, p.185; the Baron print is not mentioned by Spinosa and was presumably unknown to the him. He refers to two other versions (but not the Mahon picture): a larger work (97 x 139 cm) apparently sold at Christie's in New York in 1986, of which he considered the Fahy painting to be the preparatory *bozzetto*, and a version of lesser quality on the Rome art market.
7 Compare the painting of the same subject by Chiari at Calke Abbey, Derbyshire, recently exhibited at the National Gallery, see London (National Gallery) 1995–6, no.70 (see also Chiari's larger version of the composition sold at Sotheby's, London, 11 December 1996, lot 88).
8 For Rossi, see Spinosa 1987, pp.61, 64, 252–60, 446.
9 See the painting of the same subject, dated to Conca's first decade in Rome, in the Hercolani Fava collection, Bologna, Gaeta 1981, no.8.
10 As early as 1704, the Abate Orlandi in his *Abecedario* refers to 'alte commissioni per oltramontani paesi, dove giunte l'opere sue, sono state accolte con sommo genio dagli Amatori della Pittura', quoted in Bologna 1958, p.204.
11 For these versions, see Christie's, New York, 10 October 1990, lot 6, oil on copper (32.7 x 39.1 cm), as 'Circle of Francesco Solimena'; that picture appeared again at auction at Christie's East, New York, 17 May 1995, lot 113, 'After Francesco Solimena'; another was at Christie's East, New York, 17 May 1995, lot 113 ('After Francesco Solimena'), copper, 32.7 x 39.1 cm; a version on copper was sold at Sotheby's, London, 8 December 1993, lot 99 (32 x 38.8 cm), as by an eighteenth-century follower of Sébastien Bourdon; a copy in reverse on panel appeared at Christie's, London, 5 February 1988, lot 138, as by Balthasar Beshey.
12 A paper label on the reverse is inscribed: 'D. of Norfolk/ South Drawing R/ N.6'.

Matthias Stom *c.*1600–after 1649

77 Salome receiving the Head of John the Baptist

Oil on canvas, 109.2 x 155.7 cm

Matthias Stom – who traditionally and incorrectly has been known as Stomer – was born in about 1600.[1] According to Houbraken, he came from Amersfoort but investigations in the Amersfoort archives have failed to confirm this. The earliest mention of Stom is in Rome in 1630 when he was sharing a house with the French painter Nicolas Provost in the Strada dell'Ormo in the parish of S. Nicola in Arcione. Paulus Bor from Amersfoort had lived in the same house five years earlier. Stom was certainly in Rome until 1632 and subsequently spent a substantial period in Naples where he painted pictures for several churches. He then travelled further south to Palermo; in the church of S. Agostino in Cacamo, near Palermo, is a painting of *Saint Isodorus Agricola* signed by Stom and dated 1641. Stom received very important commissions in Sicily: Giovanni Torresiglia, who from 1642 was Archbishop of Monreale, ordered an *Adoration of the Shepherds* from him for the high altar of the Capuchin Church in Monreale; Antonio Ruffo, the great collector in Messina who owned

paintings by Rembrandt, Guercino and many other distinguished contemporary painters, bought three paintings by Stom in the period 1646–9. The sales are recorded in Ruffo's account book, which informs us that in these years Stom was living in Palermo. It is not known when or where Stom died. In the Italian documents Stom is invariably referred as 'fiamingo' or 'Flandriae': the name is more frequently found in the South rather than the North Netherlands and it is possible that Stom was in fact from Flanders. The style of his early paintings, as Nicolson has argued,[2] suggests training with Honthorst in Utrecht and a period in Antwerp, where he became acquainted with the work of Rubens, Van Dyck, Jordaens and Abraham Janssens.

A substantial number of paintings by Stom are known but very few are dated and there are considerable difficulties in creating a convincing chronology.[3] Indeed the present painting provides one of the few dates for the construction of a chronology as there is a copy of it by the

English painter William Dobson (1611–46) which was probably made in London in about 1640 (fig.46).[4] It follows Stom's original closely, although the flame from the boy's candle is less stylised in form and the head of Salome is given greater liveliness and individuality. There are also small changes to the jewellery that Salome wears. The Stom (or a copy of it) was presumably in London in a private collection or on the art market.[5] The *Salome receiving the Head of John the Baptist* is therefore likely to be an early work, probably painted during Stom's Roman years, although Nicolson raised the possibility that it was in fact painted in Antwerp before Stom left for Italy and that it reached England from there shortly after it was painted.[6]

The bearded executioner stands on the left holding up the head. His powerfully muscled body and the elaborate folds of his shirt are thrown into rich shadows by the candle held by the boy in the foreground. Salome, seen in a strict classical profile[7], holds out the plate on which the head is to be placed and gazes at it as if mesmerised. Herodias, her mother, stands behind her and raises her hand to register her horror. Stom's style was later to become somewhat mannered: he invariably used a highly characteristic way of modelling in broken planes. At this moment, however, his careful study of the paintings by Caravaggio in San Luigi dei Francesi is evident in the statuesque figure of the executioner, while the boy seems to step from the work of one of the Utrecht Caravaggisti such as Hendrick ter Brugghen or Dirk van Baburen. The head of Salome, drawn in such strict profile, reveals Stom's familiarity with Rubens. Such eclecticism appears to be typical of the early works he painted in Italy.

CB

Fig.46 William Dobson, *Salome receiving the Head of John the Baptist*, *c.*1640. Oil on canvas, 110 x 129.5 cm. Liverpool, Walker Art Gallery (National Museums and Galleries on Merseyside).

TECHNICAL NOTE
The support is a coarse plain-weave canvas and there are horizontal seams running the length of the canvas 3 cm from the top edge and 4 cm from the bottom edge. The painting is lined and the stretcher is not original. Irregular tacking edges survive on all four sides. The picture is in reasonable condition. The blue of the executioner's breeches, probably smalt, has degraded and appears grey. The blue robe of the boy has sunk considerably and been retouched. There is some retouching in the craquelure on the highlights of the orange cloak draped over Salome's arm. There are no obvious pentimenti but there are minor adjustments made in brown pigment to Salome's profile intended to soften and refine the contour. The ground is a warm ochre.

PROVENANCE

The picture (or a copy of it) was in Britain from an early date and was copied by William Dobson (see above); Earl of Malmesbury, Hurn Court, Christchurch, Hants, until 1950; sold Christie's, London, 3 November 1950, lot 20 (as Honthorst), and bought by Murphy; Christie's, London, 23 November 1951, lot 81 (as Honthorst), and bought by Colnaghi; acquired by the present owner in 1952.

EXHIBITIONS

London (Colnaghi) 1952, no.14; London 1960, no.17.

1 See the biography of Stom (by Marten Jan Bok) in the catalogue of the exhibition held in Utrecht and Braunschweig 1986–7, pp.333–4. A chronology of Stom's work was proposed by Pauwels (1953), and subsequently refined by Benedict Nicolson in 1977. Nicolson lists 150 paintings by Stom and places them in four principal periods. See also Nicolson 1990, I, pp.179–88. The present painting is no.19 in Nicolson's 1977 article and it appears on p.185 of his 1990 lists.
2 Nicolson 1977, p.240.
3 See note 1 above.
4 Provenance: Collection of the Earls of Pembroke, Wilton House, by 1731; Christie's, London, 22 July 1951 (Pembroke sale), lot 34; Arcade Gallery, London; Sir Thomas Barlow, by whom sold to the Walker Art Gallery.

Literature: Gambarini 1731, pp.lx, 79; G.Vertue, *Notebooks*, 6 vols., *Proceedings of the Walpole Society*, I, p. 135 (vol.18, 1930), IV, pp.2, 19 (vol.24, 1936); Walpole 1862, II, p.352; Spencer 1937 (unpublished) no.3; Millar 1948 (rejecting the attribution to Dobson); London (Tate Gallery) 1951, no.26 (reinstating the attribution to Dobson); Nicolson 1979, p. 46; London (National Portrait Gallery) 1983–4, no.4; Nicolson 1990, I, p.103, no. 1569.
5 Vertue records that Isaac Fuller made a copy of Dobson's copy (see note 4 above) but this has not been traced.
6 Nicolson 1977, p.240 and cat.19.
7 Briganti notes this allusion to classical sources in support of Nicolson's dating of the picture early in Stom's career (Briganti 1953, p.11 and no.48, p.18; Nicolson 1952, p.251–2).

Bernardo Strozzi 1581/2–1644

78 Horatius Cocles defending the Bridge

Oil on paper attached to canvas, 24 x 35.5 cm (paper size)

The painting is a preparatory oil sketch, or *bozzetto*, for a ceiling fresco by Strozzi in the Villa Centurione-Carpaneto in Sampierdarena, near Genoa (fig.47).[1] Strozzi painted three ceilings in the villa, all of Roman subjects: the other two show *Marcus Curtius leaping into the Abyss* and *Dido and Aeneas at the Cave*.[2] The frescoes were commissioned by Filippo Centurione (died 1649), one of the wealthiest financiers in the city and a prominent figure in the political life of the Republic.[3] Their subject matter emphasises the virtues of self-sacrifice or self-abnegation for the greater good: Horatius Cocles held off the Etruscan army single-handed, while his fellow soldiers destroyed the Sublician Bridge over the River Tiber, so saving the city of Rome;[4] Marcus Curtius flung himself into the abyss, which had mysteriously opened up in the forum of Rome, when the oracles demanded that a sacrifice should be made to redeem the city;[5] and Aeneas later abandoned Dido in order to fulfil his destiny and found Rome.

Strozzi was born in Genoa and trained under the Sienese painter Pietro Sorri, who was in the city in 1596–7. He became a Franciscan Capuchin in 1598 but continued painting and became known as 'Il Cappuccino' and, after his move to Venice in 1630/1, as 'Il prete genovese'. His early works show the influence of Tuscan Mannerist painting and Lombard painting, especially that of Giulio Cesare Procaccini.[6] In 1608/9 he was permitted to leave the friary to take care of his mother, and never returned. The increasing naturalism of his work in the latter part of the 1610s has led to the suggestion that he may have visited Rome and studied the work of Caravaggio and his followers. He painted frescoes and altarpieces as well as portraits, genre pictures and still lifes. After his mother's death he moved to Venice and shortly thereafter left the Franciscans to become a Lateran Canon Regular. In Venice his style became more painterly and his palette much brighter. He was prolific and judging from the uneven quality of his later works he appears to have had an active workshop.

The *bozzetto* has an undeniably Mannerist character, apparent above all in the elongated proportions and complex pose of the archer on the left, but also in the stage-like setting.[7] This is carried over into the frescoes and has led to them

being dated early in Strozzi's career, in the mid-1610s, when his art shows the influence of painters like Ventura Salimbeni (1568–1613) and Giovanni Battista Paggi (1554–1627).[8] The traditional dating of *c*.1623–5 seems more accurate, however,[9] and a statement made by Filippo Centurione before the ecclesiastical tribunal which tried Strozzi in 1626 affords indirect evidence for this. He declared that he had known the artist for three or four years, which, even allowing for imprecise recall, means that the decoration of his villa could not have begun before 1620.[10] A careful reading of Ratti's expanded version of Soprani's 1675 biography of Strozzi also supports this later dating, since Ratti notes that the painter began the decoration of the Villa Centurione after executing the frescoes in the apse of San Domenico in Genoa, for which the final payment was made in 1622.[11]

Strozzi seems to have made frequent use of preparatory oil sketches, often painted in monochrome, and sometimes, like this one, executed on paper.[12] The handling here is remarkably spontaneous and confident, and the composition elegant and dynamic.

TECHNICAL NOTE
The painting is executed on paper stuck down on canvas attached to a stretcher. Strips of wood approximately 5 mm wide have been attached to the left and right sides. The paper has tended to delaminate from the canvas, resulting in some raised areas, and evidence of earlier attempts at consolidation can be seen in the numerous pinpricks made to introduce the glue. The only retouching worthy of note is in the area of the hip of the soldier brandishing a shield and spear on the left side of the bridge where there is a paper insert. A pentimento is apparent in the figure of Horatius Cocles: he appears to have originally held the shield above his head.

PROVENANCE
Acquired by the present owner at Sotheby's, London, 8 February 1950, lot 37 (as by 'Van Lint' (sic!)).

EXHIBITIONS
Zurich 1956, no.247; London 1960, no.388; Dayton/Sarasota/Hartford 1962–3, no.52; New York (Knoedler) 1962, no.26; Genoa 1995, no.32.

Fig.47 Bernardo Strozzi, *Horatius Cocles defending the Bridge*, *c*.1623–5. Fresco. Sampierdarena, Genoa, Villa Centurione-Carpaneto.

1   The ceiling is reproduced in colour in Genoa 1995, fig.36, p.62.

2   See Genoa 1995, figs.34–5, pp.60–1.

3   Filippo Centurione was closely linked to Spain, where his brother, Ottavio, was ambassador. Filippo stood as a candidate for Doge of Genoa in 1617 and 1621, see Bitossi 1995, p.332. He was a generous supporter of Strozzi and in 1626 spoke in his defence when he was tried for bringing priestly dignity into disrepute through his activities as a painter, see Assini 1995, especially p.372. Strozzi painted frescoes of the *Four Seasons*, now lost, for another of Filippo's brothers, Battista, in the Centurione family palazzo in Piazza Fossatello in Genoa, see Soprani/Ratti 1768–9, I, p.191, note (a), and also Galassi 1995, pp.42–3 and 53, note 24.

4   The episode is recounted in Livy, Book II, chapter X.

5   Livy, Book VII, chapter VI.

6   On Strozzi's early years, see Algeri 1992, and the same author's essay in Genoa 1995, pp.21–38.

7   Strozzi made no use of *sotto-in-sù* perspective in any his three Roman scenes. In treating them like easel paintings in fresco he was probably conforming to a Genoese decorative tradition.

8   See the essay by Algeri in Genoa 1995, p.26, and the 'Bernardo Strozzi' entry by Chiara Kravietz in the MacMillan *Dictionary of Art*, 1996, vol.29, p.783.

9   Fiocco 1921, p.7, and Mortari 1966, p.172.

10 Assini 1995, p.372; see also Galassi 1995, pp.40–1.

11 Soprani/Ratti 1768–9, I, p.191; for the payment, see Galassi 1992, p.51, note 12.

12 See Ferrari 1990, pp.53, 56, 235, 242. For two sketches on paper, studies for lunettes showing subjects from the *Iliad*, see Mortari 1966, p.174, figs.249–50. Various '*abbozzi*' and '*abbozzadure*' are referred to in Strozzi's post-mortem inventory of 1644, some of them in monochrome, see Genoa 1995, pp.376–8, especially p.377.

Pierre Subleyras 1699–1749

79 The Holy Family with Saint Elizabeth and Saint Zacharias and the Infant Saint John

Oil on canvas, 63.5 x 48.7 cm

Saints Elizabeth and Zacharias, here shown at the left of the picture, were, according to the Gospel of Saint Luke (chapter 1), the aged parents of Saint John the Baptist. When an angel of the Lord told Zacharias that his wife would have a son, Zacharias expressed doubt and, as punishment, was struck dumb. Luke's account was elaborated in the *Golden Legend*, a thirteenth-century compilation of stories of the saints by Jacobus de Voragine. Joseph, at the right, appears to express surprise as the infant Saint John, shown dressed in animal skins as tradition required, kisses the foot of Christ. Below Saint John is a simple cross. The snake-like cartellino wound around the cross is not inscribed.

The composition of the painting has been carefully calculated. One diagonal links the heads of Saint John, Christ and Saint Joseph, another the heads of Saint Zacharias (at the left), the Virgin and Saint Joseph. The head of Saint Elizabeth, which appears from a pentimento to have originally been lower, is parallel with that of her son, and his head is on the same central vertical axis as that of the Virgin. A multi-figural composition is thus given considerable stability, itself reinforced by the emphatic verticals and horizontals of the architecture. Even the voluminous red drapery at the top of the picture underlines this structural approach, the diagonal of its central part paralleling the diagonal arrangement of the heads of Saint Zacharias and Saint John, while at the right a finger of drapery points directly at the infant Baptist.

If in terms of composition, and for that matter colour, the dominant figure is the Virgin, the iconographical importance of the Baptist is suggested by the direction of the participants' gazes. All look at the infant Baptist, except the Virgin who looks at Saint Elizabeth, so indicating the Baptist as the psychological link through which the others connect. This, and his central position in the composition, emphasise his New Testament role as the immediate precursor of Christ, perhaps further alluded to by the Baptist's face being turned away from the viewer and towards Christ.

The attribution of this painting to Subleyras was first made by Hermann Voss (an oral opinion), and has been accepted by Pierre Rosenberg.[1] The latter has proposed that it is an early work executed before Subleyras left Toulouse for Paris in 1726, placing it with a group of works characterised by strong contrasts of light and shade and by a rapid and vigorous execution. However, the relatively even lighting and carefully structured composition of the Mahon picture seem to exclude it from the Toulouse period, and its assured handling with touches of red in the shadows of the flesh and its convincing treatment of space suggest, as Mahon has proposed, a later work dating from Subleyras's early years in Rome, where he settled in 1728 following his success in the previous year's Prix de Rome.

HW

TECHNICAL NOTE
The support is a coarse plain-weave canvas which has been lined with a glue-paste lining. The stretcher is twentieth century. The ground is a warm pink buff colour. Although there is some wear and retouching at lower right, and some abrasion bottom left, the painting is in good condition and retains considerable impasto. There are a number of pentimenti. In particular the figure of Saint Elizabeth was probably once lower in the painting.

PROVENANCE
Given to Sir Denis Mahon in 1972.

EXHIBITIONS
Not previously exhibited.

1 Paris/Rome 1987, p.138, where illustrated.

Catalogue of Drawings by Guercino

Denis Mahon

The forty-six drawings by Guercino collected by me have been since 1986 on long-term deposit at Oxford's Ashmolean Museum, to the authorities of which the National Gallery and I myself are grateful for their willingness to co-operate on the present occasion. Since the exhibition space in the Sainsbury Wing galleries was not sufficient, after accommodating my paintings, to show all the drawings it was decided with my approval to show a selection. And the choice of such drawings as could conveniently be fitted in was entrusted to Gabriele Finaldi, who has been responsible overall for the exhibition, and who has also written the entries for the majority of the paintings in so exemplary a manner. Though my drawings have been catalogued and exhibited several times in the past, the entries for the thirty sheets thus chosen naturally require bringing up to date, a task which Dr Finaldi requested me to undertake.

The first time the whole collection was shown was in 1967 in an exhibition which took place at the Pinacoteca Civica at Cento, the artist's birthplace, in commemoration of his death in 1666. Entitled *Omaggio al Guercino*, the exhibition included a number of paintings which had recently been restored, as well as my drawings, for the cataloguing of which I was responsible. The drawings section was at once reprinted, embodying corrections, as a separate volume entitled *I Disegni del Guercino della Collezione Mahon*. This provided a considerable amount of basic information on the subject. When the collection was exhibited in 1968 in London at the Colnaghi Gallery and in Sheffield at the Graves Art Gallery these findings were merely summarised. Thirty-five of my drawings were shown as part of the big Guercino exhibition at Bologna in 1968. My catalogue of all the drawings in that exhibition, with rather full entries, was published in 1969. When the collection was deposited at the Ashmolean Museum in 1986, the drawings were shown in an exhibition there and at Messrs Hazlitt, Gooden & Fox's gallery in London, together with the Museum's own notable holdings of drawings by Guercino. The accompanying catalogue was substantially compiled by me in so far as my collection was concerned, and by David Ekserdjian for the Ashmolean's own drawings. It was also published in *The Burlington Magazine* as a supplement to the issue for March 1986. The scope of the entries was fully explained in a short preface by the then Keeper of Western Art at the Ashmolean, Dr Nicholas Penny, but the order in which the drawings were catalogued there has been broadly followed here.

In 1991 a number of exhibitions were staged in celebration of the fourth centenary of Guercino's birth. Twenty-nine of my drawings were lent to the British Museum for an exhibition entitled *Drawings by Guercino from British Collections*, with careful catalogue entries by Nicholas Turner and Carol Plazzotta which on occasion provided significant facts not previously published. The exhibition at Bologna in the same year included a drawings section for which I was responsible. But, as I had lent thirty-five drawings to the exhibition there in 1968, a loan from me was not repeated in 1991, though the exhibition included sheets related to certain drawings in my collection, and my catalogue entries listed other related sheets known to me (and so is often cited here). On the other hand, my entire collection of drawings by Guercino was lent, with my approval, by the Ashmolean Museum to the exhibition of paintings and drawings by Guercino held at the Schirn Kunsthalle at Frankfurt-am-Main in 1991–2. Catalogue entries of my drawings were on this occasion updated in a particularly thorough manner by Sybille Ebert-Schifferer.

In compiling the present entries I have endeavoured to take due account of all the existing literature, though I have not entered into much detail as regards the sources on which the provenance information is based, a great deal of which will be found in my original 1967 catalogue. Most of that information remains valid, but one recent new discovery of the greatest interest should be indicated here.

As explained in the introduction and entries of the Cento catalogue of 1967, many of the artist's drawings were traceable back to the immense collection which he had preserved in his house in Bologna, which, because it was inherited by his nephews Benedetto and Cesare Gennari, is known as the Casa Gennari. And the fact is that British collectors were particularly active in the eighteenth century in acquiring drawings thence.

Apart from the enormous quantity obtained on behalf of George III by his librarian, Richard Dalton, an equally spectacular purchase in numbers and quality was that which became known as the Bouverie Collection. Until quite recently it was assumed that the collector concerned had been the Hon. Edward Bouverie, MP (1738–1818), brother of the first Earl of Radnor. But, as Nicholas Turner has shown (Turner/Plazzotta 1991, pp.23–6), he was John Bouverie, a member of the same family of an older generation, who died young in 1750, but was evidently a collector of drawings of the very first importance (see Turner, 1994). Accordingly, the appropriate changes have been made here to the entries for the ten drawings to which apply the now established provenance from John Bouverie, his heir in this respect (his nephew, Chrstopher Hervey), and their later successors.

Perhaps I may be allowed to insist that this adjustment should not be taken to imply the invalidation of the facts adduced in general in support of the provenances given in my 1967 catalogue. Indeed, I was gratified to receive a friendly accolade from Sybille Ebert-Schifferer in connection with my detective work in establishing in 1967 'mit kriminalistischem Spürsinn' the particularly distinguished provenance of cat.106 in this exhibition.